Organizational
Symbolism

**MONOGRAPHS IN
ORGANIZATIONAL BEHAVIOR AND
INDUSTRIAL RELATIONS, VOLUME 1**

Editor: Samuel B. Bacharach, *Department of Organizational Behavior,
New York State School of Industrial Relations, Cornell University*

MONOGRAPHS IN ORGANIZATIONAL BEHAVIOR AND INDUSTRIAL RELATIONS

Edited by Samuel B. Bacharach,
*Department of Organizational Behavior,
New York State School of Industrial
Relations, Cornell University*

Organizational Symbolism

Edited by LOUIS R. PONDY
University of Illinois
at Urbana-Champaign

PETER J. FROST
University of British Columbia

GARETH MORGAN
York University

THOMAS C. DANDRIDGE
State University of New York
at Albany

 JAI PRESS INC.

Greenwich, Connecticut   London, England

Library of Congress Cataloging in Publication Data
Main entry under title:

Organizational symbolism.

  (Monographs in organizational behavior and industrial
relations ; v. 1)
  Includes bibliographies and index.
  1. Symbolism in organizations—Addresses, essays,
lectures. I. Pondy, Louis R. II. Dandridge, Thomas C. III. Series.
HD30.3.073 1983   302.3'5   83-13542
ISBN 0-89323-366-3

Copyright © 1983 JAI PRESS INC.
36 Sherwood Place
Greenwich, Connecticut 06830

JAI PRESS INC.
3 Henrietta Street
London WC2E 8LU
England

ISBN NUMBER: 0-89232-366-3
Library of Congress Catalog Card Number: 83–13542
Manufactured in the United States of America

CONTENTS

MEDIATORY MYTHS IN THE SERVICE OF
ORGANIZATIONAL IDEOLOGY

LIST OF CONTRIBUTORS

Harry Abravanel   Department des Science Administration,
Université du Quebec

John A. Y. Andrews   Graduate School of Business,
University of Chicago

Richard Boland   Department of Accountancy,
University of Illinois at Urbana

Richard L. Daft   Department of Management,
Texas A & M University

Thomas C. Dandridge   School of Business,
State University of New York at Albany

Carson Eoyang   Department of the Navy,
Naval Postgraduate School

Roger Evered   Department of the Navy,
Naval Postgraduate School

Peter J. Frost   Faculty of Commerce and
Business Administration,
The University of British Columbia

Paul M. Hirsch   Graduate School of Business,
University of Chicago

Raymond Hoffman   Graduate School of Business,
Washington University

Anne Sigmismund Huff   Department of Business Administration,
University of Illinois, Urbana

Meryl Reis Louis   Department of the Navy,
Naval Postgraduate School

Joanne Martin   Graduate School of Business,
                                Stanford University

Gareth Morgan   Faculty of Administrative Studies,
                                York University

Louis R. Pondy   Department of Business Administration,
                                University of Illinois at Urbana

Melanie E. Powers   Graduate School of Business,
                                Stanford University

Linda Smircich   Department of Management,
                                School of Business Administration,
                                University of Massachusetts

Gordon A. Walter   Faculty of Commerce and
                                Business Administration,
                                University of British Columbia

Mark N. Wexler   Faculty of Business Administration,
                                Simon Fraser University

Alan L. Wilkins   Graduate School of Management,
                                Brigham Young University

Acknowledgements

This volume has benefited from the help of numerous people. In particular, we wish to extend our thanks to the authors of the contributions in the volume, and to William Cats-Baril, David Cray, Tim Davis, Bob Hogner, Nancy Kaible, and Pat Templin who participated in early meetings that served to stimulate and focus interest in this field of study.

Financial and administrative support for the project was provided by the Social Sciences and Humanities Research Council of Canada, the Distinguished Visitor's Fund of the Faculty of Commerce and Business Administration, University of British Columbia and the Research Projects Fund of the College of Business Administration, The Pennsylvania State University.

Thanks are due to Larry Cummings and John Van Maanen who offered encouragement and helpful comments on a number of papers in this volume, to Peter Frost who coordinated editorial activities, to Susan Heming, Ulrike Hilborn, Gail Robertson and Nancy Schell and her staff for administrative and secretarial services, to Sam Bacharach and finally, to Sue Openheim and her staff at *JAI Press* for their excellent editorial contributions to the production of the volume.

Introduction

This volume finds its origins in a small informal conference on Organizational Symbolism, held at the home of Lou Pondy in Urbana, Illinois, on 4–6 May, 1979. The conference was organized by Tom Dandridge and Bob Hogner, and brought together a number of people interested in exploring the implications of symbolism for the study of organization. Those present came from a variety of academic backgrounds, and attended for a variety of reasons. Some had been formally invited to attend and others, hearing about the event, had just asked if they could come along.

The group assembled on the afternoon of 4th May with no formal agenda to pursue, other than a commitment to learn more about symbolism and its possibilities. The conference was allowed to evolve, its structure and content being shaped by the interests and wishes of those present. Discussion focussed on a wide range of topics and issues in a way that at times forged common ground, and at others, created polite division between those present. Interest, excitement, frustration, curiosity, energy and weariness, combined in various ways at different times to create a rich context of inquiry in which the idea of organizational symbolism was thoroughly explored.

The conference established many bonds and commitments between those present. One such bond resulted in a series of exchanges between Peter Frost and Gareth Morgan, and a commitment to meet in Vancouver, Canada, in June 1979, to discuss some of the themes emerging from the conference. Both felt that conference discussion had raised a number of intriguing issues that could prove of central importance for the future study of organization. However, while it was clear that the idea of "organizational symbolism" identified a focus of interest, it was also clear that the term signified different things to different people. Organizational symbolism was interpreted in a way that focussed attention on the use of symbols in organizations (e.g. logos, status symbols), on symbolic activities (e.g. organizational rituals, and ceremonies), on symbolic imagery (e.g. as expressed in language, stories, myths, sagas and ideologies), as well as on the idea that organization, in all its aspects, was itself a symbolic activity of deep psychological significance.

Organizational symbolism seemed to present itself as a potentially rich and diverse field of study, that could be approached from many different perspectives, utilizing many different kinds of research methodologies. Questions arose. Was it possible to produce a monograph on organizational symbolism that would represent this richness, and communicate the potentialities that an understanding of symbolism can have for the way we understand and manage organization? Was it possible to counterpose different approaches to the study of symbolism in a way that would stimulate some basic questions, and hence continuing inquiry about the nature of the phenomenon? Was it possible to make the study of organizational symbolism something which it deserves to be—a central rather than peripheral aspect of the study of organization?

The present volume represents an attempt to respond to these questions and concerns. With the support and encouragement of Lou Pondy and Tom Dandridge, it was decided to use the May conference as a means of launching the project. Conference members were invited to elaborate and illustrate their favored approach to organizational symbolism in a way that would illustrate its significance and potential for future research. Other researchers interested in this area of study were also invited to make contributions along similar lines. The result is a collection of papers that serve to capture some of the breadth, diversity and potential of organizational symbolism as an emerging field of inquiry.

We hope that the volume will be read in the spirit in which it is offered—as a document which seeks to be exploratory rather than definitive, and which provides no more than a hint of what is possible in future research. The various papers do not attempt to provide definitive "state of the art" accounts on the nature of organizational symbolism, or to provide "blue-prints" for the conduct of future research. Their concern is to present preliminary thoughts, ideas, and approaches to research, which may serve as useful points of departure for future inquiry.

The reader will find in the different chapters many ways of approaching the study of symbolism and of appreciating its significance. As our overview in chapter one suggests, the perspectives represented in the volume by no means exhaust the full range of possibilities. However, they do provide a good indication of the rich potential which awaits the organizational researcher who appreciates the significance of symbolism in organizational life. We hope that the volume will have an effect that is greater than the sum of its parts, symbolizing the importance of organizational symbolism, as well as making substantive contributions to developments within this field of inquiry.

March, 1981

Part I

OVERVIEW

ORGANIZATIONAL SYMBOLISM

Gareth Morgan, Peter J. Frost and
Louis R. Pondy

Symbolism is no mere idle fancy or corrupt degeneration: it is inherent in the very texture of human life. A. N. Whitehead (1927)

The purpose of this volume is three-fold:

1. To bring together in one convenient place a number of papers that examine formal organizations from a "symbolic" perspective.
2. To argue that the symbolic perspective has a legitimate and important role to play in organizational analysis.
3. To lay out the elements of organizational symbolism for others to follow, criticize and build upon.

Traditional organization and management theory has for the most part failed to grasp the full significance and importance of the symbolic side of organizational life, because of its overwhelming commitment to models based upon mechanical and organismic metaphors of organization. Such models over-simplify the nature of organizations in creating a focus upon their formal and intendedly rational aspects, rather than upon their character as complex patterns of human activity. The rationale for studying organizational symbolism stems from recognition of this all important fact: that organizations are not simple systems like machines or adaptive organisms; they are human systems manifesting complex patterns of cultural activity. The core of the argument involved here has been fully developed by Pondy and Mitroff (1979). Members of an organization are able to use language, can exhibit insight, produce and interpret metaphors, are able to vest meaning in events, behavior, and objects, seek meaning in their lives—in short, can act symbolically. This symbolic capacity is enhanced by their association in formal organizations so that institutions develop a history, a common point of view, and a need to process such complexity through symbolic means. Organizations are by their very nature symbolic entities, and a fully adequate theory of them must perforce also be symbolic in its content.

THE NATURE OF ORGANIZATIONAL SYMBOLISM

The topic of symbolism has long attracted a great deal of attention in a variety of fields concerned with understanding human activity. In anthropology, linguistics, literary criticism, psychoanalysis, many branches of sociology, and in all the arts, the symbolic nature of human action is seen as being of central importance. Developments in organizational symbolism thus have a rich source of relevant theory and research upon which to draw. The works by Barthes (1964), Blumer (1969), Burke (1968), Duncan (1953), Jung (1964), Langer (1957), Meltzer, Petras and Reynolds (1975) and Sperber (1975) are representative of a number of approaches in the above areas.

In a volume such as the present, it is impossible to treat the subject of symbolism in the depth and breadth that it deserves. As a result our object is more limited, being to set out a basis for understanding, and to identify some possible issues and directions for future research. We start in this chapter with a consideration of the nature of symbols and symbolism, proceed to discuss organizational symbolism and some approaches to the study of this field, and then to an assessment of the challenges and possibilities which organizational symbolism presents as a field of inquiry.

SYMBOLS AND SYMBOLISM

The word *symbol* derives from Greek roots which combine the idea of sign, in the sense of a mark, token, insignia, means of identification, with that of a throwing and putting together. A symbol is a sign which denotes something much greater than itself, and which calls for the association of certain conscious or unconscious ideas, in order for it to be endowed with its full meaning and significance. A sign achieves the status of a symbol when it is interpreted, not in terms of strict resemblance with what is signified, but when other patterns of suggestion and meaning are "thrown upon" or "put together" with the sign to interpret it as part of a much wider symbolic whole. Symbols are signs which express much more than their intrinsic content; they are significations which embody and represent some wider pattern of meaning.

An important characteristic which distinguishes signs from symbols is that all symbols are created subjectively and are invested with a particular kind of subjective meaning. Signs merely indicate or signify a relationship among different elements. While all symbols are signs, not all signs are symbols. It is possible for signs to be devoid of intrinsic subjective meaning, to be merely relational. Thus heavy dark clouds may merely signify the onset of rain; smoke may merely signify fire. As such they are signs. Yet vested with particular meaning they become symbols. Heavy clouds may symbolize the approach of a rain god for an isolated tribe of people, smoke may signify for them a fire god. Invested with subjective significance of this kind, signs become symbols which can be woven into complex cultural patterns.

The role of symbols and symbolism (the practice of symbolic representation) within the more sacred and highly ritualized realms of human life is well recognized. Indeed, these realms are distinguished by the conscious use of symbolism as a means of expressing and sustaining valued patterns of activity and belief. Thus within the sphere of religion and the customs and activities which sustain traditional ways of life, the use of symbols is both obvious and clear. The cross as a symbol of Christianity, the crown as a symbol of monarchy, the graduation ceremony as a symbol of learning, can be used in various ways to affirm and sustain the wider images and pattern of belief that give the Christian religion, the role of a particular monarch, or a university's claim as a seat of learning, an enduring and recognizable form.

What is less well recognized is that symbols also pervade the secular sphere, and influence virtually every aspect of human existence. Given the definition of symbol offered above, this should come as no surprise, since symbolism is a generic process rather than a narrowly defined and specialized activity. For symbols are created and recreated whenever human beings vest elements of their world with a pattern of meaning and significance which extends beyond its intrinsic content. Any object, action, event, utterance, concept or image offers itself as raw material for symbol creation, at any place, and at any time.

The following examples will serve to illustrate the rich range of possibilities.

An Object

At a closing session of the Illinois conference on "Organizational Symbolism" Lou Pondy sought to focus the attention of those present upon a bird's egg found in his garden earlier that week. The egg was hollow, and open at one end, revealing the exit through which a young fledgling had made its entrance into the world. The egg was presented by Lou as a symbol of the Conference, illustrating the "hatching of a new field of inquiry"—that of organizational symbolism.

An Action

When two people shake hands, the action symbolizes their coming together. The hand-shake may also be rich in other kinds of symbolic significance. Between free-masons it reaffirms a bond of brotherhood, and loyalty to the order to which they belong. Between politicians it is often used to symbolize an intention to cooperate and work together. To members of the counter-culture of the 1960's and early 1970's, their special hand clasp and cry of "Right On!" affirmed a set of divergent values and opposition to the system. The handshake is more than just a shaking of hands. It symbolizes a particular kind of relationship between those involved.

An Event

A birthday anniversary is more than just a cyclical event. Sometimes it is a day which the birthday person may wish to forget or keep secret. Sometimes it is a day which no one must forget, and be celebrated with vigor and glee. Anniversaries are rich in different kinds of symbolic significance, and as events may seal or break a whole network of interpersonal relations.

An Utterance

Most team supporters (e.g., in football, ice hockey, baseball) have a special kind of cheer or chant ("war-cry") used to encourage their team's effort. The symbolic significance of the cheer to the players may urge them on to do great things in attack, or sustain their energies under pressure in defence. The cheer shouted in another context, e.g., at an office party, may serve to evoke special kinds of response from fellow supporters. The cheer binds together. Like the coloured scarves, hats, badges and other regalia which people wear in support of their team, the cheer says more than "I support you". It also says that we are together;

we are part of the same team, community, grand family or whatever; win so that I can also win!

An Image

Dream images are rich in symbolic significance, as are the ideas which people invent in the waking world. Dreams convey messages in symbolic form, express restrained feelings, and allow the dreamer to explore realms of consciousness alien to daytime existence. Ideas which people generate consciously in relation to their home, their work, their family, also carry hidden symbolic meaning. The idea of changing homes, jobs, or even families may symbolize a deeper concern to change oneself, to be born again, to fulfill some distant dream or ambition. The dream or idea stands for much more than its intrinsic content.

These examples, drawn from different spheres of everyday life, have been selected to illustrate the ways in which different kinds of phenomena can be vested with symbolic significance. As stated earlier, any phenomenon can be vested with such symbolic status, and human beings in all spheres of life create and inhabit milieux which are rich in symbolic significance, much of which may not be clearly or directly appreciated. In attempting to understand the nature of this symbolism it is important and helpful to be aware of at least three broad issues. First, symbols vary quite considerably in their degree of complexity. Second symbols may be created consciously or unconsciously. Third, symbols vary in the extent to which they are shared, and can be symbolic in different ways to different people, sometimes being vested with contradictory meanings. In the following discussion we illustrate how the issues involved here can help us unravel the symbolic nature of organizational life.

ORGANIZATIONAL SYMBOLISM

Simple Symbols: Conscious and Unconscious

From the moment one enters the bounds of an organization, one quickly becomes directly exposed to relatively simple modes of symbolic expression which have been consciously contrived to create a desired effect. The accounts of work experience given by managers and workers frequently reveal how the reality of organization is rife with symbolic activity (see, for example, Frost, Mitchell, & Nord, 1978; Kanter & Stein, 1979; and all the chapters in this volume). When one walks into the office of a senior executive, for example, the size, layout and decor often shout out symbolically "I am the boss". The office is designed to impress upon all who enter that a person of importance works there. Such symbols and trappings of status may be visible throughout the organization, from the boardroom to the shopfloor, in the staff dining rooms, the carpark and the washrooms.

In one corporation the nature and status of different organizational members is directly reflected in the physical shape and layout of the building, which has been designed as a pyramid. The president's office occupies the top floor; the vice presidents are located on the floor below, with offices on a grand but more modest scale; and so on down the hierarchy to the bottom floor. In other organizations, such symbolism may be used to create different effects—of equality, frugality, tradition, modernity, a sense of security, or whatever. Sometimes well-recognized symbols are used to serve ends other than those which are most often associated with them. In at least one organization for example, a budget officer deliberately chooses to occupy a small and cramped office with trappings of a standard well below that which is expected of a person of his senior status, so that his situation reinforces the fact that he often has to say "No" to budget requests, and means what he says. His office is used to symbolize his intent to ration, control and curb expenditures whenever he can.

On the shop-floor work may stop for the presentation of a gold watch to an employee with long service. The ceremony and object is used by management to symbolize values and behaviors that it wishes to foster, as do the large performance charts which may decorate the wall providing a background for the ceremony. The corporation's honor lists, "employee of the month" awards, glossy brochures and financial statements presented to year-end share-holder meetings, and the public at large, again are consciously used to symbolize and reinforce valued organizational characteristics. In addition to whatever instrumental ends they serve, they also have a symbolic status in that they embody and convey particular images and patterns of meaning to those who encounter them.

Such simple modes of symbolism, consciously constituted to create a particular image and effect, are easy to detect throughout organizational life. So too are the relatively simple but unconscious modes of symbolism which tell us much about organizational milieux, though without the explicit recognition of those who create and sustain them. Obvious examples here are the so-called Freudian slips, those unintended words and actions which destroy a surface appearance and reveal some underlying and hidden intention or meaning. Thus, the manager who announces to employees that any worker not complying with company regulations on theft and security will be "persecuted", instead of saying prosecuted, as consciously intended, is perhaps telling a great deal more than he or she would wish about an underlying attitude to staff. The actions of a manager in drawing up a particular set of plans for dealing with unexpected events, may tell much about his or her general nature and ability to handle difficult problems and situations. Objects, actions, events, utterances and images may serve as the medium through which organizational employees symbolize unconscious concerns about themselves and their work situation. An understanding of the symbolic projections which underlie such phenomena can tell the sensitive researcher much about the situation being researched.

Other simple types of unconscious symbols are often created as an unintended consequence of action oriented to the achievement of fairly instrumental ends. Bureacratic routines and decisions for example, are loaded with such symbolic content, the routine and decision implying much more than may have been consciously intended. The bureaucratic concern for rule-following and documentation presents a good example here. Most people at some time or another have been in a situation where they are able to confront a bureaucrat with evidence of a material fact or situation, but which they cannot support with the required form of documentation. Thus one's presence at a business conference may not be admissable evidence that one is entitled to appropriate attendance and travel expenses; one has to produce an official receipt. Bureaucratic modes of organization are not geared to deal with factual realities; they deal with what is symbolically acceptable as evidence, which usually means a piece of paper carrying an appropriate signature, date, and so on. The important requirement for the bureaucrat to take action is that the action can be shown to be symbolically correct. The operation of even the simplest bureaucratic routines are rich in symbolic significance of some kind, vested with an important pattern of meaning by the bureaucrat (e.g., of security, power, importance) and also by those subject to the rules (e.g., of frustration, futility, anger). The symbolic significance may be very different according to whether one is the bureaucrat, or the one subject to the rules.

Complex Symbols: Conscious and Unconscious

As one penetrates deeper into the nature of organizational life, conscious and unconscious forms of symbolism of a more complex kind come to view. Organizational life is rich in various forms of ritual activity, tradition, patterns of humour, story-telling, and various kinds of metaphorical imagery which contribute to the development of distinctive kinds of cultural milieux within the organization. Such activities may be consciously contrived to produce certain effects within the organization, or may arise spontaneously to give shape and form to significant patterns of meaning in areas of work life which are otherwise devoid of valued intrinsic content. Thus, organizational traditions and stories may be consciously developed as a means of achieving improved managerial control. (The papers by Wilkins, and Martin & Powers specifically address this issue.) The managerial style of a chief executive may be shaped in many diverse ways to evoke feelings of paternalistic loyalty from employees, or to create a system of attitudes and beliefs which foster a competitive, aggressive organizational atmosphere (see the paper by Smircich). On the other hand, the symbolic character of organizational life may take form in opposition to managerial values, providing an escape route from the toil imposed by formal organizational requirements.

The avoidance of work may be developed into a highly accomplished skill, rich in intrinsic significance, for the worker may feel that he or she is beating the system as well as avoiding the drudgery of work. The form of machine-shop humor discussed in the paper by Boland and Hoffman, is also rich in this kind of symbolic significance.

In the use of language we find another very pervasive and symbolically significant activity which influences every area of organizational life. Here again, its use may be conscious or unconscious, and exercise an influence in a variety of ways. Evered's paper on the use of language in the U.S. Navy provides us with a splendid example here, emphasizing how the reality within an organization may be shaped by its language. It is of course an extreme example, since the language of the Navy with its various codes, acronyms, and metaphors is so complex that it has to be learned on special courses and training programmes. To the non U.S. Navy member it is likely to prove completely unintelligible. However, the general point being made is of much wider significance. The language of organization, in the board-room, on management courses, on the shop floor, etc. is also full of specialized jargon and distinctive concepts, which may be incomprehensible to the uninitiated. But, it is the language which shapes organizational reality. The shop floor worker who attends a financial planning meeting for the first time may quite understandably find the language of the accountants a very foreign one. And even after learning that language, he or she may well still find that the concepts and jargon used, define a "reality" which is contrary to that which is sought for. The language of profit and loss, return on investment, etc., may not facilitate a decision consistent with the reality which the people on the shop floor wish to enact. The use of language is rich in symbolic significance. It carries patterns of meaning which do much to evoke and define the realities of organizational life, and is a topic central to the analysis of organizational symbolism.

Individuals in organizations frequently encounter symbol systems which they do not recognize as symbolic, and with which they do not know how to cope. A detailed example of this kind of experience can be found in the account by Jones (1973), who describes his own experiences as the only black manager in an organization. His success in the company came only after an extended period of time during which he was unhappy, frustrated and confused as to what it was he was doing, which earned him mediocre performance evaluation and negative feedback from other managers. He observes in retrospect that many of his problems occurred in effect because he failed to unravel the symbol system, (e.g., as to what constituted the correct tone of voice when communicating with others, what constituted an appropriate level of assertion), and because he placed a literal interpretation upon symbolic gestures. The supervisor's (symbolic) suggestion that Jones should "just ask" for help when needed, leads to a reprimand for Jones when he subsequently takes up the offer. While there may be a measure of real prejudice underlying and distorting the process of communications involved here, such distortion revolves around the interpretation and manipulation of symbols.

Such situations in which individual organizational members may often be living within symbolic structures which they simply do not know how to interpret or understand becomes of increasing relevance in an age when organizations are becoming multi-national in terms of the structure of the work-force, and in the scale of international operation. Many Western managers visiting their clients and counterparts in other cultures, as in the Middle East, find themselves negotiating symbol systems which define quite different realities from those characteristic of the West. Ethnic groups in Western organizations have long experienced the kind of problems involved here, their inability to cope with the dominant symbol system presenting important barriers to their ability to operate effectively within the organizations in which they are employed.

It is important to note that the kinds of problems of symbol interpretation referred to above, may occur in symbol systems which exist at an unconscious rather than conscious level of awareness. And they may be all the more difficult to deal with for this reason, because they are not even clear to those who sustain the symbol system. Many of the problems encountered by Jones in the example presented above may have been of this kind, his difficulties created by the unconscious symbolization of prejudice by others. Concerns emanating from the unconscious mind can lead an individual to enact a social reality which causes great difficulties both for him or herself, and those with whom he or she interacts. A manager or employee may enact symbolic structures which embody paradoxes, inconsistencies, traps and double binds, which make it virtually impossible for others to create room for meaningful and effective action within the pattern of expectations and meaning thus produced. Many an organization has no doubt been effectively crippled by senior executives who for unconscious reasons enact an organizational climate which makes effective action difficult, and at times impossible.

The unconscious modes of symbolism that permeate organization may well in the end prove to be one of the most challenging realms within which the organization theorist can work. For the phenomenon of organization itself can be seen as having deep symbolic significance, as the paper by Walter in this volume suggests. He focuses on the symbolization of narcissism in organizational life as a reflection of unresolved unconscious processes in the psyches of organizational members. Modern organization, though perhaps consciously designed in specific ways, can be seen as giving concrete form to a much deeper unconscious set of concerns that embody significant structural relationships. Just as work can be seen as having some form of unconscious symbolic significance for the modern workaholic, so too the general phenomenon of organization for those concerned to organize. In its Western form organization embodies a concern to dominate and order the world in a way in which humans are in control. As we will discuss later, the work of psychoanalysts such as Freud and Jung have much to contribute to our understanding of the status of organization and various modes or organizational symbolism from this point of view.

Interpretations of Symbols May Not be Shared

The above discussion of organizational symbolism already points to the importance of the idea that symbols may be very elusive and ephemeral, because they may not always be shared. The centrality of this point is obvious from our definition of symbolism, which stresses the importance of subjective meaning, but it is as well that it be given specific attention. Symbols may be highly individualized, capturing a significant pattern of meaning for perhaps just one or two people; on the other hand, they may have an almost universal symbolic significance. A souvenir which is kept as a reminder of a particular organizational experience provides us with an example of a symbol which may be symbolic for just a single person, evoking personal images of the experience; an organizational logo or motto provides an example of a symbol conveying a meaning that is more widely shared. Symbolic meaning may be created on an ad hoc basis, e.g., through a person inventing an excuse or story to account for why he or she was not able to be present at a given meeting, or may have more enduring form, e.g., a ritual kind of excuse or story that is frequently summoned by people to justify action. We are identifying here a dimension which relates to whether symbols are private or public, an issue which is further explored in the paper by Wexler.

Symbols may also convey different and sometimes contradictory patterns of meaning to different people. This is an important point which must always be borne in mind in symbolic analysis, and one which re-emphasizes the fact that symbols are socially constructed as symbols. As our earlier definition suggested, symbols arise when individuals vest aspects of their world with a particular pattern of subjective meaning. It follows quite logically from this that individuals may vest the same phenomena with different patterns of meaning. Thus, to return to an example presented earlier, the gold watch presented by management to a long serving worker in order to symbolize a good record of service, may be seen in the eyes of others as a symbol of subservience and excessive loyalty to the organization; it may symbolize the way in which the worker has been exploited by the organization—"25 years of bondage for a gold watch!". Again, the manager who goes out of his way to extend an untypical degree of cordiality to his workers, e.g., by visiting the factory floor and shaking hands in a spontaneous act of good feeling, may be seen quite differently by others. The handshake which he uses to symbolize goodwill may be perceived by others to symbolize the onset of some form of manipulative ploy.

Many patterns of symbolic construction have this contradictory character, created to express one pattern of meaning but reconstituted in the eyes of others to conform with other patterns of meaning. Many organizations consciously attempt to create complex symbol systems which are intended to signify the desirability of engaging in rigorous patterns of rational, instrumental and pragmatic action. Symbols reinforcing the pursuit of excellence, achievement, aggressiveness, competitiveness and intense commitment to organizational ends provide good examples here. While intended by management to symbolize the characteristics of success, and to encourage pursuit of success, for some organizational members they may stand as a symbolic structure which expresses their perceived inferiority and inability to cope. When constituted in this way, the dominating nature of the symbol system may encourage the individual to withdraw from the organization (which may be what management wants), to acquiesce, or attempt to subvert and change the symbol system. In some cases, the effects of such symbol systems may be constituted as so domineering that they have tragic personal consequences for the individual dominated by them, resulting sometimes in suicide (Cohen, 1973), the most extreme form of withdrawal from domination. Arthur Miller (1949) in *Death of a Salesman*, dramatizes most eloquently this response to domination.

The experiences of minority groups within organizations also provide graphic illustrations of the way symbol systems may have a many-sided character, and serve to reinforce traditional patterns of social domination. A good example here is presented by Schrank (1977) who describes the experiences of two women and three men on a raft which travelled down the Rogue River in Oregon. Though he does not fully unravel the symbol structure of male dominated organizations, he provides a very insightful description of the way in which the male members of the raft team (of which he was a member) created an organization in which the female members were unable to function as equal members and eventually fell back upon passive, dependent roles. Schrank describes how the males through actions, gestures, and language (e.g., holding the arms of the women to help them up river banks despite protestations of "not being helpless," grabbing travel bags from the women and telling them not to carry the *heavy* stuff, undermining the leadership role when the women were at the helm through "humorous" put-downs, for example, "why don't we write on the back of your hands 'right' and 'left'?") serve to enact a reality which makes effective action difficult. Schrank points out in his article that it was only after the group was disbanded and he was back in his working organization, reflecting upon why the group failed to function effectively, that he recognized the subtle domination of the women which had occurred in the system the males constituted on the raft.

Similar processes occur within organizations on an ongoing basis, in relation to all kinds of employees. The symbol system which managers may constitute in the interests of rational, efficient operation, may be constituted by others as a source of oppression and domination. We will return to this point later.

Another issue which must be borne in mind when addressing the intersubjective aspect of symbolism, is that symbols may not be seen as symbolic, and interpreted in almost a literal way far removed from the meaning intended by their creator. In many respects, this is a special case of the point made above, but one worth examining on its own account. In order to do so let us leave the bounds of the organization for a moment, and consider the case of the Japanese garden, which is consciously created to convey a symbolic pattern of meaning. The Japanese symbolize through their circulating gardens the journey of life. Those who understand its symbolic significance can begin their walk on the island of creation, pass along the tree-shaded path of birth into an open and sunny area of childhood. From there the walker is offered a choice of paths, some easy, others difficult, leading to places for mid-life contemplation giving a view of what has already been passed, and to a final resting place in a small forest of miniature shrubs where one's soul can rise above the tree-tops.

The Japanese garden, though rich in symbolic significance, means different things to different people. It generates a distinctive kind of experience for those who understand the symbols, and a pleasant garden walk for those who see, inspect and enjoy it "as a garden". Unlike the splendid office of the senior corporation executive, it does not "shout out" its message in any clear-cut and obvious way. Its significance depends upon one learning to interpret its detailed pattern in the appropriate manner. One can constitute all the different elements in a fairly literal way, e.g., a beautiful waterfall, an elegant bridge, a lovely miniature tree, and even impose some personal pattern of subjective meaning upon these detailed elements, but one misses their more fundamental meaning. So too within the context of organizational symbol systems. An ability to understand organizational life often depends upon one being able to unravel a particular code of interpretation. The simple and obvious organizational events and activities may on detailed examination be seen as part of a much more complex symbolic system expressing a pattern of meaning as rich as that embodied in the Japanese garden.

SOME APPROACHES TO THE STUDY OF ORGANIZATIONAL SYMBOLISM

As will no doubt be clear from the above analysis, the topic of organizational symbolism constitutes a rich and challenging field of inquiry. A recognition that there is a symbolic aspect pervading all organizational life opens the door to so many questions and forms of investigation, that it is likely to be difficult to know where to begin. The organization theorist is presented with a problem akin to that faced by a person who wishes to understand the symbolic significance of say, a piece of poetry, a story he or she has read, or who is concerned to unravel the significance of some form of life experience. Upon what should the task of interpretation focus? In what direction should it move?

1. Should it focus upon identifying and classifying the symbols being used?

2. Should it be concerned to identify the functions which the different symbols are intended to serve?

3. Should it focus on the information content of the different symbols, and attempt to map them in some way?

4. Should it be mainly concerned with understanding the effect which the symbols are likely to have on the state of mind, feelings and behavior of those who encounter the symbolism?

5. Should it be concerned with seeing and understanding the use of symbolism as a reflection of the cultural milieu to which the symbol creator and user belongs?

6. Should it be more concerned with the pattern of subjective meaning to which the symbolism is attempting to give form?

7. Should it be more concerned with understanding the symbolism as a lived experience—something which has deeply influenced its creator and which he or she is now attempting to evoke and share with others?

8. Should it be concerned with understanding the rule-like nature of the symbolism and the methods through which the symbols are used to sustain a particular mode of experience?

9. Should it be more concerned with understanding the way in which the symbolism creates an opportunity for its "readers" to re-interpret the symbols and recreate their own individual patterns of significant meaning?

10. Should it be more concerned with understanding the deep structural significance of the symbolism and attempt to reveal the way in which the symbols used express universal images or archetypes emanating from the unconscious mind, amenable to some form of psychoanalytic interpretation?

11. Should the symbolism be viewed as an ideological statement, utilizing different kinds of symbolic imagery as a means of extolling the virtues, or expressing and transcending the anguish and trauma inherent in a particular mode of life?

12. Should the symbols be viewed as mystifying delusions, expressions and signs of a disturbed mind?

Our intention in focussing upon this illustration is to identify some of the problems which arise when an attempt is made to analyze symbolic constructs of any kind. As will be clear from the questions posed above, many different approaches are open to those who wish to understand symbolism, each of which raises different sorts of issues and guides attention in different ways. So too in relation to the study and interpretation of modes of organizational symbolism. Organizational symbols can be seen, defined and studied in different ways, according to the orientation which the researcher brings to bear upon the subject of inquiry. The study of organizational symbolism is rich in possibilities, some of which may have more to commend themselves than others, but all of which succeed in throwing some light upon the subject of investigation. For the researcher interested in the study of organizational symbolism, as indeed any other area of social inquiry, the message is that there are many legitimate ways in which he or she can proceed.

As a means of formalizing some of these ways here, the remainder of this section will identify a number of different perspectives providing alternative frameworks for organizing the researcher's approach.

Figure 1 presents a model suggesting that symbols and symbolism can be studied on the basis of different assumptions (or paradigms), shaped into specific theoretical form on the basis of different kinds of metaphorical insight. The rationale for examining social phenomena in this way has been fully developed by Burrell and Morgan (1979), and Morgan (1980). The core of their argument is that whenever a social scientist studies the social world, he or she does so upon the basis of assumptions which, though often implicit and taken for granted, shape the kind of questions which are asked, and define the mode of investigation adopted. The functionalist, interpretive, radical humanist, and radical structuralist paradigms favor different kinds of metaphors as a basis of theory building, posing different kinds of research question, and generating very different kinds of insight. A functionalist approach to symbolism encourages a view of symbols as carriers of information and meaning, and places emphasis on discovering the spontaneous functions which they play in the maintenance of social order. From an interpretive perspective symbols are viewed as the essential medium through which individuals create their world, and theory and research is oriented towards understanding the processes through which this occurs. The radical humanist approach focuses on how this process may have pathological tendencies, with individuals enacting their realities through the medium of symbolic forms in ways that are oppressive and alienating. The radical structuralist theorist interested in symbolic forms studies the way in which symbolic constructs are utilized as forms of ideological control in the interests of ruling elites, and sustaining the status quo against the pressure of inherent system contradictions favouring radical forms of social transformation. The following review seeks to identify how these perspectives can help us understand symbols and symbolism, and to indicate some of the research which already exists.

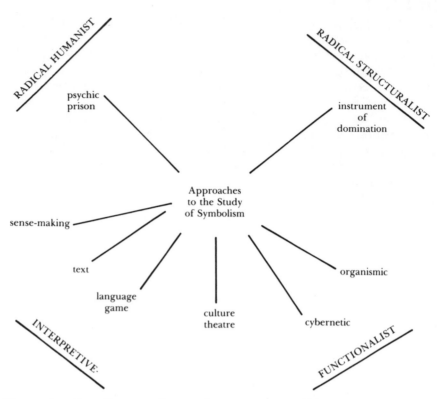

**Figure 1.   Paradigms and metaphors: some possible approaches to the
study of organizational symbolism.**

Functionalist Approaches

We will begin our review of possible approaches with a focus on some
of the insights generated by the *culture* metaphor. Developed primarily
within the realm of anthropology, this metaphor draws attention to the
way in which organizations can be seen as miniature societies with a
distinctive social structure, reflected in various patterns of action, language, discourse, laws, roles, ritual, custom, ceremony, norms, folklore,
stories, beliefs, myths, etc. These patterns of activity constitute symbolic
constructions which embody significant networks of meaning, through
which patterns of social life are enacted, understood and sustained.
When organizations are studied as cultures, attention is thus drawn to a
set of features which may escape the attention of the researcher who
views the organization as a formal structure designed to achieve rational

ends. The culture metaphor emphasizes that organizations are full of social life, and encourages the researcher to study them from this point of view.

Two broad approaches may be adopted here, one drawing upon assumptions characteristic of the functionalist paradigm, the other upon the interpretive paradigm. Both approaches seek to identify and document the various symbolic forms through which the culture of an organization expresses itself, and identify the patterns of subjective meaning embodied in the content and context of cultural practice. The functionalist researcher then typically seeks to discover the role which each aspect of cultural practice plays in sustaining the culture as an ongoing system, placing a great deal of emphasis upon the functions which meaning systems perform. This perspective is inherited from anthropology, which in its early days modelled its theories upon organismic metaphors. The interpretive approach on the other hand takes the existence of all aspects of the culture as problematic, and seeks to understand the methods and practices by which its elements are created and sustained through ongoing interpretive processes, which construct and reconstruct the culture as a realm of significant meaning. From the interpretive point of view significant meaning is embodied in the symbolic actions which create the culture; from the functionalist perspective these symbolic actions are viewed as means oriented to the wider end of system survival. While this point may seem a very fine one when viewed in the abstract, it is of great significance insofar as the conduct of research practice is concerned. The distinctions are well illustrated in the functionalist approach of Firth (1973) and the interpretive approach of Geertz (1973). Within the field of organization studies the work of Turner (1971) and many of the papers in this volume give general indications of what may be possible using this metaphor.

The *theatrical* (or *dramaturgical*) metaphor can also be used as a basis for the study of organizational symbolism from functionalist and interpretive perspectives. Here, attention is focussed on how human beings utilize symbols as a means of dramatizing the ritual and routine of everyday interaction. Human action is viewed as unfolding through theatrical modes of presentation to an audience of some kind, either real or imaginary. Goffman (1959) presents the outstanding functionalist exposition of the manner in which the theatrical metaphor can serve as a model for this kind of social analysis. Numerous studies of symbolic action building upon a somewhat behavioral interpretation of the ideas of G. H. Mead (see, for example, some of the readings in Manis & Meltzer 1967; Rose 1962) also provide useful examples of how the use and manipulation of symbols underlie the management of affairs in many walks of social life. Young, (1965) has presented an analysis of ritual in similar terms, emphasizing how continuing patterns of social life have to be conspicuously affirmed through dramatized modes of performance. It is often not sufficient for activities to be performed, so that given ends are fulfilled; it is the nature of the way in which they are performed that is sometimes all important, for the manner of performance reinforces or contravenes a whole range of symbolic meaning associated with the event in question. The relevance of such approaches to the analysis of organizational symbolism should be clear. For organizations are pre-eminently involved with the business of impression management, in relation to the general public, other corporations, consumers, employees, government, and other significant actors capable of influencing their well being. Individuals too are required to produce and sustain appropriate symbolic images of their relation to "the organization", their managers, colleagues and the like. Modifying the words of the well known song, the theatrical approach to organizational symbolism suggests very clearly that "There's no business *without* showbusiness".

The more phenomenological approach to symbolic interaction characteristic of the interpretive paradigm also has much to offer, since this is primarily concerned to show how action is *always* symbolic, and depends upon the use of symbols for its very existence. Illustrated in quite different ways in the work of Blumer (1969) and Burke (1968), it tells us much about the process through which action is constructed and made meaningful, rather than simply how action can be managed and manipulated, which tends to be the main concern of the functionalist theorist. It may thus contribute a great deal to our knowledge of the underlying structure of organizational activities and the way they are sustained through the use of various modes of symbolic action.

A *cybernetic* approach to the study of symbolism tends to place principal emphasis upon symbols as codes for the transmission of information within society. In this sense, symbols are treated as signs which convey significant messages to the individuals which use and interact with them. Considerable emphasis is placed upon the role which the transmission of information plays in the creation of negative feedback, as a basis for self regulation and control. This perspective is well illustrated in the analysis of ritual offered by Rappaport (1971), who offers a cybernetic interpretation of the manner in which the performance of symbolic rites and ceremonies contribute to the creation of social systems which enjoy a harmonious balance both internally, and in relation to their ecological context.

The special significance of the symbols utilized in ritual here, lies in the importance of their message for the creation of negative feedback. A ritual may serve to emphasize, for example, the danger associated with a particular kind of social action, thus contributing to its elimination. Different kinds of ritual and symbolic forms are seen as transmitting different kinds of such functional messages, as a means of fostering a balanced state of social affairs. The cybernetic approach to symbolism is also well illustrated in a growing body of psychological research which has concerned itself with the role which symbols play in human memory. Paivio (1971) provides a good illustration of the perspective involved here, focussing upon the way in which verbal and non-verbal symbolic images act as memory codes and mediators of behavior, offering a modified form of behaviorism which tends to view human beings as information processors, receiving signals from their environment in the form of stimuli, storing information through the means of appropriate imagery, drawing upon the stock of information (experience) thus stored in memory, and aligning action accordingly. Cybernetics, the key perspective underlying the development of electronic computers, within the realm of psychology leads to a view of "computer man" with a data bank of significant symbols. Clearly, both kinds of cybernetic approaches described above lend themselves to applications within organizational contexts. The symbolic aspects of information systems, and the information aspects of symbolic systems both can be analyzed in cybernetic terms as can the role played by symbols in organizational decision making.

Approaches to symbolism based upon the *organismic* metaphor tend to focus upon the role and functions which symbols play in the survival and effective operation of the system of which they are part. As noted earlier, this metaphor has had a large influence on early developments in anthropology, giving rise to the classic "functionalist perspective". As such the organismic metaphor is often closely linked to the culture metaphor; the culture metaphor focusses attention upon the importance of symbolic discourse, and the organismic metaphor is implicitly used to study the nature of that discourse.

The organismic metaphor has also influenced psychological approaches to the study of symbolism concerned with the explanation and prediction of behavior. These approaches often treat symbols as being equivalent to signs, under-emphasizing the significance of the subjective meaning embedded in the symbols and the role which this may play in sustaining a cultural pattern. This is well illustrated in the classic study by Morris (1946), who argues that all that needs to be done to determine the meaning of any sign is determine what habits it produces. Symbols, as a variety of sign, are from this perspective to be described and differentiated in terms of the dispositions to behavior which they cause in their interpreters. In other words, the symbolic world provides another source of stimuli, of causal influences upon behavior.

The implication of organizational symbolism when interpreted from this perspective, is that it is likely to identify new explanatory variables which can be used within the context of orthodox behavioral models. While there can be little doubt that such an approach would enrich traditional behavioral approaches to the study of leadership, motivation, organizational control, effectiveness and the like, by building from concepts grounded in work experience rather than those generated by the researcher, this approach does not capture the full significance and implications of symbolism insofar as symbolism is concerned with the way in which human beings *create* and sustain significant patterns of meaningful action, rather than simply "behave". The central message of symbolism is that humans *act* (symbolically); organisms behave!

The functionalist metaphors considered above approach the study of symbolism from a perspective which is concerned to identify and categorize symbols, the functions they perform, the way they can be manipulated and controlled, the significance of symbolic activity as part of a wider cultural milieu, and the way in which it contributes to the functioning of a wider system, such as an organization. These approaches show ways in which symbolism can contribute to organizational analysis in a very direct and practical way.

Interpretive Approaches

As our discussion of interpretive approaches based upon the culture and theatre metaphors has already begun to show, the interpretive perspective is concerned with questions relating to how symbolic activity is created and sustained as a means of giving shape and form to human life. It is concerned to unravel and understand the way in which social life is constructed as an ongoing activity. It is concerned with understanding the genesis of meaningful action, how individuals make sense of their situations, and thus come to define and share realities which may become objectified in fairly routinized ways. In short, to understand how the objective, taken for granted aspects of everyday life are constituted and made real through the medium of symbolic processes.

The *language game* metaphor provides one important way in which the issues identified above can be addressed. In essence, the metaphor presumes that all forms of symbolic activity can be studied as if they are a form of language, and encourages the researcher to unravel the meaning and significance of the symbols and forms of discourse embedded in different cultural patterns. Language use has a game-like quality, in that it is governed by specific rules and conventions. The metaphor of the language game thus suggests that reality emerges as a rule-governed symbolic structure as individuals engage their worlds through the use of specific "linguistic" codes and practices. This metaphor, which has been brought into prominence through the work of Wittgenstein (1958), has been extended under the influence of Winch (1958, 1964) to cover other forms of non-verbal action, such as ceremony, ritual, law, role activity, etc., which can be seen as possessing similar-rule-governed characteristics. One of the principal features of this metaphor is that it emphasizes the internal coherence of language games, and how the various symbolic practices which they embody must be understood within the context of the game as a whole.

Symbols assume their particular significance and meaning in terms of the wider context of which they are part. Social life, from this point of view, is based upon a whole network of symbolic games which define many different modes of reality. Individuals are to be seen as engaging in different games at different times, thus passing from one mode of reality to another. The task of symbolic analysis when approached upon the basis of the language game metaphor, is to understand how social reality is enacted through different verbal and non-verbal "linguistic" frames of meaning, and through which human beings communicate with one another, and create and sustain shared views of reality. Witherspoon's anthropological work on the Navajo Indians (Witherspoon, 1977) provides us with a clear example of the kind of interpretive approach which is required here. Approaches to the study of organizational symbolism focusing upon the rule governed nature of the verbal and non-verbal languages which sustain particular patterns of organizational activity, are likely to contribute much to our understanding of the multiple realities within and among organizations of all kinds.

The metaphor of the *text* urges that social scientists should view and 'read' social life as if it were a living document. Texts are built up through the use of various kinds of language game, and make much use of various modes of metaphorical expression to convey significant patterns of meaning. They are produced within a historical context, give form to various patterns of subjective meaning which often stem from deep unconscious concerns on the part of the author, expressed in terms of some form of surface discourse—the written words upon a page. The metaphor of a text identifies a number of features which can be seen in social life—surface action within a social context, expressed through various modes of symbolic discourse, shaped and formed through conscious and unconscious patterns of meaning. Social life is in essence an acted text.

This metaphor for social analysis stems from the hermeneutic school of thought, with the work of Ricoeur (1971) providing the clearest statement of what is entailed. The structuralism of Lévi-Strauss, who has concerned himself with understanding how the structure of the symbolic world (as reflected in language, myth, totemism) can be related to the nature of the unconscious mind, is also relevant here. The social world from this point of view reflects a deep structure of ideas of considerable significance for understanding both the nature of human mind and its reflection in the sphere of social action (e.g., Lévi-Strauss, 1963, 1966; see also, Leach, 1970, 1976; Rossi, 1973; Staude, 1976).

Methods of literary criticism also have a great deal to contribute here in showing the way in which the various patterns of symbolic meaning present themselves as a social document for in-depth analysis. Embracing, but in many respects going beyond the metaphor of a language game, the idea of text offers a powerful new perspective for the analysis of organizational symbolism.

The *sense-making* metaphor focuses attention upon the idea that the reality of everyday life must be seen as an ongoing "accomplishment", which takes particular shape and form as individuals attempt to create order and make retrospective sense of the situations in which they find themselves. Drawing upon the core notion of "reflexivity", as emphasized in the phenomenologically oriented work of G. H. Mead (1932, 1934, 1938), Schutz (1964, 1966, 1967a, 1967b), and the ethnomethodology of Garfinkel (1967), individuals are seen as engaged in ongoing processes through which they attempt to make their situations rationally accountable to themselves and to others. Weick (1977) has developed certain implications of this general approach in his discussion of enactment processes in organizations. Symbols, when approached upon the basis of this perspective, assume principal significance as constructs through which individuals concretize and give meaningful form to their everyday lives. The sense-making metaphor encourages an analytical focus upon the processes through which individuals create and use symbols; it focuses attention upon the study of the symbolic process through which reality is created and sustained. Individuals are not seen as living *in*, and acting out their lives in relation *to*, a wider reality, so much as creating and sustaining images of a wider reality, in part to rationalize what they are doing. They realize their reality, by "reading into" their situation patterns of significant meaning. This metaphor has much to tell us about how individuals constitute symbols in different ways.

Much has been made of this point in the discussion of organizational symbolism earlier in this chapter. The same symbols can mean different things to different people, because they are used to make sense of the world in different ways. The meaning rests not in the intrinsic content of the symbol, but in the way in which it is constituted as a symbol.

Radical Humanist Approaches

Approaches to the study of symbolism characteristic of this paradigm draw, in one way or another, upon an image expressed in the metaphor of a *psychic prison*. Human beings are seen as creating and sustaining a world of symbolic form which has alienating properties. This image has been developed in a variety of ways, each of which has distinct implications for the study of organizational symbolism. First, there is a perspective deriving from the "critical theory" tradition originating in the early work of Marx (1975), and Lukács (1971), and developed in the work of theorists of the so called Frankfurt school, such as Fromm (1942, 1962), Marcuse (1955, 1964) and Habermas (1972).

In essence, these theorists view the symbolic world created by modern man as a form of self-laid trap, which channels human consciousness in service of demands imposed by an industrial society dominated by perceived needs to produce and consume as much as possible. Social organization is seen as being created and sustained through a blind adherence to socially created concepts which become concretized and objectified and viewed as imperatives, which are independent of the individual. This process of over-concretization, or reification, is seen as an aspect of the alienation of modern human beings, cut off from their nature and potentialities as members of the human species. Trapped by projections of their own consciousness, their minds in psychic chains which form a conceptual prison from which there seems no escape, the plight of modern human kind is, from the viewpoint of critical theorists, one from which he or she must be set free.

The focus of the critical theory tradition rests upon a "critique" of modes of symbolic domination. Language, rationality, logic, and other modes of symbolic discourse which express the culture of modern industrial societies, both East and West, are scrutinized for their dominating properties, with a view to making human beings more aware of the way in which they are dominated by the modes of discourse in which they are engaged. The modern women's movement provides a good example here, with its emphasis upon consciousness raising as a means of understanding and overcoming the way in which women are exploited in male dominated societies. The language games which humans play (verbal and non-verbal) are from this point of view, "games" of domination. Interpretive metaphors acquire in the radical humanist perspective, an overtly political dimension; the "text" of social life is to be seen as a political document.

The implications of this approach for the study of organizational symbolism are profound. For they urge the social researcher to study organizational symbols with a view to revealing their power dimension, and the process of social domination to which they give form. We have cited above an example relating to the role of women in organizations. As the womens' movement has already begun to show, the language of traditional organization (e.g., *man*ager, chair*man, man*power) transmits codes of expectation as to who is equipped to do what, and an awareness of this process raises consciousness with regard to these processes of domination within organizations which are at least partially sustained through the language used. As suggested earlier, all patterns of cultural activity can be seen as expressing a form of language, and modes of domination may be reflected in many of the less obvious patterns of culture. As an example here, we may cite the way in which "helping" behaviors may serve to define patterns of helplessness, as illustrated in the tale of Schrank (1977) discussed earlier.

The scope for critical analysis of organizational symbolism is wide ranging. The ways in which verbal and non-verbal language defines the role of minority groups in organizations, the relations between managers and managed, white collar and blue collar, all lend themselves to similar consideration as that identified in our example relating to the role of women in organizations. In addition, the "language" of rationality and all its manifestations, from the perspective of the critical theory tradition can be seen as lying at the heart of the process through which power-relationships are sustained in modern industrial society (e.g., Marcuse, 1964).

A second interpretation of the psychic prison metaphor is evident in various psycho-analytic approaches to the study of social life, as reflected in the work of Freud (1922), Jung (1953–1965), and their respective followers. (see, for example, Grotjahn, 1971; Jones, 1917; May, 1960; Whitmont, 1969). The symbolic world from their point of view is to be understood principally in terms of the workings of the unconscious mind, and each have offered rival theories developing the links between the unconscious and the everyday world (Freud, 1930; Jung, 1964). For both Freud and Jung symbols are to be understood as metaphorical constructs, the meaning of which resides not so much in the specific *content* of the symbol, as in its relationship to the unconscious. Thus for Freud, human thought and action gives specific shape and form to the demands of unconscious needs, many of which are set in early childhood.

Freud's theorizing has much to offer in the analysis of organizational symbolism. For example, the unconscious meaning of the manifest actions of organizational members who are preoccupied with rules, control, and relentless programming of activity may perhaps be explored through Freud's personality types—in particular the anal-compulsive type. Formal organization itself from this point of view, may be seen as an objectification of unconscious anal preoccupations. In a similar way, the contemporary social trends towards narcissism noted by some psychoanalysts (Lasch, 1979) can be seen as another expression of deep unconscious concerns that have implications for the role and nature of organizations in modern society. The image underlying these and related ideas is that conscious human activity is trapped, channelled and ultimately controlled by the operation of unconscious processes. This image points towards an important perspective for the understanding of organizational symbolism, which seeks to unravel the relationships between concrete organizational activities and the hidden unconscious concerns to which they give form.

Similarly, Jung's notion of "archetype", used to depict unconscious tendencies or predispositions to enact a reality in accordance with a particular mold or form, may also prove immensely valuable in understanding the unconscious reasons why humans pattern their world in distinctive ways. In creating formal organizations human beings may be merely providing a specific content to an underlying archetype which embodies a predisposition to organize. The specific acts through which we give organizations concrete form, e.g., in defining roles, rules, authority patterns, may, from this point of view, be merely determining the content and conscious detail of an underlying archetype (Jung, 1967, p. 213).

We can illustrate the essentials of the point being made here by returning to the example of the Japanese garden presented earlier, but this time asking the question What about French gardens and English gardens? Unlike the Japanese, the English and French do not consciously vest the design of their gardens with symbolic significance. Nevertheless, they are no less symbolic. Such gardens clearly reflect the Anglo-French pre-occupation for order and method in their neat and open arrangement of paths, borders, trees and shrubs. The English rose garden presents a splendid example of a concern for detailed empiricism—different kinds of roses are clearly named so that the observer can know what he or she is looking at. Interpreted from a Jungian perspective, the English and French may be giving content and concrete empirical form to an unconscious archetype. The same archetype reflected in the gardens can be seen underlying the detailed content expressed in patterns of formal organization. The process of organizing and ordering from this point of view is itself a symbolic act, reflecting deep unconscious concerns to create a particular relationship with the material world.

Jung's work may provide a rich source of inspiration for the theorist who wishes to understand the deep structural significance underlying various patterns of organizational life. We have outlined the possibilities here in the broadest of terms suggesting that the tendency to organize may itself be the manifestation of an archetype. The various modes of symbolic representation which are used to structure the detailed content of organizational life—the myths, stories, folklore, ceremony, tradition, etc.—may themselves also give form to other archetypal modes of experience. The Jungian perspective thus lends itself for the analysis of organizational symbolism in a wide variety of ways.

Radical Structuralist Approaches

The perspective characteristic of this paradigm draws upon various Marxist and radical Weberian approaches to the study of society, discussed in detail in Burrell and Morgan (1979). As in the case of the radical humanist paradigm, human beings in modern society are viewed as being opressed by the nature of the social organization within which they live. For the radical structuralist, this domination is *real*, and not just symbolically constructed as in the case of the radical humanist and interpretive paradigms. Modern organizations are viewed as comprising an important means through which the wider mode of social organization, reflected for example in class structure, is sustained. Organizations are viewed as instruments of domination, manipulated and controlled by ruling interests who dominate other sections of society in pursuit of their own ends, particularly those relating to the accumulation of wealth and power.

Within the context of this domination metaphor (which presents but one aspect of the radical structuralist point of view), symbol systems are viewed and studied as constituent features of social ideology. The metaphor focuses attention upon the way in which a dominant ideology is fostered, manipulated and controlled by those in power, to sustain the socio-economic mode of production upon which the society is based. The radical structuralist message is that all symbols have ideological significance—whether embodied in language, patterns of religious belief, scientific knowledge, patterns of education, political rhetoric, custom, ritual, or whatever. The whole sphere of human culture is seen as a reflection of demands stemming from the nature of the society's underlying mode of productive activity. Ideology seeks to legitimize, and encourage patterns of activity which ensure that a particular set of social relations continue to be produced and reproduced.

This perspective stresses that the social scientist interested in the study of symbolism should focus upon the link between the mode of production and patterns of ideology, with a view to understanding the relationships between them, and the precise mechanisms through which changes in dominant symbol systems are brought about, as part of a wider process of social control. For example, a change in the mode of production upon which a society is based—such as a transition from a domestic to industrial system of production requires that certain changes be achieved in patterns of values, attitudes and behaviors on the part of those who are to work within the new production system. How is this brought about? How are values regarding the importance of regular work, good time keeping, diligence, etc., fostered in the working population? This is the sort of problem which attracts the attention of the radical structuralist interested in the role of ideology, and has been addressed in a number of classic studies. Weber's work on the relationship between capitalism and the protestant work ethic provides an excellent example (Weber, 1958). Bendix's study of the managerial ideologies which support different types of industrial system provides another (Bendix, 1956). Other theorists approaching the subject have focussed upon the way in which ideology may be manipulated by ruling interests (e.g., Schiller, 1973).

Translated to the level of organizational analysis, the perspective has an important role to play in demonstrating the detailed manner in which symbol systems are used to manipulate and shape attitudes of the workforce in the service of organizational ends. As Braverman (1973) has suggested, social science research in the human relations tradition can be seen as having played its part here, not in a philanthropic sense, as its practitioners would have it, but in a more manipulative sense. Braverman sees the human relations movement as a servant of management ideology, working to increase the pleasantness of the cage in which workers are trapped. Others have addressed the way in which ideology supporting the industrial system may be manipulated by the media. The work of the Glasgow University Media Group (1976) which focuses upon the ways in which labour-management relations are handled on television, provides a good illustration.

The way in which managers may consciously manipulate symbols to sustain their power base is well illustrated in Royko's (1971) biography of

Chicago mayor, Richard Daley. Daley's tactics when attacked by minority members of the City Council included waving his arms, shaking his fists, shouting abuse, and invoking Robert's Rules of Order, which he regarded the greatest book ever written. When these tactics failed, he would signal for the critic's microphone to be cut off. Modern managers often work through more subtle methods, but the example serves to make the point. Studies such as Royko's and that of O'Day (1974) on intimidation rituals involving the manipulation of symbols for purposes of domination and control, indicate fruitful avenues for research here.

The symbolism within organizations, and within society as a whole, can be viewed from a radical structuralist perspective in a way which generates many powerful insights. Organizations of all kinds (the media are but a special and very important case example) do much to shape social ideology, and they do so symbolically. The instrument of domination metaphor contributes an approach to organizational symbolism with a special focus upon the political-economy of cultural creation.

ORGANIZATIONAL SYMBOLISM: PROSPECTS AND POSSIBILITIES

The central message of our overall analysis is loud and clear. The subject of organizational symbolism presents the interested theorist and researcher with a rich and open field, and there are many different ways in which it can be approached. The process of symbolization is a widespread generic activity which characterizes the very nature of being human. Human beings are distinguished from all other living species by their ability to create and use symbols as a basis of discourse, and as a means of forging their individual lives. As such, it would seem that any social science concerned to do justice to the fact that it is dealing with the study of human beings, should accord the subject of symbolism a high place in their interests and concerns. So too in relation to the study of organization.

Our analysis suggests that symbolism pervades every aspect of organizational life, for it is through the medium of symbolic processes that humans engage and give form and meaning to their world. Even in those realms of life which are frequently identified as having a purely literal or instrumental significance, some form of underlying symbolic structure is evident. We have illustrated this point in many ways, e.g., through the English and French gardens, which reveal an underlying preoccupation for order and method; through the routine organizational activities which may symbolize patterns of domination for those working under their influence; through the language of organizational life which though seeking to convey literal meanings, also serves to constitute a particular pattern of symbolic meaning—the reality which it defines and sustains.

The implication of this point may be boldly stated. Every topic which the organizational researcher studies has a symbolic aspect of some kind. Whether approaching the study of leadership, motivation, communication, control, politics and power, organization structure, organizational change, or whatever, symbolic processes are at work. As such, they need to be taken into account.

The perspectives presented earlier in this chapter introduce a number of possible ways in which this can be done. The orthodoxy within organization studies has largely been developed upon the basis of mechanical, organismic and cybernetic metaphors characteristic of the functionalist paradigm. One obvious way in which symbolism can begin to be brought into account is by devoting attention to it within the frameworks defined by these traditional metaphors. Thus, it may be possible to treat symbols and symbolic processes as variables within established modes of analysis, and no doubt enrich these modes in significant ways. For example, behavioral models could take more account of the creation and use of symbols in attempting to understand patterns of behavior. Open systems models could pay more specific attention to the function which symbols play in adaptive processes. Cybernetics could give more attention to the study of symbol systems from an information processing point of view. These areas of study have over the last few years become increasingly aware of the need to take more account of the subjective meaning conveyed in patterns of verbal and non-verbal action. An awareness of the nature and importance of symbolic processes would help them to formulate the issues involved here in a clear and consistent way.

However, the real challenge goes well beyond this sphere, for the very existence of symbolism as a generic human process questions the adequacy of metaphors drawn from the natural sciences as frames of inquiry in the human sciences. If we take our earlier analysis of the nature of symbolism seriously, then we need to develop theoretical schemes which are capable of unravelling the complex way in which social life is constructed and sustained through the medium of symbolic forms. Mechanical and organismic metaphors may be extended to focus attention upon what we have described as simple conscious and unconscious symbols, as variables, but they are not so well-equipped for dealing with the more complex conscious and unconscious sets of symbols which manifest themselves throughout organizational life in the most intricate and subtle of ways. Such manifestations of the symbolic process do not lend themselves for treatment as variables which can be plugged into traditional models of analysis. They call for new approaches, based upon metaphors capable of capturing the way in which symbolism defines the very nature of human life.

Earlier analysis has identified a number of different approaches which can contribute here. The culture, theatre, language game, text and sense-making metaphors generate theoretical and practical insights relevant to understanding the way in which humans utilize symbols to create meaningful organizational realities. They offer different perspectives upon symbolism, which start from the premise that humans are preeminently the creators and users of symbolism in organizational life. They allow the researcher to go beyond the idea that symbols are variables influencing human behavior and the functioning of a wider social system, to explore the idea that such behavior and system characteristics represent no more than enacted symbolic forms.

The metaphors characteristic of radical humanist and radical structuralist paradigms also open important new directions for the analysis of organizational symbolism. Paying particular attention to the way in which symbols concretize social forces emanating either from the unconscious mind, or the power structure of the culture in which they are expressed, these perspectives offer powerful new modes of organizational analysis. In an era when the legitimacy of so many established symbol systems characteristic of the Western way of life are being challenged in fundamental ways, e.g., those relating to the role of rationality, the work ethic, of women, of consumerism, of managerial prerogatives, the relevance and importance of these perspectives is clear. They open up important new avenues for research, which encourage the organization theorist to extend his or her focus of analysis to understand the symbolic significance of the broad structure or mode or organization through which social relations are given form. Whereas perspectives within the interpretive and functionalist paradigms are often exclusively concerned with understanding the detailed empirical content of organizational forms, the radical humanist and radical structuralist approaches draw more attention to the symbolic significance of the broader social framework in which the details of content are set.

Hopefully, our discussion of these different perspectives for the study of organizational symbolism will serve to provide the interested theorist and researcher with a concrete point of departure, and identify some of the different directions in which he or she can go. Some of the perspectives which we have identified, particularly those which are inclined to treat symbols as variables, lend themselves to development through the use of fairly conventional methodologies. However, it is important to emphasize that it is not possible to tap the rich and full potential which the study of symbolism offers through such means. Insofar as one recognizes that social life is primarily a symbolic activity, then a logic of inquiry based upon the discovery of lawful relations between "objectively" defined variables becomes problematic. For clearly the research process itself must be recognized as being a symbolic activity. Theorists and researchers of all kinds are architects of symbolic schemes, through which they attempt to understand the reality to which these schemes are applied. Empirical research based upon scientific techniques of investigation are no exception here, producing in Langer's words "a structure of facts that are symbols and laws that are their meanings" (Langer, 1957, p. 21).

The logic of symbolism points towards the importance of adopting modes of inquiry which are interpretive rather than law seeking, and for the researcher to be fully aware of the significance of the role which he or she is playing in the research process. Fortunately, research experience outside the realm or organization theory is well-versed in the problems involved here. One of the important challenges to the researcher interested in organizational symbolism will be to tap and make good use of this experience. Modern research within the fields of semiology, linguistics, hermeneutics, psychoanalysis, critical theory, interpretive sociology, interpretive anthropology and the like, will be highly relevant, as will the better known and more accessible qualitative research techniques of ethnography and symbolic interactionism (See Morgan, 1983).

The researcher interested in studying organizational symbolism thus faces the dual challenge of adopting theoretical and methodological approaches to analysis which are true to the nature of symbolism as a generic social process. The possibilities are rich, and the prospects encouraging for researchers with the imagination, inventiveness, and dedication necessary to make the study of organizational symbolism their own. We hope that the papers presented in this volume will contribute in some way towards a richer and more realistic understanding of the symbolism inherent in the very texture of organizational life.

REFERENCES

Barthes, R. *Elements of semiology*. London: Jonathan Cape, 1964.

Bendix, R. *Work and authority in industry*. New York: Wiley, 1956.

Blumer, H. *Symbolic interactionism: Perspective and method*. Englewood Cliffs, N.J.: Prentice-Hall, 1969.

Braverman, H. *Labour and monopoly capital*. London: Monthly Review Press, 1974.

Burke, K. Dramatism. In David L. Sills (Ed.), *International encyclopedia of the social sciences*. New York: Macmillan and The Free Press, 1968.

Burrell, G., & Morgan, G. *Sociological paradigms and organizational analysis*. London and Exeter NH: Heinemann, 1979.

Cohen, P. *The gospel according to The Harvard Business School*. New York: Doubleday, 1973.

Duncan, H. *Language and literature in society*. Chicago: University of Chicago Press, 1953.

Firth, R. *Symbols: Public and private*. Ithaca, N.Y.: Cornell University Press, 1973.

Freud, S. *A general introduction to psychoanalysis*. New York: Liveright, 1922.

Freud, S. Civilization and its discontents. In *The complete works of Sigmund Freud* (Vol. 21). Toronto: Hogarth Press, 1930.

Fromm, E. *Fear of freedom*. London: Routledge & Kegan Paul, 1942.

Fromm, E. *Beyond the chains of illusion: My encounter with Marx and Freud*. New York: Trident Press, 1962.

Frost, P. J., Mitchell, V. F., & Nord, W. R. (Eds.). *Organizational Reality*. Santa Monica: Goodyear, 1978.

Garfinkel, H. *Studies in ethnomethodology*. Englewood Cliffs, N.J.: Prentice-Hall, 1967.

Geertz, C. *The interpretation of cultures*. New York: Basic Books, 1973.

Glasgow University Media Group. *Bad news*. London: Routledge & Kegan Paul, 1976.

Goffman, E. *The presentation of self in everyday life*. New York: Doubleday, 1959.

Grotjahn, M. *The voice of the symbol*. Los Angeles: Mara Books, 1971.

Habermas, J. *Knowledge and human interests*, London: Heinemann, 1972.

Jones, E. W. What it's like to be a black manager. *Harvard Business Review*, 1973, (July–August), 108–116.

Jones, E. The theory of symbolism. *British Journal of Psychology*, 1917, *9*, 181–229.

Jung, C. G. *Collected works*. London: Routledge & Kegan Paul, 1953–65.

Jung, C. G. *Man and his symbols*. London: Aldus Books, 1964.

Jung, C. G. *Memories, dreams, reflections*. London: Routledge & Kegan Paul, 1967.

Kanter, R. M., & Stein, B. A. *Life in organizations: Workplaces as people experience them*. New York: Basic Books, 1979.

Langer, S. K. *Philosophy in a new key*. Cambridge: Harvard University Press, 1957.

Lasch, C. *The culture of narcissism*. New York: Warner, 1979.

Leach, E. *Lévi-Strauss*. London: Fontana, 1970.

Leach, E. *Culture and communication*. London: Cambridge University Press, 1976.

Lévi-Strauss, C. *Structural anthropology*. New York: Basic Books, 1963.

Lévi Strauss, C. *The savage mind*. London: Weidenfield & Nicholson, 1966.

Lukács, G. *History and Class Consciousness*. London, Merlin Press, 1971.

Manis, J. G., & Meltzer, B. M. (Eds.). *Symbolic interaction*. Boston: Allyn & Bacon, 1967.

Marcuse, H. *Eros and civilization*. Boston: Beacon Press, 1955.

Marcuse, H. *One dimensional man*. Boston: Beacon Press, 1964.

Marx, K. Economic and philosophical manuscripts. In *Early writings*, Harmondsworth: Penguin, 1975.

May, R. The significance of symbols. In R. May (Ed.), *Symbolism in religion and literature*. New York: George Braziller, 1960.

Mead, G. H. *The philosophy of the present*. (A. E. Murphy, Ed.) Chicago: Open Court, 1932.

Mead, G. H. *Mind, self and society*. (Charles Morris, Ed.) Chicago: University of Chicago Press, 1934.

Mead, G. H. *The philosophy of the act*. (Charles Morris, Ed.) Chicago: University of Chicago Press, 1938.

Meltzer, B. M., Petras, J., & Reynolds, L. *Symbolic interactionism: Genesis, varieties, and criticism*. London: Routledge & Kegan Paul, 1975.

Miller, A. *Death of a salesman*. New York: Viking-Penguin, 1949.

Morgan, G. Paradigms, metaphors and puzzle-solving in organization theory. *Administrative Science Quarterly*, 1980, *25*, 605–622.

Morgan, G. (Ed). *Beyond method: Strategies for social research*. Beverley Hills: Sage, 1983.

Morgan, G., & Smircich, L. The case for qualitative research. *Academy of Management Review*, 1980, *5*, 491–500.

Morris, C. *Signs, language and behavior*. Englewood Cliffs, N.J.: Prentice-Hall, 1946.

O'Day, R. Intimidation rituals: Reactions to reform. *Journal of Applied Behavioral Science*, 1974, *10*, 373–386.

Paivio, A. *Imagery and verbal process*. New York: Holt, Rinehart & Winston, 1971.

Pondy, L. R., & Mitroff, I. Beyond open system models of organization. In B. M. Staw (Ed.), *Research in organizational behavior* (Vol. 1). Greenwich, Conn.: JAI Press, 1979.

Rappaport, R. A. Ritual, sanctity, and cybernetics. *American Anthropologist*, 1971, *73*, 59–76.

Ricoeur, P. The model of the text: Meaningful action considered as a text. *Social Research*, 1971, *39*, 529–562.

Rose, A. *Human behavior and social processes*. London: Routledge & Kegan Paul, 1962.

Rossi, I. The unconscious in the anthropology of Claude Lévi-Strauss. *American Anthropologist*, 1973, 20–48.

Royko, M. *Boss: Richard J. Daley of Chicago*. New York: Dutton, 1971.

Schiller, H. I. *The Mind Managers*. Boston: Beacon Press, 1973.

Schrank, R. Two women, three men on a raft. *Harvard Business Review*, 1977, (May-June), 100–106.

Schutz, A. *Collected papers II: Studies in social theory*. The Hague: Martinus Nijhoff, 1964.

Schutz, A. *Collected papers III: Studies in phenomenological philosophy*. The Hague: Martinus Nijhoff, 1966.

Schutz, A. *Collected papers I: The problem of social reality* (2nd ed.). The Hague: Martinus Nijhoff, 1967. (a)

Schutz, A. *The phenomenology of the social world*. Evanston: Northwestern University Press, 1967. (b)

Sperber, D. *Rethinking symbolism*. Cambridge: Cambridge University Press, 1975.

Staude, J. R. From depth psychology to depth sociology: Freud, Jung and Levi Strauss. *Theory and Society*, 1976, *3*, 303–338.

Turner, B. A. *Exploring the industrial subculture*. London: Macmillan, 1971.

Weber, M. *The Protestant Ethic and the spirit of capitalism*. (Talcott Parsons, Trans.) New York: Scribners, 1958.

Weick, K. E. Enactment processes in organizations. In B. M. Straw & G. R. Salancik (Eds.), *New directions in organizational behavior*. Chicago: St. Clair Press, 1977.

Whitehead, A. N. *Symbolism: Its meaning and effect*. New York: Macmillan, 1927.

Whitmont, E. C. *The symbolic quest: Basic concepts of analytical psychology*. New York: B. P. Putnam & Sons, 1969.

Winch, P. *The idea of a social science*. London: Routledge & Kegan Paul, 1958.

Winch, P. Understanding a primitive society. *American Philosophical Quarterly*, 1964, *1*, 307–324.

Witherspoon, G. *Language and art in the Navajo universe*. Ann Arbor: University of Michigan Press, 1977.

Wittgenstein, L. *Philosophical Investigations*. (G. Anscombe, Trans.) Oxford: Basil Blackwell, 1958.

Young, F. W. *Initiation ceremonies: A cross cultural study of status dramatization*. New York: Bobbs Merril, 1965.

Part II

ORGANIZATIONS:
A CULTURAL PERSPECTIVE

In Part II we present two discussions of an approach to the study of organization based on the culture metaphor. Meryl Louis in *Organizations as culture-bearing milieux* argues for the development of a broad conceptual framework for the study of cultural processes *in* organizations, and of cultural aspects *of* organizational phenomena. She presents a sociological and a psychological context for the study of organizational culture, and discusses several ways in which organizations can be seen as culture-bearing milieux.

In *Organizations as shared meanings,* Linda Smircich provides an empirical analysis of the organizational culture in an insurance company. She discusses the way shared meanings develop and are sustained in organized contexts through the use of various symbolic processes, such as organizational rituals, vocabulary, slogans, and presidential style. She argues that common grounds for organized action and inaction rest in the beliefs of organizational members and the patterns of meaning which these sustain.

ORGANIZATIONS AS CULTURE-BEARING MILIEUX

Meryl Reis Louis

Any social group, to the extent that it is a distinctive unit, will have to some degree a culture differing from that of other groups, a somewhat different set of common understandings around which action is organized, and these differences will find expression in a language whose nuances are peculiar to that group. Members of churches speak differently from members of tavern groups; more importantly, members of any particular church or tavern group have cultures, and languages in which they are expressed, which differ somewhat from those of other groups of the same general type (Becker & Geer, 1970, p. 134).

My aim in this paper is to present a view of organizations as culture-bearing milieux, that is, as distinctive social units possessed of a set of common understandings for organizing action (e.g., what we're doing together in this particular group, appropriate ways of doing in and among members of the group) and languages and other symbolic vehicles for expressing common understandings. The timeliness of such a view is indicated in several trends in the organizational sciences. First, there has been a growing dissatisfaction with traditional research efforts, especially those grounded in essentially positivistic views of organizations. Many have become disillusioned with fundamental inadequacies in traditional methods and the meager grasp and leverage on organiza-

39

tional phenomena they have provided (Silverman, 1970; Burrell & Morgan, 1979; Pondy & Mitroff, 1979; Van Maanen, 1979b; Evered & Louis, 1981).

Simultaneously, there has been a groundswell of interest in things cultural in organizations. Organizational researchers have undertaken studies of symbols, myths, legends and metaphors, of language systems and other artifacts of organizational cultures (Clarke, 1970; Mitroff & Kilmann, 1976; Wilkins & Martin, 1979; Dandridge, Mitroff & Joyce, 1980; Evered, in this volume, pp. 125–143). Additionally, there has been an increasing concern with cognitive processes of individuals in organizations, with issues of how individuals make meaningful their interactions and encounters in daily organization life (Van Maanen, 1979a; Weick, 1979; Louis, 1980b).

A final impetus for developing a cultural view of organizations stems from a practical problem faced by increasing numbers of organizational participants. With the rising rate of voluntary turnover at all organizational levels has come a greater appreciation for cultural aspects of organizations by participants. Specifically, recognition of the need to become acculturated, to "learn the ropes," when entering an unfamiliar organizational setting suggests that some cultural stratum is present in any organization, and that its mastery is critical for the well-functioning of new organizational members (Schutz, 1964; Van Maanen, 1977; Louis, 1980a, 1980b).

The concept of culture is not new. It has long been used by anthropologists, among others, in studying ethnic and/or national groups through ethnographic and cross-cultural research. For example, Beres & Portwood (1979, p. 141) have proposed a comprehensive model of the influence of ethnic/national culture in the development of an individual's frame of reference and, in particular, orientations to work. They define culture as a "cognitive frame of reference and a pattern of behavior transmitted to members of a group from previous generations of the group," emphasize the role of socialization in the transmission of culture, suggest the need to consider psychological, social and historical dimensions, review deficiencies in cross-cultural research, and provide results of a test of one segment of the model. Although organizational (versus ethnic) culture is not considered per se, their paper offers a recent perspective on cross-cultural research and a conceptualization of cultural influence processes (or, more appropriately, factors in the process) directly relevant to work on organizational culture.

What is new and what is my particular aim here is to map dimensions of culture relevant in organizations and to suggest that researchers incorporate a cultural view of organizations into the repertoire of perspectives on organizations. The discussion will focus on several questions: What constitutes a cultural perspective? What are psychological and sociological processes and contexts of cultural phenomena in organizations? And in what ways are organizations culture-bearing milieux? While this effort is necessarily exploratory (we are just beginning to map the territory and this will be a brief essay), the purpose is to broadly consider what a cultural view of organizations might entail.[1]

A CULTURAL PERSPECTIVE

The idea of culture rests on the premise that the full meaning of things is not given a priori in the things themselves. Instead, meaning results from interpretation. Consider, for instance, a hiker encountering a fallen tree. The significance to the hiker of a tree laying across the trail depends on whether he is idly strolling through the morning woods, scouting ahead for hazards for other hikers on a pack train, making a getaway from a minimum security prison, or surveying drought damage in the forest. Whether the hiker views the fallen tree as the result of drought or of prison guards and, more basically, whether causes of the tree falling are relevant, depend on the larger historical and situational contexts of the hiker. The meaning as the significance of some event, utterance, etc. may derive from any of several aspects of the situation in which meaning is to be assigned. Meaning may involve definition, consequence, antecedents, and/or intention (Black, 1962, p. 193), as the example of the hiker demonstrates.

In a cultural view, meaning is produced through an *in situ* interpretive process. The process encompasses universal, cultural and individual levels of interpretation. The universal level refers to the broad set of objective or physically feasible meanings or relevances of each thing. For instance, universally speaking, dogs can be eaten, worshipped or befriended, but not flown. These basic physical constraints are what Weick (1979) referred to as "grains of truth."

The cultural level refers to the set of potential meanings or relevances indigenous to the local social group. In one sense, this local code is a subset of the universal set of feasible relevances. In another sense, the local code is an elaboration of the universal set. Each of the objective or physically feasible meanings may be exploded into a whole range of meanings. For instance, consider the myriad social meanings of dog in our society—companion, family member, guide dog for the blind, shepherd, guard dog, drug detective. This array of meanings derives less from objective features or universal meanings of the creature dog and more from the creative differentiation from universal meanings into contextually relevant cultural meanings. The cultural code describes the repertoire of meanings that may appropriately be assigned to a thing by members of the particular social system. That, strictly speaking, dogs are befriended, but not eaten or worshipped in 1980 America reflects the code of relevances for dog in our Western culture.

The final level in interpretation is the individual one. Here the person's idiosyncratic adaptation of cultural codes leads to a set of personal codes of relevance. In turn, personal codes are applied in the moment of encountering a thing and meaning is produced. Whether you greet or run from the dog in front of you at this moment depends on your history with dogs and your recognition of this one as your neighbor's friendly puppy.

So, from the universe of feasible relevances of any thing, a cultural set of possible meanings appropriate through time and space for the social group is carved out, and based on this cultural code, social system members derive their own codes of relevance. As I have indicated in Figure 1, the universal can be thought of as an objective realm. Only at the universal level is meaning given a priori. The cultural stratum can be thought of as an intersubjective realm. And the individual stratum is most nearly a subjective realm, studied through clinical means.

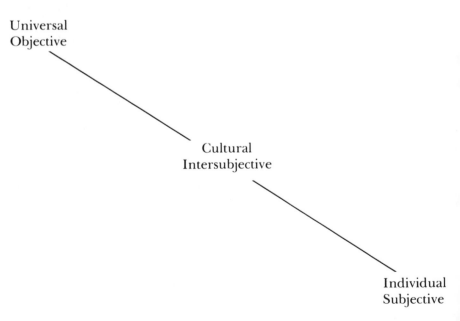

Universal
Objective

Cultural
Intersubjective

Individual
Subjective

Figure 1.   Levels of interpretation in producing meaning.

With few exceptions researchers in the organizational sciences have proceeded as if study of the universal stratum *alone* were sufficient to produce understandings of organizational behavior; organizational phenomena have been studied implicitly as universal matters devoid of any cultural component.[2] It is time to begin studying cultural phenomena as distinct aspects of organizational life. It is increasingly clear that much of what matters in organizational life takes place at the cultural level. From the "informal organization" first recognized in the Hawthorne studies to the "organizational politics" currently in vogue among researchers, cultural phenomena pervade organizational life. Yet, by and large, cultural phenomena seem to elude, be overlooked by, and/or remain on the fringe of mainstream organizational science. I suspect this is due in part to the lack of a coherent integral image conveyed in symbols and language sufficient to distinguish it from other images (e.g., culture versus machine). And so, in the following pages, I will begin to flesh out and give language to such an image. (The paradox is that traditional images, ideals and language of organizational science [i.e., our culture] tend to blind us to supplementary images of organization phenomena.)

The next two sections will consider aspects of culture relevant to a view of organizations as culture-bearing milieux. For purposes of discussion, a distinction is made between what goes on inside any one individual vis-à-vis cultural processes and what goes on outside the person; that is, between persons or, more generally, within the social system. The former is termed the psychological context and the latter the sociological context of culture.

CULTURE IN ORGANIZATIONS: THE SOCIOLOGICAL CONTEXT

In a brief but classic statement, Kroeber and Parsons (1958) define culture as the ". . . transmitted and created content and patterns of values, ideas, and other symbolic-meaningful systems as factors in the shaping of human behavior . . ." as distinct from social system, or ". . . the specifically relational system of interaction among individuals and collectivities" (pp. 86–87). As discussed above, the codes of meaning or relevance indigenous to a social system serve as behavior-shaping social ideals (i.e., "thou shalt", "thou shalt not"). Social ideals constitute a system of values and relevances by which individuals and institutions set goals and aspirations, sanction behavior and judge performances. A set of social ideals is represented in a kind of hierarchy or prioritization of meanings, a coherent meaning system. A cultural view then encompasses the system of social ideals and the set of symbolic devices (i.e., myths, rituals, signs, metaphors, special languages) that embody and are used to convey the ideals. While these symbolic devices are used to convey the local culture, they are simultaneously the artifacts of that culture.

Culture provides for social system continuity, control, identity and integration of members. The stability (through time) of shared ideals across generations of social system members provides continuity and serves a homeostatic function.[3] The stability (through space) of the standards or goals conveyed in the commonly-held set of ideals serves the control function of deviance detection and reduction.[4] Ouchi's (1979) work on control by clan illustrates this function. Further, ideals shared among members provide for the integration of individuals into the social group, a kind of individual-to-institution linking. Etzioni's (1961) work on moral involvement of organization members illustrates the integrating function of culture.[5]

More diffusely, culture embodies the identity of the social group. What we, as members, stand for and how we deal with one another and with outsiders is carried in and through our culture. Discussions of corporate personality are concerned at least implicitly, with the identity aspect of organizational culture (O'Toole, 1979).

CULTURE IN ORGANIZATIONS: THE PSYCHOLOGICAL CONTEXT

At the indiviudal level, ". . . human beings act toward things on the basis of the meanings that the things have for them . . ." (Blumer, 1969, p. 2). And those meanings, or significances, are the products of an in situ interpretive process. Meaning is essentially and endlessly negotiated by social system members. In one sense of negotiated, meaning production represents navigation of an experiential landscape by which one controls one's course or position. In the other sense of negotiated, it represents bargaining among alternative meanings differentially preferred by the various parties to an interaction.

At the micro-interactional level, the navigational aspect of cultural processes produces the individual's definition of the situation.[6] Features as landmarks are identified and interpreted in light of present sociological position and destination. In an interaction, the person's individualized version of the local set of social ideals (i.e., personal code of meanings or frame of reference), guides perception, interpretation and action. Through a series of steps, it allows the individual to assess whether, for instance, a particular performance constitutes a job well done. First, one's culturally derived meaning system facilitates the iden-

SOCIOLOGICAL CONTEXT
SHARED IDEALS   SYMBOLIC DEVICES
Cultural system
of relevances
Through the functions of culture,
  social systems achieve:
  Continuity—transtemporal stability
  Control—contemporaneous stability
  Integration of individual members
  Identity of social group

PSYCHOLOGICAL CONTEXT
INTERPRETIVE SCHEME
Personal system
  of relevances

Within a culture:
  Meaning is emergent and intersubjective
  Individuals negotiate meaning

  Negotiation as: Navigation
                    Bargaining
The in situ interpretive process:
Perception → Negotiation → Meaning ⇾
  Definition of situation → Behavior

Figure 2.   Aspects of a cultural perspective.

45

tification of a performance from a continuous stream of experience, or parsing as Weick (1969) refers to it. What is noticed is, to a great extent, given in our cultural set. Second, it directs attention to certain features of the performance considered worth assessing. Third, it provides the yardstick for assessing those features of the performance. Fourth, assessment or interpretation guides action; or, as W. I. Thomas (1928, p. 584) has phrased it, "If men define situations as real, they are real in their consequences." Responses are made in terms of features assessed and assessments of those features.

The psychological context of cultural processes has been discussed at length by Schutz (1964, 1970b) who has shown how the individual's interpretive scheme or meaning system is embedded and operational in a particular culture. As a result of this communal embeddedness of members' meaning systems, meaning produced in situ is extensively intersubjective. Discussions of specific subprocesses in which individuals make meaning in social interaction based on an intersubjective perspective are found in McHugh (1968) and Louis (1980b).

Figure 2 reviews the aspects of a cultural perspective outlined so far.

CULTURE IN ORGANIZATIONAL SETTINGS

Ways in which organizations can be viewed as culture-bearing milieux and critical issues encountered in doing so are explored in this section. In addition, we will consider defining characteristics of cultural participation (e.g., physical vs. psychological connection, self-perception, competence) and issues of boundary and perspective in studying culture in organizations.

Organizations provide regularly-convening settings in which cultures may develop; thus, an organizational setting is analogous to a petri dish. Whether or not, or, more precisely, the extent to which, a particular organizational setting fosters the development of a local culture depends on a great many factors, only a few of which seem apparent at this stage of study. Some organizational settings may "bear" (in the sense of supporting the development of) elaborate cultures, while, in others, no appreciable culture may develop. In the latter case, the settings may be characterized by more purely instrumental involvement of members and individually-oriented behaviors. This is analogous at the organizational level to what Hall (1976) has referred to at the societal level as a "low-context" setting. Further, multiple nested and/or overlapping cultures may be borne by any given organization in correspondence to the potential multitude of physical/sociological/cognitive settings convened within the bounds of organizational activities. For example, somewhat distinct local cultures may form in each of several departments within a division of an organization, and at the level of the division as an organizational setting. In this view, then, the organization provides the setting or milieu in and through which cultures may develop; thus, the phrase, "organizations as culture-bearing milieux".

Several features of organizational settings are hypothesized to contribute to the development of local cultures, regardless of the organizational level at which culture is investigated (e.g., whether we consider organization-wide culture or the work-group culture). For instance, more extensive cultures are expected to be associated with: stability of membership; the extent to which key members "consistently point to (a set of) general ideas or frameworks (Wilkins, in this volume, pp. 81–92); "members' perceptions of the relative youth and smallness of the organization; identification of human qualities of key people (i.e., idiosyncracies, personal values, interpersonal style); impermeability of organizational boundaries (e.g., for purposes of product secrecy in an R&D lab or societal privacy in a nudist colony); membership restrictions (essential acquired or innate attributes, e.g., education or experience, sex or race). There are undoubtedly other features of organizational settings that contribute to the development of local cultures which remain to be identified through further study.

I believe we will discover in future studies that patterns of features, the relative importance of some over others, will differ depending on the organizational level (e.g., organization-wide versus work-group) at which we are investigating cultures in organizations. Additionally, I believe we will discover different cultural processes and culture-shaping processes in operation depending on the developmental stage of the organizational unit qua setting under study. For instance, in entrepreneurships (organizations in early stages of development), culture-creating processes are expected to be in evidence. Stories and the values they convey are being shaped from the actions of key people. In contrast, cultural revitalization in mature or stagnating organizations (mid and late stages) may be fostered through the development and dissemination of new images and accompanying rationales for breaking with the past. The literal bringing in of "young blood" in the form of new leadership is often used to symbolically represent a new "life for the organization."

Changes in organizational settings can alternatively disrupt or support local cultures. For instance, the imposition of new technology may disrupt the local culture. Witness the example documented by Trist and Bamforth (1951) in their coal-mining studies. Previous to the change, task planning, coordination and control, interpersonal bonds and interfamily relationships were facilitated and mediated by the work-group culture. The new technology imposed a different set of interpersonal relationships and externalized planning and control. The basic features of the work-group setting were altered; the structural arrangements in and of the work-group were dismantled and re-assembled. Like a spider's web between garden tools resting against the walls of a shed, the web of the work-group culture was torn when the tools were rearranged.

Changes in organizational settings can also foster new cultural developments. For instance, establishing an identified task team creates a setting in and through which a local culture may develop. Creation of project teams, new geographically distinct divisions, and even matrix structures all represent the convening of potentially culture-bearing milieux. Each "new" unit created in an organizational change effort (e.g., adding project teams) may be new "in name only;" that is, it may be made up of people who have been members of the organization doing tasks done before in buildings and at desks long familiar. But, what matters is the "name." Organizational settings refer essentially to sociologically and cognitively identifiable spaces, not merely or even necessarily to physical aspects of setting; identifiability is facilitated by shared namings of space and/or by physical bounding of space. So, in a number of ways, organizational settings represent milieux which may foster, enhance, hinder, and/or disrupt the development of local cultures, depending on specific features of the setting.

In terms of membership in a particular organizational culture, an individual may be a member of a social system and its culture by virtue of regular ongoing physical presence and participation in face-to-face interactions with other members. One may also be a member of a culture by virtue of affiliation without necessarily being physically present in a face-to-face interaction system. For instance, being a member of the Academy of Management constitutes membership in a social system which convenes in the strict physical sense only once a year. Yet the culture of the Academy of Management seems clearly distinguishable from the culture of the Association for Humanistic Psychology or other professional groups. Further, membership by affiliation may be purely informal, as in the case of "regulars" at the culture-rich Monterey Jazz Festival, which convenes 3 days per year and has done so for more than 25 years. Thus, in two distinct ways, as opportunities for affiliation and as physically convening social systems, organizations can be seen as culture-bearing milieux.

An individual may be a member of a social system and participate superficially or deeply in the local culture. What determines the level of cultural membership is the individual's self-perception. This is particularly true when we consider cultures in work organizations as opposed to national and ethnic group cultures. In contrast to participation in a culture of birth, participation in an organizational culture is more temporary or transitory and more a matter of voluntary choice (though not necessarily the product of a conscious rational decision process). Ultimately, one is a participant in a particular culture to the extent that one considers him or herself to be a member.

In addition to self-perception as a factor in cultural participation, the competence of the participation must be considered. Competence is more at issue in organizational culture than societal culture in part because of the relative frequency with which individuals change organizations and therefore have an opportunity and an attendant need to master a new culture. Has the person sufficiently internalized core ideals and values, and appreciated key symbols? Adequate grasp of the local intersubjective or social reality is necessary in order for the individual to function within the culture.

In an organizational setting, the definition of a situation by an individual may be guided by several nested and/or overlapping cultural systems. These may be differentially dominant depending on the individual, his or her tenure in the social system, the congruence among cultural systems, the situation to be defined, etc. For instance, incongruence between overlapping cultures may result for individuals who have both professional and organizational affiliations (e.g., an attorney or CPA working at GM corporate headquarters). Similarly, nested cultures can exert incompatible pulls on individuals. This is illustrated in the case of the division manager torn between loyalty to his division and loyalty to the company, particularly when performance is assessed at divisional profit centers. Such situations have been studied in terms of role conflict and organizational commitment without adequate attention to relevant cultural elements.

The prevalence of nested and overlapping cultures (by affiliation and/or physical colocation) and the self-perceptual nature of cultural membership indicate the need to clarify issues of boundary and perspective in conducting organizational research. In studying culture, especially when organizations are studied at a distance, from the outside (Evered & Louis, 1981), one can't tell whether a particular boundary—e.g., the IBM culture as a whole—is a meaningful level of analysis, a substantially rich culture in comparison with other nested or overlapping cultures— e.g., the culture of IBM systems engineers in which individuals are simultaneously members. As well, different members of IBM may consider different boundaries relevant; they may consider their dominant affiliation at the organization-wide, or subunit or functional specialty level.

The challenge, then, is to identify which culture(s) is being studied and from whose points of view.

In addition to the organizational phenomena previously identified (e.g., control systems, nature of involvement, role conflict, organizational/professional commitment), a number of other phenomena (e.g., organizational climate, goal setting/performance feedback) imply that cultural processes are present in organizations and suggest vehicles for studying culture in organizations. Organizational climate has dealt at least conceptually almost directly with culture in organizations. Goal setting and performance feedback, which serve to guide and assess actions of organizational members, can be seen through a cultural view as the formalization and individualization of shared social ideals.

CONCLUSION

In this essay I have proposed that organizations be viewed as culture-bearing milieux. Essential ingredients of a cultural perspective were outlined and a number of organizational phenomena implicated in a cultural perspective were identified. A key premise of a cultural view is that meaning is emergent and intersubjectively negotiated. It was proposed that shared social ideals, frames of reference and symbols for conveying them are indigenous to social systems in organizations, as elsewhere; and that these aid members in interpreting experience and that they facilitate expression and guide behavior.

Conceptual development is needed to flesh out a cultural perspective. For instance, it may be useful to develop what seem to be natural categories of cultural facets. Prescriptive, descriptive, and expressive facets correspond on first glance to the cultural manifestations of, respectively, shared ideals, present images of local life, and symbol sets. And, by viewing culture as the context of individual action, the temporal/real-time, self-referencing, context-embedded, and actionable qualities of culture could be studied in much the same way that discourse is studied distinctly from language (Ricoeur, 1971).

Traditional analytic, etic-oriented research strategies (e.g., survey research) must be supplemented with more synthetic emic-oriented strategies in order to tap contextual aspects of phenomena and the perspectives of system members. Ethnography, participant observation and intensive case study techniques may be appropriate. Certain types of interaction analysis may also be appropriate in that they reveal communicative codes (e.g., sociolinguistics), native knowledge (especially as in Frake's work [1964] on elicitation frames), and information management schemes (e.g., Mehan, 1978) constituting the underlying structures by which people organize each other and build environments for one another. (See McDermott & Roth [1978] for a review of interactional approaches and Cicourel [1978] for a comparative illustration of three models of discourse analysis.) Whatever specific methods are used, appropriate study of cultural phenomena requires that researchers avoid objectifying intersubjective phenomena and consider critical issues of boundary and perspective.

Culture in organizations needs to be studied both as a primary focus (i.e., cultural processes in organizations) and as an additional level of analysis (i.e., cultural aspects of organizational phenomena). There are abundant opportunities to study culture as a primary focus. For instance, at the sociological level, evolution of culture could be examined by studying the initial convening and early history of a social system, its shared ideals, metaphors and symbol systems. Pettigrew's (1979) work in tracing the development of a newly established organization illustrates this type of study. The start of a project team, the commissioning and initial staffing of a new ship in the Navy, and the beginning of classes each semester are all situations in which the evolution of culture in organizations can be studied. And what happens during a corporate takeover, the shifts in priorities, images, and even languages reflect sometimes massive and sudden alterations of culture.

I close this essay by suggesting a final rationale for adding a view of organizations as culture-bearing milieux to our repertoire of perspectives on organizations. Historically, organizational scientists have adopted a reductionistic approach in studying organizational phenomena. Parts and pieces have been studied; 2 to 5 variable causal models have predominated (e.g., in studies of leadership, technology, structure). Results and conclusions about organizational functioning drawn from such research have been weak and necessarily tentative. Perhaps progress in the organizational sciences has suffered due to a pattern of pursuing the whole by exclusively examining the parts, without a balanced recognition that the whole, especially in the case of organizations, is greater than the sum of the parts. In contrast to the traditional reductionistic approach, considerations of culture require, support and themselves imply a more holistic and integrative approach to studying organizational phenomena. The themes and images characterizing particular cultures are lost when examined piecemeal. When considered as a whole, the character of a culture is rather readily detected, for instance, through its imprint on social system members. In sum then, a cultural perspective might help us to move from a fairly exclusive reliance on a reductionistic approach to more diverse and, in particular, more holistic approaches to organizational inquiry.

NOTES

1. This paper was completed in 1980. Since then, organizational scientists have written much on this subject; my thinking has evolved; I have become concerned that our pursuit of culture may not prove fruitful (Louis, 1983). My notions of culture in organizational settings have been influenced by writings in cultural anthropology, sociology, linguistics, and philosophy. The works of Schutz (1964, 1970a, 1970b), Berger and Luckmann (1966), Geertz (1973), Thomas (1951) and Ball (1972) have been particularly influential. Basic material on anthropological approaches to meaning and culture, can be found in Hammel and Simmons (1970), Spradley (1972), Gamst and Norbeck (1976). Nida (1964) provides a helpful and detailed discussion of linguistic, referential and emotive meanings.

2. A detailed critique of deficiencies arising from the exclusive use of universalistic approaches in organizational research is found in Louis (1981). Discussions in Ritzer (1975), Burrell and Morgan (1979), and Pondy and Mitroff (1979) provide other characterizations of limitations of traditional perspectives on organizations.

3. See Buckley (1967, p. 206) for a discussion of systemic origins of this function.

4. McHugh's (1968) temporal and spatial themes are analogous at the individual psychological level to what is suggested here at the social systems level.

5. This emphasis on stabilizing functions of culture is not meant to suggest that cultural systems are static. On the contrary, they are more appropriately viewed as in-process, evolving and emergent. For example, the changing attitudes toward career/family trade-offs that are being reflected in changes in work cultures in America illustrate the evolving character of culture.

6. "The definition of the situation" is used here to refer to the meanings given by the individual to particular experiences in an immediate sense, that is, in the moment of experience; the interpretive scheme refers to the meaning set that the setting and social system typically has for the individual, across particular situations.

REFERENCES

Ball, D. W. 'The definition of situation': Some theoretical and methodological consequences of taking W. I. Thomas seriously. *Journal for the Theory of Social Behaviour*, 1972, *2*, 61–82.

Becker, H. S., & Geer, B. Participant observation and interviewing: A comparison. In William J. Filstead (Ed.), *Qualitative methodology*. Chicago: Rand McNally, 1970.

Beer, M. *Organization change and development: A systems view*. Santa Monica, CA: Goodyear, 1980.

Beres, M. E., & Portwood, J. D. Explaining cultural differences in the perceived role of work: An intranational cross-cultural study. In George N. England, Anant Negandhi, & Bernhard Wilpert (Eds.), *Organizational functioning in a cross-cultural perspective*. Kent, Ohio: Kent State University Press, 1979.

Berger, P., & Luckmann, T. *The social construction of reality: A treatise in the sociology of knowledge*. New York: Anchor Books, 1966.

Black, M. Meaning. In Dagobert D. Runes (Ed.). *Dictionary of philosophy*. Patterson, N.J.: Littlefield, Adams & Co., 1962.

Blumer, H. *Symbolic interactionism: Perspective and method*. Englewood Cliffs, N.J.: Prentice-Hall, 1969.

Buckley, W. *Sociology and modern systems theory*. Englewood Cliffs, N.J.: Prentice-Hall, 1967.

Burrell, G., & Morgan, G. *Sociological paradigms and organisational analysis*. London: Heinemann, 1979.

Cicourel, A. V. *Three models of discourse analysis: The role of social structure*. Unpublished paper, Department of Sociology, University of California, San Diego, 1978.

Clarke, B. *The distinctive college: Antioch, Reed and Swarthmore.* Chicago: Aldine, 1970.

Dandridge, T. C., Mitroff, I. I., & Joyce, W. F. Organizational symbolism: A topic to expand organizational analysis. *Academy of Management Review,* 1980, *5,* 77–82.

Etzioni, A. *A comparative analysis of complex organizations.* New York: The Free Press, 1961.

Evered, R., & Louis, M. R. Alternative perspectives in the organizational sciences: 'Inquiry from the inside' and 'Inquiry from the outside.' Under review with the *Academy of Management Review,* 1981, *6,* 385–395.

Frake, C. O. Notes on queries in ethnography. *American Anthropologist,* 1964, *66,* 1323–1145.

Gamst, F. C., & Norbeck, E. *Ideas of culture: Sources and uses.* New York: Holt, Rinehart and Winston, 1976.

Geertz, C. *The interpretation of cultures.* New York: Basic Books, 1973.

Hall, E. T. *Beyond culture.* New York: Anchor Press, 1976.

Hammel, E. A., & Simmons, W. S. *Man makes sense: A reader in modern cultural anthropology.* Boston: Little, Brown, 1970.

Harrison, R. Understanding your organization's character. *Harvard Business Review,* 1972, *5*(3), 119–128.

Kroeber, A. L., & Parsons, T. The concepts of culture and of social systems. *American Sociological Review,* 1958, *23,* 582–583.

Louis, M. R. Career transitions: Varieties an commonalities. *Academy of Management Review,* 1980, *5,* 329–340. (a)

Louis, M. R. Surprise and sense making: What newcomers experience in entering unfamiliar organizational settings. *Administrative Science Quarterly,* 1980, *25,* 226–251. (b)

Louis, M. R. Culture in organizations: The need for and consequences of viewing organizations as culture-bearing milieux. *Human Systems Management,* 1981, *2,* 246–258.

Louis, M. R. Prerequisites for fruitful research on organizational culture. Unpublished paper.

McDermott, R. P., & Roth, D. R. The social organization of behavior: Interactional approaches. *Annual Review of Anthropology,* 1978, *7,* 321–345.

McHugh, P. *Defining the situation: The organization of meaning in social interaction.* New York: Bobbs-Merrill, 1968.

Mehan, H. Structuring school structure. *Harvard Educational Review,* 1978, *48,* 32–64.

Mitroff, I. I., & Kilmann, R. On organizational stories: An approach to the design and analysis of organizations through myths and stories. In R. H. Kilmann, L. R. Pondy & D. P. Slevin (Eds.), *The management of organization design: Strategies and implementation.* New York: Elsevier, 1976.

Nida, E. A. *Toward a science of translating.* Leiden: E. J. Brill, 1964.

O'Toole, J. J. Corporate and managerial cultures. In C. L.Cooper (Ed.), *Behavioral problems in organizations.* Englewood Cliffs, N.J.: Prentice-Hall, 1979.

Ouchi, W. G. A conceptual framework for the design of organizational control mechanisms. *Management Science,* 1979, *25,* 833–848.

Pettigrew, A. M. On studying organizational cultures. *Administrative Science Quarterly,* 1979, *24,* 570–581.

Pike, K. L. *Language in relation to a unified theory of the structure of human behavior.* Glendale, CA: Summer Institute of Linguistics, 1954.

Pondy, L. R., & Mitroff, I. I. Beyond open system models of organization. In Barry M. Staw (Ed.), *Research in organizational behavior* (Vol. 1). Greenwich, Conn.: JAI Press, 1979.

Ricoeur, P. The model of the text: Meaningful action considered as a text. In P. Rabinow & W. M. Sullivan (Eds.), *Interpretive social science: A reader.* Berkely: University of California Press, 1979. (Reprinted from *Social Research,* 1971, *38.*)

Ritzer, G. *Sociology: A multiple paradigm science.* Boston: Allyn & Bacon, 1975.

Schutz, A. *Collected papers II: Studies in social theory.* (Arvid Brodersen, Ed.) The Hague: Martinus Nijhoff, 1964.

Schutz, A. *On phenomenology and social relations.* (Helmut R. Wagner, Ed.) Chicago: The University of Chicago Press, 1970. (a)

Schutz, A. *Reflections on the problem of relevance.* (Richard M. Zaner, Ed.) New Haven, CT: Yale University Press, 1970. (b)

Silverman, D. *The theory of organizations.* New York: Basic Books, 1970.

Spradley, J. P. *Culture and cognition: Rules, maps, and plans.* San Francisco: Chandler, 1972.

Thomas, W. I. *Social behavior and personality: Contribution of W. I. Thomas to theory and social research.* (Edmund H. Volkart, Ed.) New York: Social Science Research Council, 1951.

Trist, E. L., & Bamforth, K. W. Some social and psychological consequences of the Long-wall Method of coal-getting." *Human Relations.* 1951, *4*, 1–38.

Van Maanen, J. Experiencing organization: Notes on the meaning of careers and socialization. In John Van Maanen (Ed.), *Organizational careers: Some new perspectives.* New York: Wiley, 1977.

Van Maanen, J. On the understanding of interpersonal relations. In W. Bennis, J. Van Maanen, E. H. Schein, & F. I. Steele (Eds.), *Essays in interpersonal dynamics.* Homewood, IL: The Dorsey Press, 1979. (a)

Van Maanen, J. Reclaiming qualitative methods for organizational research: A preface. *Administrative Science Quarterly,* 1979, *24*, 520–526. (b)

Weick, K. E. *The social psychology of organizing.* Reading, MA: Addison-Wesley, 1969.

Weick, K. E. Cognitive processes in organizations. In Barry M. Staw (Ed.), *Research in organizational behavior* (Vol. 1). Greenwich, Conn.: JAI Press, 1979.

Wilkins, A., & Martin, J. *Organizational legends.* Unpublished paper, Stanford University, 1979.

ORGANIZATIONS AS SHARED MEANINGS

Linda Smircich

The overall purpose of this paper is to illustrate how organizations exist as systems of shared meanings and to highlight the ways in which shared meanings develop and are sustained through symbolic processes. The paper is derived from an ethnographic study of the executive staff of an Insurance Company. It describes the system of meaning the group members used to make sense of their experience and traces its emergence from their interaction and its influence on their further interaction. The paper shows how such symbolic processes as organizational rituals, organizational slogans, vocabulary, and presidential style contribute to, and are part of, the development of shared meanings which give form and coherence to the experience of organization members.

The stability, or organization, of any group activity depends upon the existence of common modes of interpretation and shared understanding of experience. These shared understandings allow day to day activities to become routinized and taken for granted. Through the development of shared meanings for events, objects, words and people, organization members achieve a sense of commonality of experience that facilitates their coordinated action.

In a particular situation the set of meanings that evolves gives a group its own ethos, or distinctive character, which is expressed in patterns of belief (ideology), activity (norms and rituals), language and other symbolic forms through which organization members both create and sustain their view of the world and image of themselves in the world. The development of a world view with its shared understanding of group identity, purpose and direction are products of the unique history, personal interactions and environmental circumstances of the group. Yet the particular world view may continue to shape organizational existence long after the key actors have departed from the scene and environmental conditions have changed. Acknowledgment of this provides the impetus for the study of the symbolic processes which facilitate the continued existence of particular organizational realities.

BACKGROUND

The Insurance Company[1] studied is one division of a Corporation that has 10,000 employees in 12 northeastern states. The Corporation was formed in 1964 as a result of a merger of three well-established regional farmer's cooperatives with the formal objective of building and maintaining a strong, diversified, cooperative business organization to improve the economic well-being of its members. Before the merger each of the three cooperatives had developed their own insurance programs to protect the lives and property of their farmer members and to provide them with lower group rates. In 1968, the Insurance division was developed out of these programs and was eventually expanded into insurance services for the general public as well as the membership. The Insurance Company employs 250 people and is housed in a modern two story building two blocks from the corporate headquarters located in a medium size northeastern city.

An agreement was reached whereby the researcher was invited to spend six weeks in the Insurance Company as an observer of the top management group. The researcher's role was negotiated as that of an observer, to learn about the organization not to serve as a consultant. There was to be no presentation of "results" to the company. The fact that the President agreed to have an observer in the organization, but did not want feedback on the experience, is itself a piece of data, and one which is consistent with much of what is said here about the ways of life in this group.

The specific techniques used in this setting were similar to those of many anthropologists and sociologists doing field work (Bogdan & Taylor, 1975; Schatzman & Strauss, 1973). The researcher maintained the work hours of the organization and was provided with office space. Early on she met individually with each of the staff members and explained the project. The researcher's activity consisted of observing the management staff in a variety of situations: staff meetings, planning sessions, interactions with their subordinates, on coffee breaks and in casual conversation. The work proceeded in a way which allowed the themes present in the setting to emerge and to be explored in cycles of data collection and analysis (Glasser & Strauss, 1968; Diesing, 1971). Towards the end of the stay in the organization tape recorded conversations/interviews were held with each of the 10 staff members including the president. The conversation was oriented around several topics or themes which appeared to be relevant to the people in the organization. The raw data from this study consist of: daily field notes, documents from the organization, tapes of conversations, and the researcher's experience.

The Ethos

The dominant interpretation that the executive staff used to account for their way of life was the belief that, in their group, differences or problems which may be difficult or painful to handle were submerged. There was widespread agreement that "if you've got anything that is controversial, you just don't bring it up."

They saw their mode of behavior as a direct result of the style and preferences of the company president. The staff claimed that the president "likes to keep it cool," "doesn't like to see any friction or animosity" and "doesn't like to hear if things are bad." Consequently, there was a belief that in the company "people say what they know everyone else wants to hear." Problems get "buried" instead of dealt with directly because "it's easier to handle that way." Staff members perceived the president as having the philosophy that "you shouldn't air problems or disagreements." They feared that if they were to surface a disagreement they would be labelled a "troublemaker" or accused of "pointing a finger." The atmosphere in the organization was described as "a fiction, not reality." The corporate secretary believed that the president was aware that the staff members did not say what they really thought but that he allowed it to continue because "he'd like to finish out his time with the company having everything quiet, without any uproar."

Thus the staff made sense of their experience in similar ways ("we maintain a smooth surface of agreement") and they shared a rationale for why the situation was as it was ("we behave this way because of the president"). It is these areas of shared meaning which give the executive group a sense of commonality and unity to their experience. These beliefs contributed to coordinated, albeit restrained, interaction and an aura of passivity among the staff members. To the outside observer the beliefs appeared to function in rule-like fashion and lent the staff member's activity a programmed character.

In private almost all the staff members complained to the researcher about their mode of behavior and the president's style. Some expressed a preference for dealing with differences directly but they felt blocked from doing so. In public they tried scrupulously to maintain a facade of agreement and politeness. They shared the perception that they were behaving according to the president's preferences and to do otherwise would invite disaster.

With the executive staff we see at least two meaning systems, the public and the private, in operation. What is striking is the high degree of overlap across executives in both public and private systems of meaning. It is also striking that even though some staff members had an awareness of the dynamics of their situation, they felt dominated by their perception of a third meaning system, that of the president, and felt powerless to change it. Through the action of the president, the participation of the staff members, and the enactment of particular symbolic forms cultivated by the president, the ethos of apparent harmony was sustained and elaborated and came to dominate the ways in which the organization members interpreted their situation.

In addition to understanding the nature of the shared meaning systems of a group it is also important to understand the ways in which they come to be shared and by what mechanisms they are perpetuated. The remainder of the paper addresses these issues.

The Emergence of the Ethos

The emergence of this dominant system of meaning can be understood as a consequence of the historical development of the company, the struggles for leadership within it, and the personal ideology of the current president.

The formative period (1968–1978) of the Insurance Company, described as "traumatic" and "chaotic" was marked by several specific events: the demotion of the first head of the company, the firing of the second, the hiring of an executive vice president, and the hiring of a cadre of insurance professionals to strengthen the staff. These events surfaced struggle and conflict in the developing company between those staff members originally employed by one of the original farmers' cooperatives and those brought in from the insurance industry.

The distinction between the outside people and the inside people was heightened by the fact that most of the new personnel came directly from the same company as the executive vice president or had worked for that company at some time in the past. Discussions would frequently involve statements such as "This was how we did it at the other company," which would further alienate the outside group from the inside group. It was perhaps awareness of the potential harmful effects of such a division which led to the creation of a ritual, a form of initiation rite, for each new member of management.

Rituals are behavior patterns which are stylized or formalized and which are repeated in that form. While it is common to assocaite rituals with events of religious significance there are also rituals carried out in everyday organizational life which are imbued with significance and which hold various meanings for the participants.

At special management meetings the staff became an Indian tribe; each new addition was given a headband with a feather and was christened with an Indian name. For example, one staff member was dubbed "Chief Running Water" because of his habitual lateness. As part of this ritual, the executive vice president instituted a 50¢ fine, levied any time anyone mentioned the name of the other firm.

Although the Indian tribe and the 50¢ fine were intended as symbols of the starting of new allegiances to a new company, the split between the people who had been associated with the corporation and those from the competitive firm was real and difficult to overcome. That the memory of the distinction between the inside and outside people was still quite vivid many years later is obvious from the talk of one executive who was with the company before the executive vice president was hired. He described the presence of a "division here in the company between that other company and the rest of us" because "if somebody wanted something and the guy was from the other company, he got it. If you weren't from there, you didn't get it." Those who came from the competitive firm to the Insurance Company seemed to remain aloof and not mingle with the others. It appeared to the veteran employees that the "executive vice-president's boys" were shown favoritism which contributed to a clandestine and political atmosphere. During this time period the executive vice president was responsible for the daily operations of the company while the president's efforts were devoted to external relationships. This arrangement came to an end in November of 1977 when the executive vice president entered the hospital with cancer. His death in January of 1978 marked the end of an era at the Insurance Company. When the executive vice president died a decision was made not to replace him; instead the vice presidents and directors began to report directly to the president.

The president was the central figure in the emergence and shaping of an ethos of apparent harmony which stood in contrast to these earlier conditions. He saw his task as the blending of the traditions and orientations of the people from inside the parent corporation with those brought in from the outside because of their knowledge of the insurance business. The desire to blend the inside and the outside was the basis upon which the symbols of the Insurance Company, connoting harmony and integration, were developed. We turn now to an examination of the symbolic processes associated with the president and the shared meanings which evolved around them.

An Organizational Ritual: The Monday Morning Staff Meeting

With the death of the executive vice president, weekly staff meetings were instituted to bring the president up to date on operations. The meanings that the executive staff members associated with these meetings were tied up with the historical context in which they began and their feelings about the president's style of management. At the time of the fieldwork the staff members shared an interpretation of these meetings. To them they appeared to represent the way their president wanted business to be conducted: calmly, coolly, politely, harmoniously with no conflict, controversy or upset, but also with an air of unreality.

The Monday morning staff meetings had very much of a ritualistic quality. "We sit in the same seats, like cows always go to the same stall" said one executive. The tone of the meetings was low key, polite, calm, restrained and seemed to reflect the president's personal style of interaction which was also calm, reserved, and restrained. There was very little discussion among staff members in the meetings, instead comments were directed to the president in one-to-one fashion. This one-to-one mode of interaction also reflected the president's favored style of management. The meetings appeared to resemble "show and tell" sessions more than anything else. They began promptly at 8:15. One member was habitually late and this was a source of humor and irritation. But although his lateness bothered some of the staff members, and was the target of covert derision, neither they nor the president said anything when he made his late entrances, instead, his entry was ignored.

The president's role at the staff meetings appeared to be that of a newscaster, funnelling information from the external environment into the system. He usually spoke about ten minutes. When he was finished each member in turn would report about the activities in his or her area. While this was being done the other staff members usually kept their eyes downcast. Only one staff member consistently took notes. There was rarely any interchange between staff members that was of a substantive nature, although there were upon occasion quick questions or minor barbs.

There was a shared belief among the staff members that these meetings were an empty formality; they consisted of "superficial" communication. Discussion was kept at a surface level. People reported how many policies were handled; but they did not "delve as deep" into what they really felt about certain things which may be going on in their own departments or the departments of others. "You'll never see the nitty-gritty in the staff meeting," one executive told the researcher. "But I think I know why (the President) does it—to keep us together." One executive said their meetings were "just like coming home and the wife says 'How was your day at the office today?'" They believed the president did not ask the staff members hard questions because "it's not his policy to say or do anything that would offend anyone or hurt anyone's feelings" which led to the opinion that "It's a real waste of time. It's a situation where you can say just about anything and no one will refute it." One member observed that people "are very hesitant to speak up, afraid to say too much." (They think) "If I say this, will this happen?" or "(the president) likes to keep it cool. He doesn't like to see any friction or any animosity." Thus, the staff members see their behavior in these meetings as superficial where they say "what everyone else wants to hear." They considered "maybe (the president) doesn't want to know." Another staff member felt sure that the president was aware of the superficiality of their behavior but that he preferred it that way.

On the other hand, the president expressed the belief to the researcher that the staff meetings were "a forum where we exchange information and keep up to date, on external and internal (issues) and on major decisions. They provide a forum for a little bit of important debate and discussion."

The staff members did not see the meetings in those terms. Instead they were seen as a ritual for bringing them together but from which nothing of any substance emerged.

An Organizational Slogan: "Wheeling Together"

Shortly after the death of the executive vice president there was a deliberate effort to create an image or symbol for the Insurance Company. It took the form of a slogan "Wheeling Together" and was represented by an actual wagon wheel mounted on a flat base. The various spokes on the wheel represented the different parts of the Insurance Company; at the center was the customer. The wheel, about 4 feet high, was kept at the top of a file cabinet and was moved around from depart-

ment to department. Lucite paper weights were produced embedded
with the wheel image. There were even "Wheeling Together" rubber
stamps for use on outgoing mail.

This image was originally created as a theme for a sales contest to
convey the relationship between the agents in the field and the people in
the home office, but was adopted by the president of the Company and
incorporated into his annual "kick off" speech. Most of the staff members believed that the president meant his symbolic message to be applied to the executive staff members because of the divisiveness and
conflicts between staff members which surfaced after the executive vice
president's death. One staff member recalled "There was a lot of dissen-
sion around the staff, a lot of disagreements, fights, an inordinate
amount of finger-pointing . . . "Wheeling Together" is a theme that developed in order to promote teamwork."

The symbol of the wheel and the slogan "Wheeling Together" were
intended to communicate a spirit of interdependence and teamwork.
But at the time of the study the symbol and its accompanying slogan
were clearly not alive as a positive image for the staff. In fact, the symbol
became a shared image but in a negative way; it gave the staff members a
common way to understand and talk about how poorly they worked
together. "Wheeling Together" was the counterpoint or antithesis of
their experience and they used it derisively to mock and ridicule their
own behavior. One staff member talking about a series of incidents
which demonstrated the hostile behavior between two departments sum-
med up his description with a sarcastic "now that's wheeling together."
For the most part the executives were sympathetic to the ideal the symbol represented but questioned its applicability to their group. "The
philosophy was that each of the departments was a spoke of this wheel
and if all the spokes were there and functioning you had a smooth-
riding trip. But some of the departments are a little splintered and as a
result the thing isn't really working together." Another staff member
joked "Actually we've got four wheel drive, but every wheel is going in its
own direction."

The image of the wheel served to highlight to the staff members that
which was absent in their organization: a sense of cooperativeness with
all parts of the company going in the same direction. Although the
symbol and the slogan were ineffective in creating a feeling of harmony,
they did capture the staff's attention, and provided a common way of
understanding their experience. They mentioned for example the belief
that one department was a "weak spoke" and therefore "the whole wheel
can break," and that the "executive staff does not wheel together."

The image was part of the president's language. In talking about his role to the researcher he said he tried to encourage people to see their interdependence, "You really don't go very far unless everybody's got their shoulder to the wheel." But he also voiced some reservations. "You can't overdo this to the point where you threaten to suppress some spirited debate . . . You could have people not speaking their minds just because they feel they might undermine the teamwork." He believed "that would be wrong," there should be "some confrontation between people as long as it doesn't get personal." He said he stressed to his staff that "you just can't get personal about these things" because "then you've injected a little poison into the outfit." He felt that "debate should be encouraged if you're going to make the best decisions." He added, "the main thing is just to keep the personalities out."

It is obvious from the behavior and talk of the staff members that they have clearly received the message about keeping personalities out. This message is so important to the president and his concern about keeping things impersonal is so strong, the staff feel that there really is no room for any confrontation or debate. Although the president says it would be "wrong to suppress debate," it appears that that is exactly what has occurred here. The president paid lip service to the belief that "debate should be encouraged if you're going to make the best decisions" but through his actions and the enactment of these symbolic forms, the ethos which places value on the appearance of harmony is sustained and remains dominant.

Organizational Vocabulary: The Meaning of "Challenge"

The executive group sustained an appearance of smoothness and nonconfrontation not only in their activities but in their choice of vocabulary as well. This was most obvious in their use of the word "challenge" as a cover up word to mask what were really problems. The inability or unwillingness to call a situation a problem was consistent with the whole interaction pattern of keeping things hidden.

The staff members privately shared the view that challenge means "a problem." Some members put it more forcefully, "It means a very goddamn severe problem—my god what a mess." Another said, "It's an excuse word, it's a soft way of putting things. We don't want to hurt each other." Even the president said to the researcher, "I think the word challenge is sometimes overused. When people have problems or when an organization has problems, it's often considered a challenge, at least that's the way everybody uses it, to put it in a better light, I guess."

In this instance the way a particular word is used is congruent with and supportive of the larger pattern of behavior. Shared meanings for other words, events, objects, can provide a sense of commonality to experience and allow for coordinated responses without a great deal of re-negotiation of meaning at each encounter. In this group the members had a shared but unspoken agreement about using the word challenge, instead of problem, to spare a person who had a "challenge" from the harsher implications of a problem.

Conclusion

Organizations exist as systems of meanings which are shared to varying degrees. A sense of commonality, or taken for grantedness is necessary for continuing organized activity so that interaction can take place without constant interpretation and re-interpretation of meanings. Much of this commonality is developed through and perpetuated by such symbolic processes as the rituals, slogans and specialized vocabularies considered in this paper. The particular set of meanings that a group evolves provides it with its own ethos or distinctive character. The ethos may reflect historical circumstances, critical events, and unique attributes and preferences of key people. It emerges from social processes and shapes their course as part of the ongoing reality of the group.

The methods which ultimately emerged in the executive group of the organization here were a product of the difficulties of the search for leadership for the new division and the need to mesh a diverse group of people into a new organization, coupled with the calm, reserved, polite style of the president. The experiences of the formative period, characterized by interpersonal conflict, worked their way into the fabric of meanings shared by the executive group, including the president. They were not mere memories or artifacts but were kept alive as part of the ongoing reality of the organization in that the prevailing ethos was designed to encourage a completely opposite form of experience. The ethos of maintaining a smooth surface of agreement and avoiding confrontation seemed to serve as both a rationale and a guide for behavior. It was sustained through the rituals of the staff meeting and the president's one-on-one style of management; it was reflected and elaborated in the "Wheeling Together" slogan and the wheel symbol, and was firmly embedded in the patterns of speech.

The case study illustrates the way organization members forge common grounds for action, although in the situation presented here, it was more often inaction. These common grounds for action stem from mutual beliefs and the enactment of patterns of meaningful activities. Some of these may be purposely designed by those with influence as in the case of the "Wheeling Together" slogan, whereas many others take their significance as a consequence of the particular context and circumstances of action. Such processes are central to the existence of organized activity, which though so often taken for granted as routine and real, rests upon a complex system of shared meaning.

REFERENCE NOTE
1. Additional analyses of the dynamics of the executive staff of this organization can be found in Smircich, L., & Morgan, G. Leadership: The Management of meaning. *Journal of Applied Behavioral Science*, 1982, *18* (3), 257–273.

REFERENCES
Bogdan, R., & Taylor, S. J. *Introduction to qualitative research methods.* New York: Wiley, 1975.

Diesing, P. *Patterns of discovery in the social sciences.* Chicago: Aldine, 1971.

Glaser, B. G., & Strauss, A. L. *The discovery of grounded theory.* Chicago, Aldine, 1967.

Schatzman, L., & Strauss, A. L. *Fieldwork.* Englewood Cliffs, N.J.: Prentice-Hall, 1973.

Turner, G. A. *Exploring the industrial subculture.* London: Macmillan, 1971.

Part III

**MANAGING
ORGANIZATIONAL SYMBOLS**

Several papers in Part III deal with use of symbols and symbolic processes for accomplishing organizational outcomes. Tom Dandridge (*Symbols' function and use*) focusses on identifying the nature and types of symbols found in organizations, and on the general functions which they may perform. He discusses the 'descriptive', 'energy controlling', and 'system maintaining' functions of symbols, and how they may be used to achieve various ends by organizational elites, organizational members, and organizational researchers.

The papers by Alan Wilkins (*Organizational Stories as Symbols which Control the Organization*), and Joanne Martin and Melanie Powers (*Truth or Corporate Propaganda: The Value of a Good War Story*) continue this functionalist theme. Wilkins discusses and describes the way stories can operate as "third order" controls in organizations, serving as symbols of meaning, and providing behavioral descriptions which people can follow to achieve organizational ends. This theme is further explored by Martin and Powers who examine the impact of organizational stories on how organizational members behave, what they remember, and what they become committed to. They describe laboratory experiments which suggest that organizational stories appear to be more powerful than statistical and distributional data in influencing organizational beliefs, memory, and commitment.

In *Symbolic transformation of belief systems*, Carson Eoyang develops the implications of a cybernetic approach to organizational symbolism. He focusses on the role of symbols in information processing, and the process of organizational transformation. He discusses how insights from this perspective can be related to leadership practice, particularly with regard to how leaders shape and alter belief systems of their followers.

SYMBOLS' FUNCTION AND USE

Thomas C. Dandridge

Past study of organizational life has concentrated principally on rational, objectively identifiable processes and relationships. From this perspective we have tried to understand and develop theories of conflict, decision making, leadership, or patterns observed in organizations. Another layer of behavior in organizations has been largely disregarded. This is the symbolism in organizational life. Examples of this symbolism surround us. A major airline recently ended a successful year by sending bonus checks to select employees, and giving them a medal at the same time. The material from which these medals were made was scrap metal parts from every type of plane the airline had ever flown, plus a part from the moon landing vehicle used by the company president, a former astronaut. A pilot remarked that it was impressive to hold in his hand the history of the whole company's development.

Employees at Hyatt Regency hotels are familiar with a phrase describing the impact of the orientation program as "being Hyattized". This indicates full acceptance of the company's philosophy, more than just learning rules or procedures.

Organizations such as Eli Lilly and U.S. Steel have produced hardbound books containing the company history. These may be presented to individuals on special occasions.

Individuals can be powerful symbols. During the Watergate crisis a congressman remarked that the American people are eager to revere the President, and they are entitled to one they can revere. In these cases and countless other examples throughout organizational life members repeat special stories, attribute unusual significance to routine acts or use selected material items as symbols.

Business executives and marketing theorists show they know the importance of such symbols by the use made of them in their trademarks or advertisements. While symbols in marketing, or external to the company, have been studied extensively and used consistently by marketing managers, the roles of symbols internal to the company are generally overlooked in organizational research. Until recently only limited related writings were important, and these came from outside the study of U.S. organizations. Thurman Arnold (1937) was one of the first to look at active symbolism in American business as he wrote of the mythology of capitalism. He cited the importance of a creed and related ritual as organizational elements. Gomersall and Meyers (1966) describe a study of the place of patterned experiences and stories in a well designed orientation, but without reference to symbolism. Rohlen (1970, 1974) uses his anthropological training for careful exploration of symbols in Japanese industry, particularly banking. Company songs, creeds, ceremonies, and stories take on great importance in teaching and maintaining company values, as well as a source of inspiration. Pettigrew (1979) draws comparable conclusions from his study in England. He describes how organizations create symbols from their own structure, activities, or environment, and that the resulting rituals or myths have great functional consequences for the organization. Clark (1970) studied the importance of a distinctive creed and history in the shaping and maintenance of three unique small colleges.

Recent articles on American business consider symbols in more depth, still focussing on stories more than other forms, and not clearly delineating functions. Mitroff and Kilman (1976), Wilkins and Martin (1979) or Dandridge, Mitroff and Joyce (1980) are examples.

Organizational research can study symbols to gain greater understanding of internal processes of organizations in much the same way that anthropologists use them to understand cultures. By using the functioning of symbols as an added lens, a deeper and more comprehensive understanding of organizations is possible.

The nature of symbolism and the relationship between symbols and signs has been discussed in the introductory chapter of this volume. Symbols comprise one category of a larger set of signs. All signs serve the static function of talking *about* something or taking the place of that for which they are a representation. Symbols go beyond this static function as they actively elicit the internal experience of meaning. Signs help a person to denote and comprehend knowledge of the external world objectively. Symbols go further as they help to translate an unconscious or intuitively known internal world of feelings into the comprehendable terms of our visible reality.

Other authors describe the symbolizing process in a similar way—Jung (1969) describes symbolizing as helping to translate the world within us into a visible reality. He states that "As the mind explores the symbol, it is led to ideas that lie beyond the grasp of reason" (1964, p. 4). A prominent anthropologist, Victor Turner (1969) describes symbols as "a set of evocative devices for rousing, channeling and domesticating powerful emotions . . ." (p. 166). Finally, Joseph Campbell (1972) well known for his many works on mythology, sums up his conception of a symbol with a quote by Thomas Merton: "The true symbol does not merely point to something else. It contains in itself a structure which awakens our consciousness to a new awareness of the inner meaning of life and reality itself" (p. 270).

In an organization, symbols carry us beneath the objective surface of organizational life, into the underlying value structure and feelings inherently there. A symbol elicits or directs individual member's feelings or values. To the extent that any element of organizational life functions in this way it acts as a symbol. A company motto or creed or the story of its founding often function as symbols. So do annual awards, banquets, or an office Christmas Party. Material items such as the company logo, a gold watch, or even ID badges may serve as symbols to some people, bringing to consciousness selected values or emotions. The story may not be factual, or the material item may not have monetary value. It is a symbol because the user believes or accepts it in a way that facilitates experiencing specific feelings or values. It provides a bridge, linking reason and emotion. The reader could use facts and surface description to convey the appearance of his or her work place to another person. However to guide the other person in experiencing what life is like there, how life *feels* there, a story may be both more efficient and more effective.

It is important to recognize that the perspective taken here views symbols as functional elements; that people make functional use of symbols and that we can recognize symbols by noting this use. Other papers in this collection consider the broad range of perspectives from which we may deal with symbols. This paper is intended to emphasize the functional perspective.

FUNCTIONS OF ORGANIZATIONAL SYMBOLS

The functions which symbols serve for organizations can be divided into the three broad categories of *descriptive, energy controlling*, or *system maintaining*. These are described below. It is not the claim of this paper that symbols are the only means of fulfilling functions such as maintaining the organization or describing it to members. Symbols are subjective means and as such they complement the rational objective means on which theorists have generally focussed.

Descriptive

In response to the question "What's this organization like? What's it like to work here?" one member may produce a string of adjectives or a few statements about pay rates, vacation policies, or management style. A second member might provide a story, using it as a symbol. The following three very brief "stories" came from three different companies. Each evokes a different experience of life in the organization as represented by the leaders.

1. The owner of the company liked to claim he was the only businessman in New York who could be driven right to his office door; the elevator in his building was large enough to accomodate his limousine which took him to the 12th floor.
2. Every Christmas season the chairman of the board, who was the grandson of the founder, used to walk through every department wishing employees Merry Christmas. He knew most of the older employees by name.
3. At a recent stockholders meeting the president arrived in bermuda shorts, riding up the aisle on a motorbike.

Either standing alone or with other responses these stories are descriptive symbols. The teller conveys information in a complex form that helps the listener grasp feelings and operative values present in the organization. Adjectives alone could be less complete or less convincing.

Energy Controlling

There are three ways in which symbols can function to control energy of organization members or of outsiders. First, they can be used to inspire members, to attract new recruits, or to repel undesired outsiders. Military organizations seem particularly adept in this use of symbols. Recruiting campaigns are rich in stories, slogans, or material elements to attract appropriate candidates (The Marines are looking for a few good men.) The manager of a toy company personnel department described how he tried to use the mystery or excitement of a new toy to inspire new employees when he learned many applicants were attracted to the company by the imagery of making toys. Similar symbols are used to repel those who don't share the desired values. Hotel employees traded stories of how bad working conditions were in other hotels as they affirmed their commitment to their present employer. The contrast present in the stories became part of the attraction of their hotel. In each of these cases a symbol has functioned as it influenced people's feelings about the organization, changing their level of energy committed or withheld.

Second, symbols facilitate re-experiencing of a feeling by the user alone. A plaque or a gold watch can be looked at by its owner or a ritual followed by the person alone to recapture feelings with which the symbol is associated. The keeper of the egg shell from the Organizational Symbolism Conference can look at this object alone for inspiration. The potency of that object as an inspirational symbol should relate to the care its keeper devotes to it.

Third, symbols serve the function of controlling energy as they provide acceptable venting of feelings for organization members. An office party or interdepartmental athletic contest can serve this function. Two offices within a Federal department in Washington have a continuing competition for departmental resources, with poorly hidden rivalry between the two leaders covered by polite distance. A softball league for the department pits these offices against each other twice a year. The turnout is noticeably higher at these games and the directors of each office are sure to play, and play very hard. Following the game derisive signs are often posted by the elevators. At no time is the work related rivalry mentioned in the game or the posters.

In each of these energy controlling functions the examples show an intent to reach beyond the simple objective presentation in order to inspire, to describe more fully, or to facilitate venting of feelings. Note that venting can also be dysfunctional for the organization, in counter-organizational symbolic acts or disparaging stories. Similarly an organization can inadvertently foster stories of how permissive or nurturant the company is regardless of employee's behavior. In such cases lower effort may result.

System Maintaining

Symbols have an important function in protecting a system, stabilizing it, or guiding change in the structure. Symbols can function to make sense of relationships between roles or to maintain these relationships. Some firms for example have official rules as to the size of office, the quality of a desk or the price of artwork which is authorized for each level in the organization's hierarchy. Informal rituals are often evident in seating at lunch or coffee break, giving symbolic messages of relationships. Company celebrations often provide an opportunity to point out long standing values or beliefs through stories or awards. Seating arrangements or stories at an annual banquet have been used to link company units which might otherwise have little contact, such as dispersed sales units. The same situation can provide symbolic messages of who the company values most. One company provides gold blazers and front-table seats to the top salespeople and their spouses.

A memo circulated among airline pilots recently criticized those pilots who cared more about their stylish hair than about their professional image, which required wearing a hat. Calling them amateurs and juveniles it claimed that ". . . it takes as much self-discipline to adhere to public appearance as prescribed in the company manual as it does to stay right side up in a thunderstorm". Such exhortation emphasizes the importance of maintaining existing values and relationships, and does so through the medium of the symbolic image of the pilot. The reasoning, or sensemaking is evident in description, going beyond the symbol to a critical element of the job.

Another way symbols function for system maintenance is during individual transitions from one role to another. New employee orientations, promotions, and termination proceedings all may be studied as rites of passage.

In one example of a promotion, the acts associated with becoming a bank officer form a ritual which symbolically transmits values of the bank and of the new role. A unique envelope is used for the letter of notification, separating this announcement from all other correspondence. The day of the announcement, existing officers take each new one to the Officers Dining Room, supposedly for the first time, to introduce him or her. The new officer is informally obligated to buy drinks for all members of his department on the first Friday after notification. These acts can be seen to emphasize the importance and elevated status of the initiate. The drinks seem to carry a message of sharing the good fortune, or of the higher status member's responsibility to the lower.

A variety of rituals accompany separations for example, and as symbols these rituals can function to reaffirm the solidarity of those left behind or to guide the transition of the person separating. A promotion or retirement may be accompanied by a party, a "roast", stories, etc. A firing may be accompanied by an exit interview with a formal opportunity to vent feelings, or by an instant stripping of all company contact. A death may produce a day off for relevant employees (for all employees if the individual's importance is to be emphasized).

Organizations themselves go through transitions. During cyclical changes in a company's fortunes, stories or rituals may stabilize commitment or organizational climate as they first provide explanation or celebrate good times, then carry memories to support the system through difficult times. The same symbol, such as an annual banquet may serve in both ways.

Multiple Functions in one Symbol

Many symbols seem to serve multiple functions. The company history provides an example. Telling the story during orientation of new employees teaches organizational values and provides a common base of "inside" information. The story functions to stabilize and reinforce the existing structure and the company-supported values in this way. At the same time the story can be inspirational, serving to arouse or direct new employee's enthusiasm or energy, creating features which can be used on future occasions to inspire these employees again. The story can function as part of the sensemaking process, explaining *why* the organization is as it is.

Telling the same history in other contexts can function to attract or screen out job applicants, or can be told to non-participants for a descriptive function, merely to let them experience more completely what life in the organization is like. Thus a distinct separation of symbols by the function they serve would be inaccurate.

THE PLANNED USE OF SYMBOLS

From the perspective of this paper, symbols serve their users through the various functions described. They often do so unconsciously with no forethought or planning by an organization. Within an organization, as within a culture, the myth is believed or the ritual enacted usually without participants' forethought or awareness of the functions being served. It is often only through the perspective of an outsider that rational intentionality in the choice and use of symbols is seen. This lack of conscious choice is not inevitable, as organization members do not always have to be victims of myths and rituals, permitting these symbols to continue without awareness of their impact and without preplanning.

It would benefit persons influenced by these symbols and persons wishing to understand or influence an organization to know how existing symbols are working or what they are communicating. This knowledge can help a manager, an observer, or an organization member to gain a better grasp of the unique totality of the organization and a deeper insight into the richness of life there.

Use by Managers

For managers, understanding active symbols provides insight into employees current values. Beyond understanding the present, symbols provide a medium for influencing or directing future activity. Business organizations go through a founding and multiple growth changes in a short period of time. Such historical stages of development have been documented and discussed by authors such as Greiner (1972) and Torbert (1976). Stories nurtured by management at each stage can emphasize desired development or make sense of the organization's present state. Public organizations such as city governments go through periodic changes as political leadership is changed. Understanding and use of symbols can facilitate these changes. Public or private leaders can exercise choice as to which stories or other symbolic elements are supported or nurtured throughout their condensed history. While we may not agree with the values he supported, Hitler provides an example of choice among potential symbols contributing to success in a modern organization. He nurtured symbols with roots primarily in Norse mythology to elicit energy, direct activity, and justify this direction. In contrast, within most of our organizations, various managers will individually support whatever is convenient and fits into his or her department, or will permit symbols to randomly emerge or die. Very little attention is paid to the congruence of various types of symbols within one manager's span of control or in connection with other parts of the organization.

Preplanning is of value not only in the choice of which symbols to support, but in providing some guidance or explanation as to the meaning which is intended to be communicated. An individual's previous cultural or organizational experience may have given a symbol a different meaning than is desired here. Orientation programs can help guide new employees to make sense of the organization's values or procedures. The important point here is that symbols can occur naturally and may influence organization members, whether consciously or not. Leaders can overlook this impact or can plan and choose what to support or neglect, with concern for the consistency and message of the elements supported.

Use by Outside Observers

An outside observer—consultant or theoretician—can use symbols as a diagnostic tool, looking at inconsistencies or bringing the central theme or core process to a level of consciousness. Careful examination of the components of an organizational story or celebration can expose congruence in messages, or internal inconsistencies. Through a comprehensive understanding of the symbolic process the consultant can make use of symbols as the organization's natural channels of change. Interventions can be chosen that match or make use of existing acts or other symbolic elements (e.g., Gomersall & Meyers, 1966). For example, existing stabilizing symbols can be nurtured as a secure base, while change is introduced in some other aspect of the organization. Knittel (1974) has discussed at length the use of essential and non-essential ritual by a change agent, including the importance of considering the effect of the vacuum left when a change attempts to kill off any existing ritual.

Christian missionaries can be seen as early organizational change agents, trying to modify the values and beliefs of an existing system. Snyder (1975) noted that in one case missionaries outlawed the extravagant gift and party exchange between competing tribes of Indians of the Pacific Northwest, an exchange known as "Potlach." This ritual was forbidden as part of the conversion of these Indians to Christianity. The missionaries described Potlach as a wasteful and pagan ritual which strengthened the authority of native leaders and thus weakened the missionaries' potential for influence. Snyder notes that this intervention was not as successful as other situations where missionaries have incorporated the existing rituals into the Christian practices, and used them together to support the new beliefs. The incidence of warfare increased significantly when the Potlach competition was destroyed.

Use by Individuals as Members

Individual members of an organization can use symbols as a valuable means to greater understanding of the relation of the organization-supported values to their personal values or goals. The person may find that his or her most important symbols are ones related to the company, to a profession, or to the world away from work. In noting this he or she may become more conscious of individual priorities and values and of means of increasing fulfillment in work. As symbols are used to attract employees they can also serve these potential members as a filter promoting accurate self-selection by prospects. As they are parts of passages within the organization they communicate important values which are part of the new role, and can smooth personal transition.

CONCLUSION

Symbols serve broad classes of functions in organizations; to describe it, to control individuals within it, or to aid in making sense of the organization and maintain it. In appreciating these functions we increase our ability to understand or to change organizations. Patterns and consistencies among the types of symbols present within the life in an organization fashion its uniqueness and continuity. From separate symbols a consistent and continuous thread may be woven into the system's fabric, to use the history of the organization to communicate specific values identified there to the future. As this thread remains whole, it carries the organization's immortality. Incongruencies or inconsistencies among the messages or impacts of different symbols produce a fraying of that thread. Major changes such as a merger or new management can discontinue support of old symbols and bring in new ones. This can also lead to a break in the thread. By increasing awareness of the presence of symbols and their impact, organization members or researchers can add another dimension to understanding feelings and individual behavior within organizations.

REFERENCES

Arnold, T. W. *The folklore of capitalism.* New Haven: Yale University Press, 1937.

Campbell, J. *Myths to live by.* New York: Viking, 1972.

Clark, B. *The distinctive college: Antioch, Reed and Swarthmore.* Chicago: Aldine, 1970.

Dandridge, T. C. *Symbols at work: The types and functions of symbols in selected organizations.* Unpublished doctoral dissertation, UCLA, 1976.

Dandridge, T. C., Mitroff, I., & Joyce, W. Organizational symbolism: A topic to expand organizational analysis. *Academy of Management Review,* 1980, 5(1).

Eliade, M. *Myth and reality.* (W. R. Trask, Trans.) New York: Harper and Row, 1963.

Gomersall, E. R., & Myers, M. S. Breakthrough in on-the-job training. *Harvard Business Review,* 1966, 44(4), 62–72.

Greiner, L. E. Evolution and revolution as organizations grow. *Harvard Business Review,* 1972, July-August, 37–46.

Jung, C. G. *Man and his symbols.* London: Aldus Books Ltd., 1964.

Jung, C. G. *The structure and dynamics of the psyche* (2nd ed.). Bollingen Series XX. Princeton, N.J.: Princeton University Press, 1969.

Knittel, R. E. Essential and nonessential ritual in program of planned change. *Human Organization,* 1974, 33(1), 394–396.

Korda, M. *Power: How to get it, how to use it.* New York: Ballantine Books, 1975.

Mitroff, I., & Kilmann, R. On organizational stories: An approach to the design and analysis of organizations through myths and stories. In R. Kilmann, L. Pondy, & D. Sleven (Eds.), *The management of organization design.* New York: Elsevier North-Holland, Inc., 1976.

Pettigrew, A. M. On studying organizational cultures. *Administrative Sciences Quarterly,* 1979, 24 (Dec.), 570–581.

Rohlen, T. P. Sponsorship of cultural continuity in Japan: A company training program. *Journal of Asian and African Studies*, 1970, *5*(3), 184–192.

Rohlen, T. P. *For harmony and strength: Japanese white-collar organizations in anthropological perspective.* Los Angeles: University of California Press, 1974.

Snyder, S. Quest for the sacred in northern Puget Sound: An interpretation of Potlach. *Ethnology*, 1975, *14*(2), 149.

Torbert, W. R. *Creating a community of inquiry.* New York: Wiley, 1976.

Turner, V. W. Planes of classification in a ritual of life and death (1969). In Lessa & Vogt (Eds.), *Reader in comparative religion.* New York: Harper and Row, 1972.

Whitmont, E. C. *The symbolic quest: Basic concepts of analytical psychology.* New York: G. P. Putnam's Sons, 1969.

Wilkins, A., & Martin, J. *Organizational legends.* Unpublished manuscript, Brigham Young University, Provo, Utah, October 1979.

ORGANIZATIONAL STORIES AS SYMBOLS WHICH CONTROL THE ORGANIZATION

Alan L. Wilkins

At Swarthmore College located near Philadelphia, it was difficult in the late 50's and early 60's for new students or faculty to spend much time on campus before they heard some part of the Swathmore saga. In this saga, Frank Aydelotte is portrayed as a charismatic president who, with his growing band of supporters, changes one aspect of the college after another to overcome a casual "Joe College" atmosphere and produce a unique, scholarly, and successful small college. For believing college participants, this saga was almost a sacred way of communicating both their vision of what their college should become and their progress at implementing the vision (Clark, 1970).

Bill Hewlett and Dave Packard at Hewlett-Packard are "legends in their own time" to the employees of that company. New employees learn from a slide presentation shown when they first arrive that "Bill and Dave" started the company in Bill's garage and made some of the first products using the Hewlett oven. They hear informally from many employees stories about how Bill and Dave expect employees to address them by their first names. Stories emphasize and legitimate the management philosophy to avoid long-term debt and to avoid layoffs. Stories also help define, in a way mere statements can't, what the "HP way" is.

Though anthropologists have found the myths and legends of primitive tribes critical to an understanding of these social groupings, students of contemporary work organizations have with few exceptions neglected related phenomena such as stories and legends (exceptions include: Clark, 1970; Dandridge, 1979; Wilkins, 1978). Employees in the organizations mentioned above ignore the contents and implications of the stories they hear at their own peril. The stories are important indicators of the values participants share, the social prescriptions concerning how things are to be done, and the consequences of compliance or deviance. The stories may also indicate the social categories and statuses which are legitimate in the organization, and are thus an important guide to what kinds of people can do what. Such information is crucial for the successful participation of organizational actors.

Indeed, stories appear to perform control functions in organizations which Perrow (1979) would label "third-order controls", or control over decision premises (Simon, 1945). Ouchi (1980) has discussed a similar form of control in organizations which he calls "clan control," or control through shared traditions. Organization theory provides us with little help in understanding how organizational participants make decisions, allocate work, and coordinate efforts based on shared perspectives, or tacit meanings rather than through rules and programs or through direct supervision (see, March & Simon, 1958; Perrow, 1979; Ouchi, 1980).

This article presents a case for considering organizational stories as an important means by which third-order controls are transmitted and reinforced in organizations. Research and argument will be presented to claim that stories are particularly effective at presenting information in a way which is concrete, vivid, and thus easily remembered. We will also discuss research demonstrating that for most people a story (N = 1) is more persuasive in making a claim than is a statistical argument based on multiple observations. In a similar vein, stories have been shown to produce at least attitudinal commitment to values or the behavioral implications which are presented in the story. Thus, our discussion will suggest that the concrete story, whether taken as a symbol or as a behavioral prescription (a "script"), is particularly well suited to present values and suggest models for action in a way which is memorable and persuasive.

Stories as Symbols or Scripts

As symbols.   Geertz (1973) defines a symbol as "any object, act, event, quality, or relation which serves as a vehicle for conception—the conception is the symbol's 'meaning' . . . tangible formulations of notions, abstractions from experience fixed in perceptible forms, concrete embodiments of ideas, attitudes, judgments, longings, or beliefs." Thus, the focus in this definition of symbol is on the communication of internal states through the means of tangible formulations (Dandridge & Pondy, 1978).

In his classic study of myth, Durkheim (1961) claims that these important tribal narratives present in concrete form the values of the society. His thesis is that the god of the society as presented in the myth is society itself divinized. He further claims that concrete symbols like myths are necessary because "the clan is too complex a reality to be represented clearly in all its complex unity," (1961, p. 220). Stories about the founding of the organization, about charismatic leaders, or about other significant events in the organization may serve a similar function of presenting an image of an organization which many participants value and which would therefore serve to unify them (Clark, 1970, 1972).

As scripts. Scholars studying the folklore of various cultures have discovered that certain tales may be used to teach vicariously approved behaviors and attitudes. Among the Jicarilla Apache, for example, grandparents or other relatives use stories to instruct the young. Not only during youth but also in adult life, it may be sufficient to "chide aberrant behavior by inquiring scathingly of the transgressor, 'Did you have no grandparent to tell you the stories?'" (Opler, 1938).

Import of Stories to Understanding Organizations

Most of the functions which have been attributed to narratives like myths, sagas, or stories have to do with the maintenance of social order. Such narratives have been associated with shared values which are used to legitimate institutional arrangements like economic systems or status hierarchies (Malinowski, 1961), or they may be used to present and resolve inherent contradictions in society (Levi-Strauss, 1963). Clark (1970) has demonstrated the association of strong organizational loyalty with the embodiment of an image of the organizational mission (Selznick, 1957) in the form of a saga (a large portion of the organization's history told in heroic style). The saga shows how the vision of a charismatic leader or an organizational elite group is translated into reality and therefore symbolizes the vision in some sense.

Wilkins (1978) and Wilkins and Martin (1979) have also argued that a developing literature on cognitive scripts (Abelson, 1976) is relevant to an understanding of organizations. Scripts are a form of cognitive shortcut in that they are an event map for routine events. They help us categorize events of "this type" so that we know what to expect and/or how to behave. My research on stories told in organizations (Wilkins, 1978) suggests that many stories are scripts for organizational participants. In one organization, many participants tell a story about how the company avoided a mass layoff in the early 1970's when almost every other company in the industry had felt forced to lay off employees in large numbers. The company had managed to avoid a layoff of 10% of their employees by having everyone in the company take a 10% cut in salary and come to work only 9 out of 10 days. This company experience is thus called the "9 day fortnight." The story is well known and it is apparently used as a script. In 1974, the company was again confronted with a drop in orders and they went to the "9 day fortnight" scheme for a short period. Recently, in the Far East a company plant was faced with a significant and unexpected drop in orders and the plant immediately applied the "9 day fortnight" arrangement. Furthermore, when other companies in the industry begin layoffs, the oldtimers use this story to quiet the anxiety of concerned newcomers. The story is a script employees use to predict the behavior of the company and which managers use to make decisions when layoff pressures mount.

Organizational Control

All of these functions mentioned seem to have implications for control in organizations. To use Perrow's terminology, the form of control suggested, looks like second- or third-order control rather than first-order control (Perrow, 1977, 1979). First-order controls refer to direct supervision or control by direct orders (or rules). Second-order controls are more remote controls deriving from an assembly line layout, or from "programs" or "standard operating procedures" (March & Simon, 1958). Third-order controls are found in the assumptions or definitions of the situation which are taken as "givens" by organizational participants.

Organizational stories that have become scripts provide the same kind of cognitive "satisficing" device that a standard operating procedure does and are therefore like second-order controls. The decision maker has only to place an incoming problem into the framework of a well-known story about how such a problem was handled to decide what should be done. Of course, the difference between scriptal stories and standard operating procedures is that the story is an informally transmitted, and subjectively interpreted event from the organization's history rather than a formally prescribed procedure or rule.

Third-order controls are even more subtle and perhaps therefore less well understood. Perrow defines this type of control as control over decision premises (Simon, 1945). This is the type of control Durkheim, Malinowski, Clark, Selznick and others refer to when they suggest that such narratives as myths, legends, and sagas are often viewed by participants as concrete instances of abstract values or implicit assumptions. An example of this form of control comes from a personnel manager in a company I studied. He told me of an experience he had while working in the Far East. He and the plant manager were confronted one day with an emergency decision and had been unable to contact headquarters in the U.S. for instructions. They sat down together and asked themselves: "Well, what would the company president do?" What occurred to them was a shared perspective which the personnel manager derived from a story the president had once told him. This rather implicit perspective made the decision clear to these men and they later found that top management agreed completely with their conclusions.

This kind of control works by restricting what decision makers consider as relevant, the form of logical reasoning that is deemed appropriate, and the kinds of solutions that are seen as acceptable. Thus, stories from the organization's history may provide not only implicit shared scripts but also a set of assumptions and implied values which guide and limit decision makers.

"Institutional" Leadership

Selznick (1957) views this kind of control from the top management perspective in speaking of the role of institutional leadership. This kind of leadership communicates a vision of the organization's mission or role in society. This vision becomes the "socially integrating myth" which, if it can appeal to a broad enough base of believers, provides energy and helps to link the differentiated parts of the organization together in achieving the vision. Clark (1970) demonstrated in three small colleges how a charismatic leader was in each case able to infuse purpose and value into the organization and how these values were passed on through the recounting of the college's saga.

In this same vein, Peters (1978) has recently argued that top management has relatively little control to change the organization through means of structural rearrangements, strategic planning programs, or organizational development efforts. His study of successful executives suggested to him that managers have more control over their organizations by means of providing a simple overarching theme or symbol like Geneen's (ITT), "search for the unshakable facts", Clausen's (Bank of America) "laying pipe" (shorthand for anticipating and preparing for events), DeButt's (AT&T) "the system is the solution", or Joneses'

(Northrop) "everybody at Northrop is in marketing." The biographies of Cordiner at GE, Vail at AT&T, Greenwalt at DuPont, and Watson at IBM all stress the quest to give operational force and meaning to a dominant, though imprecise, idea (Peters, 1978, p. 19).

My research (Wilkins, 1978) in two electronics firms suggests that when (1) top executives consistently point to general ideas or frameworks and (2) organizational membership is relatively long term, the participants begin to have time and the "material" with which to fashion stories. They also have time to pass on stories told by management. In either case, the stories may become symbols and provide the social integration and committed energy that Selznick, Clark and Peters describe. In one company, company Z, the CEO wrote in 1956 to his employees about his philosophy of avoiding layoffs and of searching for products which have immediate profitability and long-term stability. Twenty years later he wrote about the "company Z way" and described the same basic ideas. In contrast, at company A, there has been considerable uncertainty about a philosophical framework or a direction. At times they have avoided layoffs and at other times they have perfected the "hire and fire" policies for which the electronics industry is well known. They have moved quickly from supplying industrial concerns to consumer markets and they have not yet developed clear themes or frameworks which help them understand their direction in these new endeavors. Executives and other participants in company A would frequently say that "the only thing that is constant in the company is change" and that "we look at the bottom line." If the bottom line looks good, no matter what your strategy, you are doing things right.

Ouchi and Johnson (1978) argue that the most important difference between a type A and type Z company is the length of employment. Employees have to be around for a while before they really understand the more subtle, third-order controls which are emphasized relatively more in a type Z company. The importance of long term employment at company Z was brought home forcefully to us in an interview with the executive vice president. Just prior to our interview he had turned away a superior division general manager prospect when he told the man that frankly it would take at least 2 or 3 years for him to know enough about the company to be an effective manager. "Why, he could go into another company and be an effective division general manager in a matter of weeks," said this executive. "That's just one of the costs of the way we run this company."

At company A, on the other hand, the president bragged about how quickly the company had been able to get into a particular business by merely buying pieces of other companies and putting them together.

Length of employment figures show a significant difference between companies, particularly among management (see, Ouchi & Johnson, 1978; Wilkins, 1978).

When I systematically interviewed participants at the middle management and operator levels of both companies, I found significantly more "shared stories" (stories told by several people) in company Z than in company A. Many of the shared stories told at Z were about ritual practices of the company like a beer bust for each division which meets its monthly production goals, a yearly company picnic using recreation facilities either owned or rented by the company, and calling people by their first names. Some of the shared stories had to do with how the company got into some market early but avoided making all the units they could sell so they wouldn't have to hire and then fire when competition came in. I also found that a significantly greater proportion (33%) of the stories told by participants in company Z were used to illustrate or legitimate the management philosophy than was the case at company A (14%). These stories were concrete symbols of how management applied their philosophy.

Apparently, company Z executives perform the role of Selznick's institutional leaders in part because they are story tellers and in part because they focus consistently on general themes which lower participants use as the theme for stories which they tell and pass on. The result at company Z is that stories are significant symbols of shared values and shared perspectives which participants must learn to function effectively.

WHY STORIES AS THIRD-ORDER CONTROLS?

But why should stories serve as the vehicle to transmit shared values, frameworks or assumptions? We will now turn to a review of some rather diverse sources which suggest an answer to this question. Though the research to be reviewed is not extensive, it is suggestive. For purposes of clarity, we will consider three general reasons why organizational stories play a significant role as third-order controls: (1) they facilitate recall (memory) of values, principles, as well as specific information; (2) they tend to generate belief; and (3) they seem to encourage attitudinal commitment by appealing to legitimate values. We will take up each of these claims in turn.

Stories Facilitate Recall

Research on memory has demonstrated that concrete words, sentences, and paragraphs of "connected discourses" were recalled more accurately than more abstract versions of these phenomena. Martin, Patterson, and Price (1979) for example, have demonstrated that the more concrete a story is, the more accurately it was recalled.

There are two types of research relevant to the function of stories in facilitating recall. The first type compares the accuracy of recall or recognition, speed of information processing or of problem solving of subjects when they have a script in mind with subjects who don't have a script. This research has for the most part supported the conclusion that the presence of a script facilitates recall or recognition (Bower et al., 1979; Hamilton, 1980), although a few contradictory findings have been reported (Taylor & Crocker, 1978).

The second area of relevant research uses an independent variable which is not necessarily a narrative. The research is relevant, however, because a case example ($N = 1$) is compared with consensus information usually in the form of statistics which indicate how a number of people react to a given situation. It seems logical that the statistical information should be useful to subjects because it is based on multiple observations. However, the single observation had significant and stronger effects on recall relative to information presented as statistics (Nisbett & Borgida, 1975; Borgida & Nisbett, 1975; McArthur, 1972, 1976; Nisbett et al., 1976). The implication of this research is that since organizational stories are similar to information about a single individual, stories would also produce similar effects on recall when compared with consensus information or merely a statement of fact. This implication was supported by the research of Martin et al. (1979) reported previously.

Stories Generate Belief

Another finding in the research which has compared consensus information with case examples is that subjects overutilize case information in making probability judgments or predictions about themselves and others (Kahneman & Tversky, 1979; Tversky & Kahneman, 1977; Borgida & Nisbett, 1975; Nisbett & Borgida, 1975; McArthur, 1972, 1974). Of course this research holds variables like the credibility of the source of information constant and recent research has begun to investigate other boundary conditions for this tendency (Ajzen, 1977; Feldman et al., 1976; Hansen & Donohue, 1977).

Malinowski (1961) observed in the Trobriand islands that the myths and legends of the natives served as the proof of claims to property, to fishing rights, or to social roles of people or communities. Apparently, the legend or myth served to "prove" that claims were valid by presenting historical "evidence" and permitting an interpretation of that "evidence."

Stories Encourage Commitment

Anthropological myths have been associated with commitment to the values of a society (Cohen, 1969; Durkheim, 1961; Malinowski, 1961). A similar association was observed between organizational sagas and a commitment to a definition of organizational mission and values (Clark, 1970).

I studied (Wilkins, 1978) stories in two organizations, one with high and the other with low commitment to the organization. In the organization with high commitment, there were significantly more stories told which were favorable to the company and which were used to justify a claim of uniqueness for the company. The anthropological studies do not, of course, have comparison populations as did my study and all of our studies demonstrate association rather than causality.

Martin and Powers (1979) have used experimental methods to demonstrate that when information is presented in story form it generates a relatively more favorable distortion in memory than do claims supported by statistics (subjects remember the information as being more favorable than it really was). Thus, it seems that as a relative matter we can conclude that stories cause at least attitudinal commitment.

Summary

My claim has been that stories may function to communicate presuppositions or values which, in subtle ways, limit and enrich what participants see and believe and feel. These shared values and perspectives are not always expressed or even expressable in merely descriptive terms (Polanyi, 1958). What is assumed here is that many of the values and assumptions of an organizational culture are often implicit, though operative in the normal conduct of affairs (Dandridge & Pondy, 1978). Many participants interviewed at company Z struggled to put into words a description of the "company Z way" and would then make a comment like the following: "Well, I can't tell you exactly what the company Z way is, but I can give you some examples." They would then proceed to tell us stories about the company and its practices.

Stories may provide a richness of detail, a vivid description, with which people can identify and even experience vicariously. Perhaps they are memorable and believable because of this potential for vicarious experience. But what is most important to us as students of organization and culture is that the story may communicate a perspective, an approach to problem solving, implied causal relationships, and deep-seated values. The implied hope in this claim is that stories may serve as a window through which we may see and better understand the tacit third-order controls of a culture.

There are, however, some caveats we should note lest we be misled in our use of stories. First, we should recognize that other symbolic forms such as rituals, concrete images or words, and magic may perform similar functions. They may also be concrete and vivid. They may also present scripts as well as presuppositions to the minds of participants. I would argue that the story seems potentially more concrete and vivid than most of these other forms. On the other hand, participation in a company ritual like a beer bust or a company-wide picnic might provide a "real" experience which has even greater concreteness or vividness than a story.

To further confuse those who seek easy categorizations, we should also recognize that one of the critical elements of many rituals is the enactment of a story or myth (Cohen, 1969). We should, then, be careful to avoid the neat conclusion that stories are the only mechanisms by which presuppositions and values are communicated. The argument here has been that they are often a convenient or a relatively more effective means of establishing or maintaining third-order controls.

Second, not all organizations approach the status of a cultural entity to the same degree. This is the clear implication of my research in companies A and Z. Ouchi (1979, 1980) has explicitly presented three ideal types or forms of control: markets, bureaucracies, and clans. His work and my research suggest that one would most likely find organizational stories associated with third-order controls in clan organizations like company Z rather than company A which uses more bureaucratic and market controls. We should recognize, however, that Horatio Alger stories and a protestant ethnic deriving from some forms of Christianity may provide the justification for a norm of reciprocity which Ouchi says is crucial to the existence of market controls. Thus, though one might expect more shared stories and a greater reliance on stories and other symbols to control the clan organization, other forms of control require some degree of shared values (and hence the potential use of stories or symbols) to undergird them.

Third, there may be something more to learning a culture than hearing stories. To be sure, one is able to pick up contextually appropriate vocabulary, scripts, tacit assumptions, and an intuitive gestalt or perspective from a collection of stories. But, at company Z, it still seems to take some time to live with the system long enough to (1) see the application of principles in varied circumstances and (2) to prove that you can be trusted (that you are "one of us"). The first point suggests that stories aren't enough—one needs experience too. Furthermore, stories are often exaggerations claiming uniqueness. They may be the ideal or preferred image of the culture requiring the participant to gain some experience at making the tradeoff between the ideals presented in the story and actual practice.

These caveats do not suggest that stories will not be useful to the participant or organizational observer but rather that they will not tell us all we want to know. However, the point of this article is that organizational stories can tell us a lot that we don't presently know because we have not been willing to take them as a serious source of data.

REFERENCES

Abelson, R. P. Script processing in attitude formation and decision-making. In J. S. Carroll & J. W. Payne (Eds.), *Cognitive and social behavior*. New York: Erlbaum, 1976.

Ajzen, I. Intuitive theories of events and the effects of base-rate information and prediction. *Journal of Personality and Social Psychology*, 1977, *35*, 303–314.

Borgida, E., & Nisbett, R. E. *Abstract vs. concrete information and persuasion*. Unpublished manuscript, University of Michigan, 1975.

Bower, G. H., Black, J. B., & Turner, T. J. Script in memory for text. *Cognitive Psychology*, 1979, *2*(2), 177–220.

Clark, B. *The distinctive college: Antioch, Reed, and Swarthmore*. Chicago: Aldine, 1970.

Clark, B. The Organizational saga in higher education. *Administrative Science Quarterly*, 1972, *17*, 178–184.

Cohen, P. S. Theories of myth. *Man*, 1969, *4*(3), 337–353.

Dandridge, T. C. *Major corporate anniversary celebrations as means of intra-organizational communication*. Paper presented at the National Academy of Management Meetings, Atlanta, Georgia, August, 1979.

Dandridge, T., & Pondy, L. *Organizational symbols in the American wine industry*. NSF grant proposal, 1978.

Durkheim, E. *The elementary forms of religious life*. (Joseph W. Swain, Trans.) New York: Collier, 1961.

Feldman, N. S., et al. Use of consensus information in causal attributions as a function of temporal presentation and availability of direct information. *Journal of Personality and Social Psychology*, 1976, *34*, 694–698.

Geertz, C. *The interpretation of cultures*. New York: Basic Books, 1973.

Hamilton, David L. Cognitive representations of persons. In E. T. Higgins, C. P. Herman & M. P. Zanna (Eds.), *Social cognition: The Ontario symposium on personality and social psychology*. New York: Lawrence Erlbaum Associates, 1980.

Hansen, R. D., & Donohue, J. M. The power of consensus: Information derived from one's and others' behavior. *Journal of Personality and Social Psychology*, 1977, *35*, 294–302.

Kahneman, D., & Tversky, A. On the psychology of prediction. *Psychological Review*, 1979, *80*, 237–251.

Levi-Strauss, C. The structural study of myth. In (C. Jacobson & B. G. Scheoff, trans.), *Structural anthropology*. New York: Basic Books, 1963.

Malinowski, B. *Argonauts of the western Pacific.* New York: E. P. Dutton and Co., 1961.

March, J., & Simon, J. *Organizations.* New York: Wiley, 1958.

Martin, J., Patterson, K., & Price, R. *The effects of level of abstraction of a script on accuracy of recall, predictions, and beliefs* (Research Paper No. 530). Stanford, Ca.: Graduate School of Business, Stanford University, 1979.

Martin, J., & Powers, L. *If case examples provide no proof, why underutilize statistical information?* Paper presented at the American Psychological Association Meetings, New York, September, 1979.

McArthur, L. Z. The how and what of why: Some determinants and consequences of causal attribution. *Journal of Personality and Social Psychology,* 1972, *22,* 171–193.

McArthur, L. Z. The lesser influence of consensus than distinctiveness information on causal attributions: A test of the person-thing hypothesis. *Journal of Personality and Social Psychology,* 1976, *32,* 733–742.

Nisbett, R. E., & Borgida, E. Attribution and the psychology of prediction. *Journal of Personality and Social Psychology,* 1975, *32,* 932–943.

Nisbett, R. E., et al. Popular induction: Information is not always informative. In J. W. Carroll & J. W. Payne (Eds.), *Cognitive and social behavior.* Hillsdale, N.J.: Lawrence Erlbaum Associates, 1976.

Opler, M. Myths, and tales of the Jicarilla Apache Indians. *Memoirs of the American Folklore Society,* 1938, *31.*

Ouchi, W. G. Markets, bureaucracies, and clans. *Administrative Science Quarterly,* 1980, *25*(1).

Ouchi, W. G., & Johnson, J. Types of organizational control and their relationship to emotional well-being. *Administrative Science Quarterly,* 1978, *23*(2), 293–317.

Ouchi, W. G. A conceptual framework for the design of organizational control mechanisms. *Management Science,* 1979, *25.*

Perrow, C. *Complex organizations: A critical essay,* Glenview, Ill.: Scott, Foresman and Co., 1979.

Peters, T. J. Symbols, patterns, and settings: An optimistic case for getting things done. *Organizational Dynamics,* 1978, Autumn, 3–23.

Polany, M. *Personal knowledge: Toward a post-critical philosophy.* Chicago: University of Chicago Press, 1958.

Selznick, P. *Leadership in administration.* Evanston, Ill.: Row, Peterson, 1957.

Simon, H. A. *Administrative behavior.* New York: Free Press, 1945.

Taylor, S., & Crocker, J. Schematic bases of social information processing. In *Advances in experimental social psychology* (Vol. 2). New York: Academic Press, 1978.

Tversky, A., and Kahneman, D. Causal schema in judgment under uncertainty. In M. Fishbein (Ed.), *Progress in social psychology.* Hillsdale, N.J.: Lawrence Erlbaum Associates, 1977.

Wilkins, A. *Organizational stories as an expression of management philosophy: Implications for social control in organizations.* Unpublished doctoral dissertation, Stanford University, 1978.

Wilkins, A., & Martin, J. *Organizational Legends* (Research Paper No. 521). Stanford, Ca.: Graduate School of Business, Stanford University, 1979.

TRUTH OR CORPORATE PROPAGANDA:

THE VALUE OF A GOOD WAR STORY

Joanne Martin and Melanie E. Powers

Many organizations have become adept at symbolic means of communicating information about their philosophy of management, the culture of their organization, and the humanistic rationale for their policies. Symbolic forms of management, discussed in the chapters of this volume, include the creation of rituals of initiation and transition, the evolution of shared jargon and special metaphors, and—the focus of this chapter—the telling of organizational sagas, myths, legends, and stories.

COLLECTING HEADS, TAMING WILD DUCKS, AND J.F.K.

One organization which has become known for its attention to symbolic forms of management is I.B.M. Under the guidance of its founder, T. J. Watson, Sr., I.B.M. developed a distinctive culture, a well-articulated philosophy of management, and a strong demand for conformity (cf. Belden & Belden, 1962; Foy, 1975; Malik, 1975). For example, the famous I.B.M. dress code required male employees to wear dark suits, crisp white shirts, and narrow black ties. The organizational culture included rules concerning sexual relations between employees (not advisable), the use of coarse language or alcohol during working hours (don't), and the way to make a speech (list key points using simple words on a flip chart). T. J. Watson, Sr. reinforced these forms of organizational control with numerous rituals and ceremonies. For example, until the company became too large, employees lived temporarily in tents on company grounds during the annual picnic. There they sang company songs and listened to speeches given with evangelical fervor.

When T. J. Watson, Jr. took over the leadership of I.B.M. from his father, he wanted to improve the functioning of the corporation and leave his personal mark on its distinctive philosophy of management and culture. One means to these ends was to change the rhetoric, and perhaps the reality, of the corporation's demands for conformity. T. J. Watson, Jr. stated this objective directly in his speeches at company functions: "I just wish somebody would stick his head in my office and say (to me) 'you're wrong.' I would really like to hear that. I don't want yes-men around me" (Malik, 1975, p. 210).

Watson, Jr. justified his encouragement of dissent by citing *The Organization Man:* "when an organization tries to get too close to its people and makes a lot of the team idea, the individual gets swallowed up, loses his identity, and becomes a carbon copy of his fellow employees" (1963, pp. 24–25). He claimed that the company already had in its ranks a number of employees who would dare express dissent:

> [Our company] has more than 125,000 employees. A substantial number of them, many of whom I could pick out by name, are highly individualistic men and women. They value their intellectual freedom and I question whether they would surrender it at any price. Admittedly, they may like their jobs and the security and salaries that go along with them. But I know of few who would not put on their hats and slam the door if they felt the organization had intruded so heavily on them they no longer owned themselves. (1963, pp. 25–26)

Such abstract, direct statements of this change in the demand for conformity were dismissed as corporate propaganda by many employees: "[Watson, Jr.] says to us to stick our heads into his office and say 'you are wrong;' you should see the collection of heads that he has" (Malik, 1975, p. 210).

Watson, Jr. seemed to recognize the difficulty of convincing I.B.M. employees that this change in policy was truthful, and not corporate propaganda. He repeatedly supplemented abstract, direct statements, such as that quoted above, with stories illustrating his point. His favorite story concerned wild ducks:

The moral is drawn from a story by the Danish philosopher, Soren Kierkegaard. He told of a man on the coast of Zealand who liked to watch the wild ducks fly south in great flocks each fall. Out of charity, he took to putting feed for them in a nearby pond. After a while some of the ducks no longer bothered to fly south; they wintered in Denmark on what he fed them.

In time they flew less and less. When the wild ducks returned, the others would circle up to greet them but then head back to their feeding grounds on the pond. After three or four years they grew so lazy and fat that they found difficulty in flying at all.

Kierkegaard drew his point—you can make wild ducks tame, but you can never make tame ducks wild again. One might also add that the duck who is tamed will never go anywhere anymore.

We are convinced that any business needs its wild ducks. And in I.B.M. we try not to tame them. (Watson, Jr., 1963, pp. 27–28)

This metaphorical story also failed to convince many employees. Indeed, some researchers (cf. Ott, 1979) expressed scepticism about it. One employee put his reaction succinctly: "Even wild ducks fly in formation" (Malik, 1975, p. 210). Watson, Jr. had another story he told which made a similar point. The main characters in this story were I.B.M. employees.

Early in 1961, in talking to our sales force, I attempted to size up the then new Kennedy Administration as I saw it. It was not a political talk. I urged no views on them. It was an optimistic assessment, nothing more. But at the close of the meeting, a number of salesmen came up front. They would listen to what I had to say about business, they said, but they didn't want to hear about the new Administration in a company meeting.

On my return to New York, I found a few letters in the same vein. Lay off, they seemed to say, you're stepping on our toes in something that's none of your business.

At first I was a bit annoyed at having been misunderstood. But when I thought about it, I was pleased, for they had made it quite clear they wore no man's collar and they weren't at all hesitant to tell me so. From what I have read of organization men, that is not the way they are supposed to act. (Watson, Jr., 1963, p. 26)

This last story was more credible than his other statements that encouraged dissent. Even self-appointed critics of I.B.M. do not usually doubt the truthfulness of this particular story (cf. Malik, 1975), although they may continue to be sceptical of the company's actual tolerance of dissent.

This scepticism is not misplaced. Even in public statements, Watson, Jr. betrayed his unchanged desire for conformity:

It's going to be a prodigious job for every one of us to make all of them look and act and have the same basic philosophies in their business lives and their community lives that all of us have . . . I wish I could put it in a page or two and hand it out and say, 'Give this to every new employee,' who will then automatically start to look and act and think as we do. (Belden & Belden, 1962, p. 249)

In this I.B.M. example, Watson, Jr.'s policy change was more rhetoric than reality. Of all the various forms of communicating this purported policy change, the story about organizational employees seemed to arouse the least scepticism. Thus, it was most likely to generate commitment to the policy. Direct statements of the policy in abstract language were apparently less effective.

If organizational stories are a particularly effective means of generating commitment, they are a potentially powerful management tool. From a management point of view, it would be useful to know whether in fact an organizational story is a more effective way to generate commitment than other forms of communicating information. It would also be useful to know the conditions under which an organizational story would lose its impact.

From an employee's point of view, different issues are salient. An employee needs to know whether to believe a given statement is true or whether to dismiss it as corporate propaganda. It is also useful for an employee to know if a particular form of communication, such as a story, is likely to be particularly persuasive. If so, the employee can be wary when information is communicated in this form. These concerns of top management and lower-level employees suggest that symbolic forms of management, such as organizational stories, are an important topic for researchers to investigate.

ORGANIZATIONAL STORIES, MYTHS, LEGENDS, AND SAGAS

Some organizational research indicates that the persuasive power of the story in the I.B.M. example is representative of other organizational settings. This research focuses on organizational stories, myths, sagas, and legends (e.g., Clark, 1970; Meyer & Rowan, 1978; Selznick, 1957). Wilkins and Martin (1979) define an organizational story as an anecdote about an event sequence, apparently drawn from an accurate version of an organization's history. The main characters are organizational participants, usually employees rather than clients.

This research on organizational stories, including some of the chapters in this volume, has relied predominantly on qualitative methods (e.g., Clark, 1970; Selznick, 1957). Researchers have found examples of organizational stories in the transcripts of open-ended interviews and in archival material, such as memoranda, brochures, letters, and records of speeches given by company executives.

This organizational research speculates that organizational stories may serve many of the same functions that anthropologists have found myths to serve in tribal societies (e.g., Cohen, 1969; Malinowski, 1948): organizational stories legitimate the power relations within the organization; they rationalize existing practices, traditions, and rituals; and they articulate through examplars the philosophy of management and the policies which make the organization distinctive. In short, this research suggests the proposition that there is an association between stories and organizational commitment. The next section of this chapter examines this proposition in detail.

STORIES AND COMMITMENT

Alan Wilkins (1978, and this volume) decided to test this proposition using a mixture of qualitative and quantitative methods. He obtained transcripts of organizational stories through interviews with employees of two companies, and measured levels of employee commitment with a survey instrument. In the organization in which commitment was stronger, a larger number of stories were told, and their content was more favorable to the organization. Thus, Wilkins' research found an association between organizational stories and commitment.

The organizational research discussed above, including Wilkins' work, raises two sets of interesting questions. The first set concerns causality. Does the telling of organizational stories increase employee commitment to the organization? Or, is the direction of causality reversed, so that committed employees are more likely to tell favorable stories? Another possibility is that there may not be a causal relationship at all between stories and commitment. The second set of questions concerns the relative impact of stories on commitment, compared to other methods of communicating information about management philosophy or policy. Such other means of communicating information might include abstract policy statements, such as corporate objectives, or a table of statistical data. Are stories a more effective means of generating commitment than these other forms of information? The types of research designs and methodologies used in the organizational research discussed above raised these questions, but did not attempt to provide answers to them (Clark, 1970; Meyer & Rowan, 1978; Selznick, 1957; Wilkins, 1978).

We decided to seek answers to these two questions by using experimental laboratory methods. This methodology is well suited to address these questions. In an experiment it is possible to manipulate the form of information presented to subjects. Potentially confounding variables such as tenure can be controlled by the design of the experimental context and by random assignment of subjects to conditions. Hence a well-designed experiment can provide a context for testing questions of causality and for measuring the comparative strength of various means of communicating information.

We designed experiments to test two propositions based on the organizational research discussed above. We proposed, first, that supporting a management philosophy statement with an organizational story would increase the subjects' commitment to that philosophy. Second, we proposed that stories would produce more commitment than other forms of information.

As we considered in more detail elsewhere (Martin, in press), a body of experimental social cognition research is relevant to these propositions. This cognitive research begins with a premise concerning sample size which is familiar to all students of statistical inference: a judgment based on multiple observations should be more reliable than a judgment based on a single observation. If data based on multiple observations are supplemented by an additional observation, then that additional data point should be treated as merely one more observation.

This premise concerning sample size raises some issues about the impact of an organizational story. A story—indeed, any case example—is based on a single observation. Therefore, if the sample size premise is followed, a story should have much less impact then would data based on multiple observations.

Considerable cognitive research suggests that people do not behave in a manner consistent with the sample size premise (Borgida & Nisbett, 1977; McArthur, 1972, 1976; Nisbett & Borgida, 1975; Nisbett & Ross, 1980; Tversky & Kahneman, 1973). Typically in this research, some subjects were given distributional data about the behavior of a number of other people (consensus information) or the characteristics of a sample (base-rate information). The remaining subjects received the distributional information, plus additional information about a single case example. In accord with the sample size premise, subjects exposed only to the distributional data based their cognitive judgments on that data. Subjects exposed both to the distributional data and to the case example, however, weighted the case example much more heavily in their judgments then they should have, had they behaved in accord with sample size considerations.

More recently, researchers have attempted to find the limits of this phenomenon. Even in these studies, though, case examples are usually given weight beyond that dictated by the sample size premise (Azjen, 1977; Feldman, Higgins, Karlovac, & Ruble, 1976; Hansen & Donoghue, 1977; Manis, Dovalina, Avis, & Cardoze, 1980; Wells & Harvey, 1977). To summarize, social cognition research provides an experimental paradigm for examining the two hypotheses discussed above. It also provides additional support for the second of the two propositions to be tested: a case example, such as an organizational story, should have strong impact on judgments, stronger than that predicted by sample size considerations alone.

These conclusions, however, assume that the cognitive research results are generalizable to organizational contexts. This assumption may not be warranted, for two reasons. First, the experimental tasks used in the cognitive research require subjects to make rational, usually statistical, judgments. In organizational contexts, judgments are usually more complex and subjective. Second, the source of the distributional and case example information appears to be objective in the cognitive research. Subjects would have little reason to doubt the truthfulness of this information. In organizational contexts, though, the credibility of the source of information is often questionable. Organizational representatives have been known to distort information about their organizations.

Both of these limitations of the cognitive research suggest the importance of exploring ideas drawn from the cognitive research in contexts which are organizationally relevant. In such contexts, experimental tasks would require complex and subjective solutions, not derivable from statistical principles. The source of the information, whether it is based on single or multiple observations, would be of potentially questionable credibility. Two experiments having these organizationally relevant characteristics are described below.

SELLING CALIFORNIA WINE WITH A STORY

In the first experiment (Martin & Powers, 1979) subjects were recruited for a study of the effectiveness of an advertisement for a winery. An abstract policy statement (an advertisement) was read by all subjects. According to this statement, the new Joseph Beaumont Winery used many of the same excellent winemaking techniques as used in the famed Chablis region of France, thus producing California wine as fine as French chablis.

The text of the advertisement contained this policy statement plus some supplemental information. The supplemental information detailed the winemaking procedures used by the Joseph Beaumont winery. Subjects were randomly assigned to receive this information in one of three forms: a story, a table of statistics, or a combination of story plus statistics. Like many organizational stories, the story concerned the founder of a business. Extracts of the story are quoted below:

> Joseph Beaumont's father spent most of his life growing grapes in Chablis, the famous winemaking area of France. . . . Before his father died, Joe promised him that someday he would make a California wine using the traditional winemaking techniques of Chablis. For ten years, Joe worked at some of the most famous vineyards in the Napa Valley, putting all his savings into a winery and vineyard, which he named Beaumont. . . .

> He ordered special Limosin oak barrels, from the same suppliers used by Chablis winemakers. He filtered his wine using natural methods—egg whites rather than the chemical filters favored by other California wineries. As Joe tasted his first vintage wine he thought, 'My father would have been proud of this wine.'

In the statistics condition, subjects were given a table summarizing information comparing the winemaking procedures (such as the types of grapes and oak barrels) used at the Joseph Beaumont Winery, at other California wineries, and in Chablis, France. In the story condition, subjects received the story, but no statistical data. In the combination condition, subjects received both the story and the table of statistics. After reading this material, subjects answered a questionnaire about the advertisement which contained the dependent measures of willingness to predict that the organization would behave in accord with the abstract policy statement; willingness to believe the policy statement; ability to recognize its content accurately; and willingness to consider the advertisement a persuasive marketing technique.

Our hypothesis, labeled the story hypothesis, predicted the same pattern of results for each of these classes of dependent variables: the story should have the greatest impact, followed by the combination condition, and then the statistics condition. An alternate hypothesis, labeled the data hypothesis, predicted the opposite pattern of results: statistics > combination > story.

In contrast to subjects in the other two conditions, subjects who read only the story were slightly more likely to predict that the winery would continue to use the winemaking procedures from France. These subjects were significantly more likely to believe that the advertisement was truthful, to believe that the Beaumont winery actually had used the French winemaking procedures, and to distort their memory of the policy statement, in a direction favorable to the winery. In summary, in accord with the story hypothesis, the story generally had stronger impact than the combination of story plus statistics; and the combination had more impact than did the statistics by themselves.

Interestingly, the subjects were apparently unaware of the strong impact of the story. In accord with the data hypothesis, subjects in the statistics condition rated the advertisement they had read as somewhat more persuasive than did subjects who had read both the story and the statistics. Furthermore, subjects in the statistics condition rated the advertisement as considerably more persuasive than did subjects in the other conditions. Thus the subjects did not realize how powerfully the story had affected their responses. It created a "true believer" reaction even in these quantitatively well-trained M.B.A. subjects.

GENERATING COMMITMENT TO A POLICY STATEMENT WITH A STORY

In the first experiment the supplemental information supported the policy statement. In this second study (Martin & Powers, 1980), the supplemental information either supported or disconfirmed the policy statement. As in the first study, three forms of that information were used: a story, a table of statistics, or a combination of story plus statistics. Thus in this second study two independent variables were manipulated, creating a two-by-three factorial design.

The M.B.A. subjects all read a policy statement. This policy, based on an actual company policy studied by Wilkins (1978), was that the company would avoid mass layoffs in times of economic difficulty by asking employees to take a temporary 10% cut in pay. In the story condition, the subjects read about a single employee, Phil Locke. The product which was produced by Phil's division was going to have to be discontinued. According to the story, extracts of which are presented below, Phil was worried:

> Phil knew he was really banking on Electrotec's layoff policy. In fact, that policy was one reason why he had come to Electrotec in the first place. Still, he knew he shouldn't depend totally on the company to protect his career and his family's welfare. . . . Phil was in the cafeteria when his secretary came after him with the news that his boss wanted to see him right away.
>
> Phil broke out in a cold sweat as he walked into his boss' office. His boss didn't say much, just something like, 'I'm sorry, Phil. I just got the news we've all been dreading; the inertial navigation products are going to be dropped from our line. You and I have been together for a long time, and I will miss you, but. . . '

Two endings for this story were prepared. Subjects in the policy supporting conditions read that:

'. . . you'll still have a job with Electrotec. I even think we'll be able to set one up for you in one of the other military hardware divisions. Of course, this means a temporary 10% cut in pay.' Not fired! Phil said later he felt as if he had been given a reprieve from a death sentence.

Subjects in the disconfirming conditions read a different ending to the story:

"'. . . I have to let you go.' Fired! Phil said later he felt as if he had been given the death sentence."

In the statistics conditions subjects were given numerical data concerning the frequencies of turnover (voluntary and involuntary) and paycuts, both before and after the products were discontinued. In the supporting conditions, the turnover data indicated that no mass layoffs had occurred and that most employees had taken a 10% cut in pay after the product was discontinued. In the disconfirming conditions, the frequency of turnover implied that a mass layoff had occurred and that pay cuts were rare. In the combination conditions subjects received either the supporting story plus the supporting statistics or the disconfirming story plus the disconfirming statistics.

When the information supported the policy statement, subjects in the story condition, in contrast to subjects in the combination and statistics conditions, were more likely to predict that mass layoffs would be avoided, to believe the policy statement was truthful, and to require a larger salary increase before they would quit for a comparable job at another company. The opposite pattern of effects was found when the information disconfirmed the policy condition. The disconfirming story had an impact equal to or less than the impact of the disconfirming statistics or the combination of disconfirming story plus disconfirming statistics.

In summary, when subjects were given information which supported a policy statement and were then asked to make predictions, to assess their belief in the truthfulness of the policy, or to indicate their commitment to the organization, the supporting story had a stronger impact than the other forms of communication. The power of a story however, is not limitless. When the information disconfirmed the policy statement, the story never had a stronger impact, and frequently had a significantly weaker impact, than the disconfirming statistics and the disconfirming combination of story plus statistics.

CONCLUSIONS: THEORETICAL, PRACTICAL, AND METHODOLOGICAL

In this final section of the chapter, the theoretical contributions of these experimental results are discussed. The practical implications for organizational employees are outlined and several ethical concerns raised. Lastly, the appropriateness of using quantitative methods to study symbolic forms of management is discussed.

The results of these two studies can be summarized in terms of the two questions raised by the organizational research. First, stories caused commitment. Second, stories caused more commitment than other means of communicating information, such as statistics.

In addition to addressing questions raised by the organizational research, these two experiments extend the results of the cognitive research. A wider range of dependent variables was considered. Whereas previous cognitive research had used dependent measures concerning cognitive judgments, these two experiments also measured belief in the truthfulness of information and commitment to the values underlying the information. The two experiments demonstrated that case examples, such as organizational stories, have strong impact on these attitudes as well as on cognitions.

The second experiment also produced a finding which was not anticipated by previous organizational or cognitive research. It demonstrated a boundary condition or limit to the powerful impact of case examples such as stories. When the content of the information disconfirmed, rather than supported, the policy statement, the story lost its potency. Disconfirming statistics had an impact on attitudes and cognitions that was equal to, sometimes even greater than, a disconfirming story. Subjects apparently dismissed the disconfirming story as the single exception to the general rule. The results of the second experiment suggest that if a story is to have strong impact, it must be congruent with previously available information.

The results of these two experiments have some clear practical implications. Frequently managers wish to communicate information about a policy change or their philosophy of management. Obviously, they want their messages to be memorable and believable, so that employees will be committed to these ideas. The studies discussed above indicate that the most effective tactic would be to support their points with an organizational story, rather than with statistical information.

Watson, Jr. of I.B.M. was using this tactic when he told the stories about the wild ducks or about the negative reaction to his speech supporting John F. Kennedy. Unfortunately, Watson ran afoul of the boundary condition discovered in the second experiment. He told stories which disconfirmed the employees' preconceptions about the I.B.M. emphasis on conformity. Consequently, these disconfirming stories were dismissed, by many employees, as corporate propaganda.

The I.B.M. example raises some ethical issues. Employees need to be wary of the potentially powerful impact that a seemingly innocuous story can have. Management, indeed anyone, could use the power of a story to manipulate beliefs about a policy and generate commitment to an organization when the information is, in fact, corporate propaganda. As this caveat indicates, symbolic forms of management, such as the telling of organizational stories, are powerful and potentially dangerous tools.

In conclusion, we shall step back from the results of these particular experiments and consider an additional issue. Is experimental laboratory methodology appropriate for the study of organizational stories? Such stories fall under the theoretical rubric of organizational symbolism. Researchers of this theoretical topic, including ourselves, generally endorse the epistemological view that reality is socially constructed (Berger & Luckmann, 1966), i.e., that human beings actively contribute to the creation of meaning. Certain researchers suggest that when this epistemological stance is taken, "The large-scale empirical surveys and detailed laboratory experiments that dominate much social research . . . become increasingly unsatisfactory and, indeed, inappropriate" (Morgan & Smircich, 1980, p. 498). Some of these researchers conclude that the study of organizational symbolism is, and perhaps should be, associated primarily with the use of qualitative methods, such as ethnography (e.g., Daft, 1980):

> Thus, within the context of organizations there may be a concern for understanding the roles that language, symbols, and myths play in the shaping of any given reality, and a concern for generating ethnographic accounts of specific situations that yield insight with regard to the way reality works. (Morgan & Smircich, 1980, p. 497)

These authors are careful to note that although the association between this theoretical topic and this type of methodology is appropriate, quantitative methods may also be of some use.

As our use of experimental methodology indicates, we believe that topics in the area of organizational symbolism, such as stories, can indeed be profitably studied using the "dominant" quantitive methodologies, such as experimental laboratory methodology. The strengths of the experimental method are familiar, but three are of particular relevance to research in this area: generalizability, causality, and control. Each of these issues is discussed below.

Even advocates of ethnomethodology seldom claim that the results of this kind of research can, or should, be generalized to other settings. For example, "The epistemology involved here does not hold that the findings thus obtained would be universally generalizable" (Morgan & Smircich, 1980, p. 497). It is not clear that one can generalize from Burton Clark's (1970) qualitative research on sagas in liberal arts colleges to other types of organizational settings. The fact that our study of organizational stories in an experimental setting found congruent patterns of results adds considerably to the potential generalizability of these earlier findings.

It is well known that causality cannot confidently be inferred from correlational data. Nevertheless, most of the organizational research on stories (e.g., Clark, 1970; Selznick, 1957) slips occasionally into language which implies a causal relationship between the telling of stories and employee commitment levels. The two experiments described above were designed specifically to address the centrally important, and previously unresolved, issue of causality.

Finally, experiments can include various types of control variables not customarily used in qualitative research. A logical inference from the organizational research is that stories have greater impact than other means of communicating information. We were able to test this inference in a controlled experimental setting in which information was presented in a variety of comparable forms.

These examples illustrate three advantages of using experimental methods to study organizational symbolism. We share the opinion of most, however, that every methodology has inherent strengths and weaknesses (cf. McGrath, 1980). Naturally, experimental methods are no exception.

For example, one important limitation of the experimental study of organizational symbols concerns the meaning of a symbol in a laboratory context. Is it still a symbol or is it a stimulus devoid of subjective content other than the social reality constructed in the laboratory? We would argue that the organizational stories in our experiments retained some of their subjective content. The effects on the subjective dependent variables, such as belief, offer some support for this point of view. A symbol taken out of context, of course, loses some of its meaning. Its impact may be weakened. Thus, it is encouraging that the impact of the story in the laboratory was even detectable, not to mention being stronger than other, less symbolic, means of communicating information.

Our position is that the "dominant" quantitative methods in general, and experimental methods in particular, have considerable contributions to make to the study of organizational symbolism. We disagree with the position that any single methodological approach is most appropriate for the study of this theoretical area. Our position is congruent with that of the numerous methodologists who advocate the advantages of triangulation and the use of multiple research methodologies (e.g., Jick, 1979; Campbell & Fiske, 1959). A uni-method approach limits the amount we can learn about this area. If symbolic forms of management, such as organizational stories, are a powerful and potentially dangerous tool, this unnecessary limitation of our knowledge may be practically, as well as theoretically, unwise.

REFERENCES

Azjen, I. Intuitive theories of events and the effects of base-rate information on prediction. *Journal of Personality and Social Psychology,* 1977, *35,* 303–314.

Belden, T. G., & Belden, M. R. *The lengthening shadow: The life of Thomas J. Watson.* Boston: Little Brown, 1962.

Berger, P. L., & Luckmann, T. *The social construction of reality.* Garden City, N.Y.: Doubleday, 1966.

Borgida, E., & Nisbett, R. E. The differential impact of abstract vs. concrete information on decisions. *Journal of Applied Social Psychology,* 1977, *7,* 258–271.

Campbell, D. T., & Fiske, D. W. Convergent and discriminant validation by the multitrait—multimethod matrix. *Psychological Bulletin,* 1959, *56,* 81–105.

Clark, B. *The distinctive college: Antioch, Reed and Swarthmore.* Chicago: Aldine, 1970.

Cohen, P. S. Theories of myth. *Man,* 1969, *4,* 337–353.

Daft, R. L. The evolution of organizational analysis in *ASQ,* 1959–1979. *Administrative Science Quarterly,* 1980, *25,* 623–636.

Feldman, N. S., Higgins, E. T., Karlovac, M., & Ruble, D. N. Use of consensus information in causal attributions as a function of temporal presentation and availability of direct information. *Journal of Personality and Social Psychology,* 1976, *34,* 694–698.

Foy, N. *The sun never sets on IBM.* New York: William Morrow & Company, Inc., 1975.

Hansen, R. D., & Donoghue, J. The power of consensus: Information derived from one's and others' behavior. *Journal of Personality and Social Psychology,* 1977, *35,* 294–302.

Jick, T. D. Mixing qualitative and quantitative methods: Triangulation in action. *Administrative Science Quarterly,* 1979, *24,* 602–611.

Malik, R. *And tomorrow . . . the world? Inside IBM.* London: Millington HD, 1975.

Malinowski, B. Myth in primitive psychology. In *Magic, science, and religion, and other essays.* Boston: Beach Press, 1948.

Manis, M., Dovalina, I., Avis, N., & Cardoze, S. Base rates can affect individual predictions. *Journal of Personality and Social Psychology,* 1980, *38,* 231–248.

Martin, J. Stories and scripts in organizational settings. In A. Hastorf & A. Isen (Eds.), *Cognitive social psychology.* New York: Elsevier-North Holland, Inc., in press.

Martin, J. & Powers, M. E. *If case examples provide no proof, why underutilize statistical information?* Paper presented at the meetings of the American Psychological Association, New York, September 1979.

Martin, J., & Powers, M. E. *Scepticism and the true believer: The effects of case and/or baserate information on belief and commitment.* Paper presented at the meeting of the Western Psychological Association, Honolulu, May 1980.

McArthur, L. Z. The how and what of why: Some determinants and consequences of causal attribution. *Journal of Personality and Social Psychology,* 1972, *22,* 171–193.

McArthur, L. Z. The lesser influence of consensus than distinctiveness information on causal attributions: A test of the person-thing hypothesis. *Journal of Personality and Social Psychology,* 1976, *33,* 733–742.

McGrath, J. *Dilemmatics.* Paper presented at the conference on Methodological Innovations in Studying Organizations, Greensboro, North Carolina, August 1980.

Meyer, J. W., & Rowan, B. Institutionalized organizations: Formal structure as myth and ceremony. In M. M. Meyer & Associates (Eds.), *Environment and organizations: Theoretical and empirical perspectives.* San Francisco: Jossey-Bass, 1978.

Morgan, G., & Smircich, L. The case for qualitative research. *The Academy of Management Review,* 1980, *5,* 491–500.

Nisbett, R. E., & Borgida, E. Attribution and the psychology of prediction. *Journal of Personality and Social Psychology,* 1975, *32,* 932–943.

Nisbett, R. E., & Ross, L. *Human inference: Strategies and shortcomings of social judgement.* Englewood Cliffs, N.J.: Prentice-Hall, 1980.

Ott, R. *Are wild ducks really wild: Symbolism and behavior in the corporate environment.* Paper presented at the meeting of the Northeastern Anthropological Association, March 1979.

Selznick, P. *Leadership and administration.* Evanston, Ill.: Row, Peterson, 1957.

Tversky, A., & Kahneman, D. Availability: A heuristic for judging frequency and probability. *Cognitive Psychology,* 1973, *5,* 207–232.

Watson, Jr., T. J. *A business and its beliefs: The ideas that helped build IBM.* New York: McGraw-Hill, 1963.

Wells, G. L., & Harvey, J. H. Do people use consensus information in making causal attributions? *Journal of Personality and Social Psychology,* 1977, *35,* 279–293.

Wilkins, A. *Organizational stories as an expression of management philosophy: Implications for social control in organizations.* Unpublished doctoral dissertation, Stanford University, 1979.

Wilkins, A., & Martin, J. *Organizational legends* (Research Paper No. 521). Graduate School of Business, Stanford University, 1979.

SYMBOLIC TRANSFORMATION OF BELIEF SYSTEMS

Carson K. Eoyang

There has been surprisingly little organizational research on the role and functions of symbols in organizational life despite common observations that symbols are virtually ubiquitous in all kinds of organizations and seem to be related to a wide variety of human behavior (Dandridge, et al., 1980). Consequently, our understanding of the creation and use of organizational symbols is not highly developed (Pfeffer & Salancik, 1978, p. 17). The primary purpose of this discussion is to explore the nature of symbols from the perspective of information processing. In the course of this exploration, I hope to propose a way of conceptualizing the symbolic character of belief systems and to suggest how belief systems can be transformed by the symbolic functions of leadership.

INFORMATION PROCESSING

A "symbol" is conventionally defined as something which represents another thing, especially an object which is used to represent something abstract. In psychoanalytic theory a symbol is defined as "a term, a name, or even a picture that may be familiar in daily life, yet that possesses specific connotations in addition to its conventional and obvious meaning" (Jung, 1964, p. 3). From an information processing perspective, symbols can be construed as the fundamental elements by which information is conveyed between people, between places and across time. The value of adopting this view is that it narrows our focus to the processes whereby information is generated, transformed, transmitted, received, translated and interpreted. As the primary medium of communications, symbols serve several important functions. First, symbols can be more concise than the meanings that they represent; that is to say that the expression of meaning can be compressed in space and time through symbolic representation. Second, symbols may be more easily manipulated than the original thoughts. Third, the physical character of symbols makes possible the storage and retrieval of information. Fourth, since symbols can be reproduced, communications can be made highly reliable. Fifth, they enable the articulation of abstract ideas. In short, the primary function that symbols serve for humans is that they facilitate communication of meaning. Parenthetically, it should be noted that symbols are not strictly necessary for communication. For example, I can get you to understand that it is raining by causing you to observe the phenomenon, to experience it directly, or to deduce it, none of which may involve the use of symbols per se. Specifically, I can direct your attention to the rain outside the window; I can physically move you under the rain; to or I can arrange to flood your house, none of which are symbolic actions.

Chunks of Information

Additional insight into the information functions of symbols can be derived from George A. Miller's (1956) classic article, on information processing. Miller demonstrated that there are limits to the number of items that can be discriminated through the senses (sight, sound, touch, taste), and that for people that limit is about seven. Miller also outlined a variety of techniques by which humans compensate for their limited capacity to receive, process and remember large quantities of information.

One of the most powerful of these techniques is the aggregation of numerous bits of information into a familiar unit, which Miller labeled a "chunk". A vivid example of how chunks work in humans is the simple experiment in which we try to recall the tenth word in the national anthem. For almost all of us we first have to remember the whole first stanza (the chunk) and count through the first ten words. Thus, any of the information residing in the national anthem (e.g., the words, the music, the meaning, etc.) is only available to us by first accessing the entire chunk. A more precise definition of a chunk is a set of cognitions that are related by at least one associational memory trace. The trace may be based upon chronology (events that happened about the same time), space (objects that share the same or similar location). logic (arguments following some sequence), similarities (words that sound the same), affect (things that arouse a common emotion), etc. Mnemonics are also examples of chunks, which have an "artificial" functional relation among the congnitions, e.g., the childhood rhyme that gives the number of days in any month of the year. With mnenomics the functional relation may be artificial in the sense that the relation is not logically relevant to the individual information bits that are aggregated. Thus, similarity of sounds (rhymes) are often used to create, store and recall chunks of information which are not poetic or literary by nature.

A theory is another example of a chunk. Just as a mathematical equation is a parsimonious representation of a set of numbers, so a theory may be a concise representation of a set of phenomena (Webb, et al., 1966, p. 29). Another example of a chunk is found in the findings that people remember human faces more accurately when faces are associated with specific personality traits (e.g., friendliness, intelligence, etc.) than when individual physical features (e.g., jaws, nose, eyebrows, etc.) were attended to. That is to say, aggregating the numerous facial features into a single gestalt or chunk seemed to aid information recall. Similarly, Miller (Hall, 1980) has implied that the use of stereotypes is cognitively easier than processing raw information. More generally, Boulding (1966, p. 111) has argued that symbols simplify the process of evaluating reality by reducing the complexity of rank ordering objects with multi-dimensional values.

Symbols as Chunks

The relevance of chunks for organizational symbols is that it suggests how symbols facilitate processing of information. More specifically, symbols can be thought of as representations of information chunks; alternately, a symbol is a set of cognitions all related by a single or several overlapping functional associations which are stimulated by a given sign. In mathematical notation, a symbol could be described as

$$S = R (x_i, f_j).$$

Thus, a sign (S) evokes a set (R), the symbol, of several cognitions (x_i) that are related by one or more functional relationships (f_j). In general there need not be any restrictions on the form or character of the sign, the kinds of cognitions, or the nature of the relations. For example, the relationship between sign and symbol need not be unique in the sense that the same set of cognitions and relations may be stimulated by more than one sign (e.g., a stop sign and a flashing red light signify the same meaning). Also, the cognitions need not be mutually exclusive, nor do each of the relations need to relate all of the cognitions, so long as any single cognition is related to at least one other cognition by at least one of the functional relations.

To illustrate, let us consider the symbolic value of the American flag. The physical object (the sign) stimulates a number of cognitions, memories, experiences, and beliefs, all of which are related by several functional relationships and associations. Hypotheically, the symbolic relationship could be described as follows:

S = American Flag (the sign stimulus)
R = Set of cognitions and associations (x_i, f_j)
        (the symbolic response)
x_i = Cognitions (parades, ball games, holidays, military, national anthem, pledge of allegiance, feeling of pride, honor, etc.)
f_j = Associations (patriotism, ceremony, devotion)

The distinction here of sign as a physical stimulus and symbol as the interpretative response differs from that made in the introduction of this book (pp. 4–5). In that view signs are visible manifestations of some literal objective meaning while symbols are representations of subjective meanings which may extend well beyond the obvious and surface interpretation of signs. Thus it is argued, signs have some innate meaning characteristic of the object alone, while symbols require subjective interpretation.

In contrast I would argue that all meaning is ultimately subjective, even if there is universal consensus of what the meaning is, as in the case of commonly understood signs. In the present context I would classify what Frost, et al. call signs as weak symbols, i.e., stimuli of interpretative responses which are narrow and superficial in meaning. I think it is more useful to think of symbols as varying on a continuum of interpretative meaning from very simple to very rich, rather than differentiating signs as weak symbols from more powerful symbols. I would rather reserve the word "sign" for the object of interpretation.

Creation, Interpretation and Elaboration of Symbols

In Miller's context, the creation of symbols can be conceived as the recoding of information bits into larger chunks to facilitate retrieval and processing. Conversely, the interpretation of symbols consists of decoding the chunks to retrieve the individual bits of information. However, both the recoding and decoding processes presume some transformation algorithms, which are analogous to the functional relationships defined above. In other words, the creation of a symbol is equivalent to constituting a set of cognitions which are related to facilitate retrieval and processing. Thus the creation of a symbol is equivalent to constituting a set of cognitions which are related by at least one functional association, and the interpretation of symbols is the decomposition of symbols into their constituent cognitions and associations. Where the two often become confused is when symbolic interpretation does not derive the original cognitions and functional relations but instead generates new or additional meanings and associations. This third process can be thought of as symbolic elaboration. Communication is most accurate when symbolic interpretation recovers from messages as precisely as possible the originally intended ideas and when symbolic elaboration is kept to a minimum. However, there are numerous instances when elaboration of symbols beyond preconceived ideas is desirable and appropriate, such as in literature, art, history, music, etc. In these more creative endeavors, fidelity of communication is less important than the aesthetic values of discovery.

Symbolic Meaning

With this conceptualization of symbols, it remains to be seen how people attribute meaning or sense to symbols, i.e., how signs come to be understood by the mind. I propose that the process of understanding is fundamentally similar to symbolization. Specifically, just as cognitions are associated into a symbol by some functional relations, so symbols themselves are incorporated into our cognitive structure, i.e., understood by our minds, when they become connected with the ideas, cognitions, beliefs, etc. that are already there (Hofstadter, 1979, p. 582). Thus, the meaning of a sign, (and the meaning of information for that matter) is generated when the sign is translated into the existing framework of previously retained knowledge and experience. When signs are not so connected they remain meaningless. Thus, it can be seen how the sign dollar ($) can take on a different meaning for a bank clerk than for a computer programmer. Also, the same sign may have no meaning to a pre-school child because it bears no relation to any of the child's previous experience or knowledge.

However, understanding signs is not only a process of evoking remembered meanings like playing a juke box (Hofstadter, 1979, p. 170).

If it was simply that, people could not increase their store of meanings and knowledge since new information could only be assimilated in terms of past understanding. Starting with little understanding as infants, they would not be able to make sense of anything new, which is clearly contrary to human experience. Hence the complete process of understanding includes not only the connection of new information to existing knowledge but, also the change and modification of existing knowledge by the very process of assimilation of new information. In other words, understanding or attribution of meaning is an interactive process in which new information and experiences are translated into the context of the familiar and the familiar is elaborated and transformed in terms of the new.

To return to the central issue of symbolic meaning, a sign takes on symbolic meaning when it is translated in terms of previously held beliefs which in turn may be modified by the sign. In cases when signs evoke weak symbolic responses, i.e., those in which the cognitions and associations are neither important nor surprising, the effects on previously held beliefs may be minimal, such as the corporate logo of an obscure company. Somewhat stronger symbols may serve to reinforce or confirm our previous understanding without substantially changing what or how we understand. For example the victory of the United States hockey team in the 1980 Olympics (the signal event) was for many Americans a symbol of moral and athletic superiority (the cognitive response). Even more powerful symbolic interactions may induce substantial changes in our past and current understanding. That is, our belief system is fundamentally the same as it was but that some major features or components have become modified in some way. Thus, a major failure in a respected leader may change our political partisanship without destroying our basic beliefs in democracy and society such as after the Watergate incidents. In the extreme some symbolic events may be so powerful as to cause major dramatic changes in our belief systems. Such symbols may be radically different from what we currently know and understand, but so compelling with the cognitions and associations that they represent, that we adapt our belief system to the symbol resulting in a different cognitive equilibrium with new levels and types of understanding. For example, religious converts presumably undergo symbolic experiences that fundamentally change their values, beliefs, attitudes, and assumptions, e.g., St. Augustine, Buddha, Mohammed, etc.

Obviously, the power of any symbol is relative to the openness to change of the focal belief system. Some symbols may constitute such a threat to present understanding that they are totally rejected. For example, ego defense mechanisms function to protect core beliefs about self by selectively buffering or interpreting information and experiences to be consistent with prior beliefs. Theories of cognitive dissonance (Festinger, 1957) address how inconsistencies are reconciled usually in favor of highly held beliefs.

Thus, we see that symbolic meaning is not an independent attribute of the symbol (Hofstadter, 1979); nor, is it a simple translation of previous knowledge into a new context. Instead symbolic meaning is an attribute of the interaction whereby the symbol is integrated into our previous body of knowledge. The process usually results in a cognitive system only incrementally different from previous ones. However, on occassion some symbols may be so powerful that major perturbations result. If we encounter symbols that seriously challenge the validity of our current beliefs, we may wind up with a disintegrated belief system causing uncertainty or anxiety in mild cases, confusion or grave doubt in moderate cases, and perhaps schizophrenia or anomie in extreme cases.

Normally, the vast majority of symbols we encounter in our lives are largely congruent with our established belief systems and thus, changes in our understanding are gradual and incremental over time. Rarely do people experience dramatic changes in their cognitive systems except perhaps in extremely turbulent circumstances such as war, disaster, personal catastrophe, etc. However, it is also possible that individuals may significantly alter their Weltanshauung as a result of some insight, revelation, mystic experience or other profound learning. Sometimes these latter types of symbolic transformations are initiated or facilitated by another person who may be exercising what James MacGregor Burns (1978) calls transformational leadership.

Symbolic Leadership

Transforming leaders according to Burns (1978, p. 425) shape, alter and elevate the motives, values, goals and I add here beliefs, assumptions and understandings of other people. This type of influence can be achieved in a variety of ways, one of which involves, "the symbolic solution of internal and external conflict" (Burns, 1978, p. 244). That is to say, transformational leadership may serve to reconcile psychological contradictions between various cognitions and experiences by providing a coherent symbolic context which incorporates the disparate elements into a meaningful and consistent gestalt. Thus, transforming leadership may provide an external symbolic framework which permits the psychological resolution of confused or ill understood cognitions and experiences.

So far I have argued that an essential characteristic of symbols is their consistency and compatibility with established beliefs and values. Normally, symbolic consistency is achieved by accepting symbols that are compatible with our beliefs and rejecting those that are not. As Miller, (Hall, 1980) has observed, "People do not usually try to disprove their own ideas." However, some transformational leaders are able to interact with their followers symbolically in ways that result in significant changes in established beliefs and understandings. How this is accomplished in practice is the next question of interest.

Symbolic Value

In answering this, let me introduce another critical dimension of symbols, i.e., symbolic value. The value of a symbol is determined by the importance attached to the cognitions and associations of the symbol by the individual evaluating the symbol. Thus, if in our personal value hierarchy we place great importance upon truth, beauty and justice, then signs of wealth and status may not have high value. With a different value structure, other preferences may result. The exact process whereby, cognitions and associations assume value or importance is exceedingly complex and not well understood (Boulding, 1956). Classical economics avoids the issue by assuming that individuals do have some preference ordering which can be inferred from observed behavior. Since these classical assumptions have recently come under substantial criticism (cf. March, 1978; Simon, 1977; Stigler & Becker, 1977), I will here explore the implications of the assumptions that tastes and value preferences are largely exogenous and stable, and then, discuss the implications of relaxing this assumption.

Initially, let us assume that inherent in every belief system is implied some value hierarchy by which new information, cognitions and experiences are assigned some degree of importance. This value hierarchy is assumed to be stable over time and exogenous, i.e., independent of the objects being evaluated. Then the value of any particular symbol is a function of the values of the constituent cognitions and associations invoked by the symbol. In this vein symbolic leadership then consists of correctly identifying the cognitions and themes that are important to people and then constructing symbols that are clearly and directly related to them (cf. Hostadter, 1979, p. 370 ff). Thus, in election years we see the politicians intensely attending to national opinion polls as they seek the image that captures the most voters. In this sense, (Burns, 1978) has observed that leaders follow the people by merely reflecting the needs and concerns of the times. Hence, leaders become symbols of their constituencies by representing to the world at large the important values and beliefs of those that follow and support the leaders. Such leaders may articulate, reinforce and perhaps amplify the established belief system held by others. The symbols they use are designed to be easily recognized and to arouse common reactions among the populace (cf. Percy, 1975). People may see a leader as an agent through which their personal and collective needs and aspirations may be fulfilled and thus, may exchange their commitment in return for realization of some expected benefit. Burns (1978), calls this type of relationship transactional leadership to reflect the reciprocal nature of interdependence between leader and followers. Consequently, if it is assumed that people's value and belief systems are stable and not susceptible to much change, then symbolic leadership is based primarily upon mediating and crystallizing the transactional relations between leader and lead. The challenge of transactional leaders is to create and manage symbolic interactions so as to engage the needs and values of high importance of those to be led.

On the other hand, if we assume that people's hierarchy of values is not necessarily stable and independent of the symbols they evaluate, then there is the possibility for transformational leadership to change the cognitive structure underlying what and how people believe and understand. In contrast to transactional leadership which reinforces these structures, transforming leadership induces cognitive changes which incorporate both old and new beliefs and values in a different equilibrium than before. Transformational symbols may create new preference orderings which then subsequently are used to evaluate future symbols, events and experiences. To illustrate, compare the symbolic interpretation of two recent events of national significance. The Olympic victory of the United States hockey team in 1980 served the function for many people of reaffirming the country's moral as well as athletic superiority over its adversaries, especially the Soviet Union. Few, if any changes, in fundamental beliefs and understandings were the result. In contrast, consider the nuclear accident at Three Mile Island. People who are complacent and secure in the safety of nuclear technology now are confronted with integrating very discrepant experience with their previous beliefs. The symbolic result may be substantial reordering of the priorities for public safety and for energy economics. Thus, the symbolic event of Three Mile Island has had the effect of transforming the belief systems for some nuclear advocates. To be sure, for opponents of nuclear technology the event served to strengthen and confirm their belief systems.

Symbolic Transformation of Belief Systems

In general, symbols may have neutral, reinforcing, or transforming influences upon belief systems. The first two effects are obvious and straightforward in terms of the interaction between symbols and beliefs. The nature of belief transformation is more complex and less clear even though examples of this phenomenon are not at all uncommon. As an initial conjecture, transforming symbols may affect the value and importance attributed to established beliefs by introducing new ideas which take on comparable if not superior importance relative to previous notions. For example, belief systems organized around self-interest and hedonism may be radically transformed after interacting with symbols promising eternal life, divine salvation etc. The experiences of Pascal, St. Augustine and others are powerful illustrations of how the recognition of a greater good transformed their views of worldly matters. On a more mundane level, individual self-interest can become subordinated to the collective welfare if people come to believe that superior social consequences will result.

The major difficulty with this type of symbolic transformation is that in the global competition of ideas and values, successful challenges to established value preferences are historically rare events. The transforming leader is hard put to discover ideas which will dominate existing beliefs; true visionaries are the exception rather than the rule. Much more common are transactional leaders who capitalize on what people already know and believe without attempting any fundamental transformations.

In addition to affecting the values of beliefs, another way in which transforming symbols can operate is to modify directly the cognitions and beliefs themselves. Specifically, established ideas may be disproved, discredited, discounted, or demolished by information that shows that such ideas are untrue, illogical, inconsistent, harmful or irrelevant. For example, if I were to discover that what I now believe to be the circumstances of my birth and heritage were completely erroneous, there would likely be dramatic changes in what I believe about myself and others. A substantial part of my cognitive and psychological structure could well be influenced by the change of a single belief. Similarly, entirely new ideas and cognitions that require integration into existing beliefs could be introduced. Thus, a cognition not previously known or understood could induce an adaptive reaction in the belief system. To illustrate, the discovery of intelligent life in other parts of the universe will have profound effects on what many people believe and understand about humanity. A more immediate example is the great attention and energy that the Communist Chinese pay to the rewriting and re-interpretation of their own history. They seem to be acutely aware of the symbolic implications of various historical events and actors (Schurman, 1971).

The third way in which symbols can transform belief systems is to change the associations and themes that relate and organize our various ideas and understanding. Earlier, I have mentioned the human memory relies upon associations or functional relations between and among cognitions in order to store and retrieve chunks of information. These associations may be based upon chronology, space, logic, similarities, affect, etc. As the chunks of information in our minds are aggregated into larger and more complex structures, additional higher order functional associations relate and organize the various components to constitute a vast inter-connected network which is our belief system (Hofstadter, 1979). It is these higher order associations themselves that may be the focus of symbolic transformation. For example, we may interpret all the success experiences in our lives as being the result of our own diligence, virtue, self-worth, etc. Similarly, we may attribute all of our failures and disappointments to bad luck. Thus, the common association among successes is virtue, and among failures misfortune. Now suppose that I experience a symbolic transformation through which I now believe that all life is determined by the will of God. What results is an entirely new association among all the events and experiences in my life, and the very meaning attributed to them has changed without any change in the individual cognitions. I merely see them in a different context recognizing new relations among them (Burns, 1978, p. 455). In general, transformation of established cognitive associations may occur when they are replaced by other associations that account for a larger number of experiences and events, account for them in a more parsimonious manner, account for them with a higher degree of accuracy, or protect and maintain the validity of strongly held cognitions.

In summary, belief systems can become modified when the importance of established beliefs changes, when the cognitions themselves change through attrition or addition, or when the functional associations become transformed. The power of a symbol to effect changes in human thought and action is directly related to the degree to which the symbol accomplishes any or all of these three transformations. Symbolic transformation of cognitive systems will be most enduring when the result is a new robust and stable equilibrium of values, beliefs, and associations. Burns (1978, p. 454) has argued that this is the essence of great leadership:

> The most lasting and pervasive leadership of all is intangible and noninstitutional. It is the leadership of influence fostered by ideas embodied in social or religious or artistic movements, in books, in great seminal documents, in the memory of great lives greatly lived.

> . . . Where leadership is necessary, Philip Selznick writes, 'The problem is always to choose key values and to create a social structure that embodies them.' . . . (The transforming leader taps the needs and raises the aspirations and helps shape the values—and hence mobilizes the potential—of followers.)

CONCLUSION

This exploration of symbolic phenomena has begun with the comparison of Miller's concept of information chunks with the properties of symbols. I have proposed that symbols consist of three basic elements, a set of cognitions aroused by the symbol, the value or importance of these cognitions, and the set of functional associations that relate the cognitions to each other. Further, it is suggested that symbolic meaning is an attribute of the process of integrating the symbol into existing belief systems, and not solely a property of the symbol alone. In addition, three mechanisms for the symbolic transformation of belief systems have been outlined.

If this conceptualization of symbols and the symbolic process has any merit, there may be significant implications for the practice of leadership. First, transformational leadership is more difficult, complex, and risky than transactional leadership. Second, decomposition of symbolic transformation processes into three distinct approaches may illuminate specific alternatives for exerting influence on the belief systems of others.

REFERENCES

Boulding, K. E. *The image.* Ann Arbor: University of Michigan Press, 1966.
Burns, J. McGregor. *Leadership.* New York: Harper & Row, 1978.
Dandridge, T. C., Mitroff, I., & Joyce, W. F. Organizational symbolism: A topic to expand organizational analysis. *Academy of Management Review,* 1980, 5(1), 77–82.
Festinger, L. *A theory of cognitive dissonance.* Evanston, Ill.: Row, Person, 1957.
Hall, E. Giving away psychology in the 80's: An interview with George A. Miller. *Psychology Today,* December 1980, pp. 38–98.
Hofstadter, D. R. *Godel, Escher, Bach: An eternal golden braid.* New York: Basic Books, 1979.
Jung, C. G. *Man and his symbols.* New York: Dell Publishing Co., 1964.
March, J. G. Bounded rationally, ambiguity, and the engineering of choice. *Bell Journal of Economics,* 1978, 9(2).
Miller, G. A. The magic number seven, plus or minus two: Some limits on our capacity for processing information. *Psychological Review,* 1956, 63(2), 81–97.
Newman, J. R. *The world of mathematics.* New York: Simon and Schuster, 1956.
Percy, W. *The message in the bottle.* New York: Farrar, Strauss and Giroux, 1975.
Pfeffer, J., & Salancik, G. R. *The external control of organizations.* New York: Harper & Row, 1978.

Rumbaugh, D. M. (Ed.). *Language learning by a chimpanzee: The Lana Project.* New York: Academic Press, 1977.

Schurmann, F. *Ideology and organization in Communist China* (2nd. ed.). Berkeley: University of California Press, 1971.

Simon, H. A. Rational decision making in business organizations. *American Economic Review*, 1977, March, 76–90.

Stigler, G. J., & Becker, G. S. De Guistibus non est Disputandum. *American Economic Review*, 1977, March, 76–90.

Webb E. J., Campbell, D. T., Schwartz, R. D., & Sechrest, L. *Unobtrusive measures.* Chicago: Rand McNally, 1966.

Part IV

SHAPING ORGANIZATIONAL
REALITY THROUGH LANGUAGE

In Part IV we focus on the role of language in organizational life. There is an important assumption in each of the four papers presented here that language plays an important role in shaping the behavior, attitudes, images and values of organizational life, and that to understand everyday organizational events, it is important, indeed essential, that we understand the use of the language on which they are based.

Roger Evered (*The Language of Organizations: The Case of the Navy*) examines language in a single complex organization. He demonstrates in considerable detail how everyday discourse in the U.S. Navy relies on a complex vocabulary, and system of signs. The paper clearly illustrates how many aspects of the reality of navy life are enacted and sustained through its language.

Paul Hirsch and John Andrews (*The Language of Corporate Takeovers*) develop a similar theme, analysing the imagery which dominates the boardroom discussion of the financial community's view of corporate takeovers. The focus is on large commercial organizations and the development of shared images of highly visible, repetitive events which occur in and among such organizations. This paper, along with Evered's, provides a useful starting point for more detailed and intensive study of the influence of language in shaping organizational reality.

Lou Pondy (*The Role of Metaphors and Myths in Organization and in The Facilitation of Change*) presents a related view. Like Hirsch, he is concerned with the emergence and influence of imagery. Pondy argues that people use metaphors and myths to make sense of their organizational experiences, to resolve paradoxes and the contradictions they encounter, suggesting that the creation of objective organizational facts are guided by underlying root metaphors.

In *A Rhetorical Examination of Strategic Change*, Anne Huff presents an analysis which, in essense, views organization as a *text*. She discusses the use of rhetorical analysis for the study of organizational reports and documents, as a means of reconstructing and understanding the process of organizational change.

THE LANGUAGE OF ORGANIZATIONS:
THE CASE OF THE NAVY

Roger Evered

It is probably safe to assume that most people of working age have had the experience (at least once) of joining a new organization, especially a different kind of organization from those they have previously encountered. The initial experience is often described as confusing, scary, surprising, unintelligible, giving rise to a need to comprehend the new and unfamiliar surroundings in order to act (Louis, 1980). New situations characterized by unfamiliar organizational terminology, data, signals and symbols are difficult to make sense of because the critical vocabulary, relational rules and translational codes are not initially known. In short, organizational events and actions have no meaning until we learn the *language* of the particular organization that provides the context for meaning.

Presumably then, every organization has its own characteristic language system(s). Organizations typically provide orientation sessions, apprenticeships, and training programs for newcomers in order to instruct the newcomer in the *language* of the organization; the unique terminologies, codes, acronyms, and sign systems, as well as the symbols and metaphors that convey the culture of the particular organization. The larger the organization, especially those which are highly differentiated and more technologically based, the more language there will be to convey, and the more extensive will be its training programs to teach newcomers the new organizational language.

The U.S. Navy offers a particularly fine example of a very large, complex and technologically sophisticated organization. It also has a massive training function with a total annual budget of approximately $3 billion, which might lead us to postulate that the Navy is a language-rich organization and worthy of study. The language used by the members of any organizational group not only characterizes that group but reveals how its members view their organizational world and how their world is construed. In short, *the language they use defines their reality.*

What follows is an exploration of characterizing language systems of one particular organization, the U.S. Navy. The underlying premise is that the distinctive real world of the Navy is defined most fully by the language systems used by its members. "Language" is here used in the broader sense, and defined as *any structured system of codifiable symbols by means of which a particular group of people communicate meaning and regulate their activities.* Of particular relevance here are the symbols, signs, and words that most Navy folk view as commonplace, and that most non-Navy folk view as largely unintelligible.

There are, or course, many other ways of defining the reality of an organization like the Navy, depending on what is meant by reality. We might, for example, define the Navy by the tangible property for which the Navy is responsible—the ships, shore facilities, buildings, etc., which may be specified with considerable precision. Alternatively, we could map out and specify the existing organization of the Navy in terms of its offices, roles, activities, tasks, reporting responsibilities, authority structures, etc. Or, we might take a more functional approach toward defining the Navy and proceed to specify the mission, purpose and function of the Navy in terms of the larger societal purposes and environmental forces.

What I want to do here, however, is to adopt an approach toward defining reality akin to that of the symbolic interactionists. From this perspective social reality is defined by the language used by the members of the social system. Language does more than communicate information and more than enable the members to make sense. Language *creates* the reality, it has been argued. The "organization" has no objective reality (in a positivistic sense), but rather *is created daily by the linguistic enactments of its members in the course of their everyday communications between each other;* that is, by the way in which its members talk, hold discourse, share meanings. The particular language of an organization has embedded within it a categorization and structuring of a world which externalizes itself by being used. The existence of a common language implies an intersubjectivity of the inherent world view. The sense of objectivity is, in truth, achieved by this linguistic intersubjectivity.

The view that language plays the critical role in the construction of the social (and hence organizational) world has been articulated by a number of writers; the socio-linguists, Sapir (1949), Whorf (1964) and Bernstein (1974); the sociologists Mead (1943), Schutz (1973), Blumer (1969), Berger and Luckmann (1966); and the philosophers, Wittgenstein (1922), Habermas (1979) and Gadamer (1975). Until quite recently, few organizational studies have been undertaken based upon this orientation.

THE NAVY

Scope and Complexity

Before exploring the linguistics of the Navy, it is necessary to outline the overall scale, organization and function of the U.S. Navy.

At the present time, (1979) the Navy has a payroll of 1,020,000 persons, including 720 thousand military; (550,000 on active duty). The Navy procures and globally operates (on a 24-hour day basis) extremely complex equipment in three media: (a) *on* the ocean surface (470 ships including 13 massive aircraft carriers), (b) *under* the ocean surface (120 submarines; 110 of which are nuclear powered, and 40 of which carry ballistic missiles), and (c) *above* the ocean surface (approximately 6000 aircraft and satellites of diverse functions). One of the Navy ships (the USS Nimitz) is a nuclear powered aircraft carrier carrying a crew of 6300 men and having a displacement of 91,400 tons—the world's largest warship. Necessarily the hardware procurement, logistic support for supplies, materials and equipment, training and R & D are on a colossal scale. The Navy's budget is currently $55 billion.

The technological sophistication of the Navy in a number of areas is equally impressive. In ship design, avionics, navigation, weaponry, telecommunications, intelligence, oceanography, inventory control, and a number of other fields, the Navy's technology is as advanced as any in existence. This implies that the specialized languages of these forefront technologies are part of the language of the Navy organization.

The organization of the U.S. Navy is extremely complex and therefore difficult to convey concisely without trivializing its richness. What follows is merely a quick sketch to aid the reader in appreciating the linguistic theme of this paper.

Since 1947 the Navy has been part of the Defense Department, along with the Army and the Air Force; the Office of the Secretary of Defense (OSD); the Joint Chiefs of Staff (JCS); the various unified commands (composed of components of two or more services, such as the U.S. European Command); and the various specified commands, such as the Military Sealift Command (MSC).

The Department of the Navy (DON) is headed by the Secretary of the Navy (SECNAV), a civilian. The senior naval officer in the Department of the Navy is the Chief of Naval Operations (CNO), who manages the operating forces (such as the U.S. Pacific Fleet, whose commander-in-chief is known as CINCPACFLT). He is also responsible for the vast Naval Material Command (NMC) which supplies the material needed by the operating forces.

The Department of the Navy is thus composed of:

1. The "Navy Department" (the central executive authority of the Navy in Washington),
2. The "Shore Establishment" (such as the 5 "systems commands"),
3. The "Operating Forces" (the "fleet" per se).

Interfaces between the Navy and other organizations (such as the Marine Corps, the Coast Guard, and the allied Navies) generate further organizational complexity.

The complexity of the Navy is also reflected in the statements of mission, effectiveness and capability. As stated in Title 10, U.S. Code, the mission of the Navy is to be prepared for prompt, effective, and sustained combat operations at sea, to help defend against all enemies in time of war, and to support the National foreign policy in peacetime. The Navy has three main roles within the national strategy: (1) strategic deterrence, (2) deployment of overseas forces, and (3) security of the sea lines of communication with U.S. overseas interests.

Measures of effectiveness for the Navy are very difficult to specify, especially under peacetime and crisis conditions. Only under wartime conditions does an effectiveness level become at all clear. Since Secretary of Defense McNamara, it has become popular to assess military effectiveness in terms of the cost to achieve a level of confidence in the accomplishment of hypothetical missions. The capability of Naval forces is measured by such features as: force structure, state of modernization, readiness level and sustainability. The process of generating Navy capability requires careful assessment of three very elusive factors: strategy, threat, and risk.

The very great difficulties in specifying the purpose and effectiveness of the Navy results in increased attention to the professionalism, ceremonies, symbols, and traditions of the Navy—in short, *the Navy culture*. In the absence of a clear bottom-line measure of performance, greater attention must be given to Navy symbols that maintain the Navy's essential functions and identity, which is perhaps best indicated by the unique language of the Navy.

Data for this section were taken mainly from US, OMB, (1979); US, OFR, (1979); and US, CNO, (1979).

Communications Systems

Language involves a set of signs (vocabulary) and relational rules (grammar) as well as the means of discourse in these signs (communication systems). The Navy is richly endowed, both with its own sign conventions and its own means of discourse. (For a useful introduction to the study of language, see Pei, 1965, 1971).

Given the global dispersion of the Navy, the importance of command and control in the military, and the variety of specialized Navy languages, one might expect that some sophisticated systems of communication have been developed within the Navy. And such is the case. Systems for communicating the various Navy languages abound in great variety, many using extremely advanced technologies. I can think of no other organization that comes close in its variety or sophistication of communications systems.

All the familiar *verbal* modes are, of course, available—face to face, messengers, bulletin boards, public telephone, memos, intercoms, mail, "passing the word", etc. Additionally, the Navy uses a variety of *sound* systems: bells, buzzers, horns, gongs, sirens, whistles, etc., as well as a variety of *visual* systems: flag hoist, semaphore, flashing lights and pyrotechnics. The Navy uses these systems on a daily basis in ways that are highly specific to the Navy. It is also worth noting here that Navy aviators who served as POW's at the famous "Hanoi Hilton" in Vietnam, used a tap-code to communicate with each other when in solitary confinement (Butler, 1977).

A variety of radio, wire, and telegraph systems have also been developed in Navy-specific ways—including the CW system (radiotelegraph), the RT system (radiotelephone), the RATT system (radioteletype), and the FAX system (facsimile). A variety of codes (such as the Morse code) and mandatory abbreviations, procedure words (pro-words), procedure signs (pro-signs), and ciphers are used—again in Navy-specific ways.

The telecommunications world of the Navy is one of great complexity, both technologically and organizationally. The Navy uses the various private transmission networks developed by the Defense Communications Agency (DCA)—AUTOVON (voice telephone), AUTODIN (digital), AUTOSEVOCOM (secure voice), DSCS (Defense Satellite Communications System), etc., etc. Additionally, the Navy has a large number of its own private networks, most notably the FLTSATCOM (Fleet Satellite Communication), the HF, VLF, and MF networks and the sophisticated NAVCOMPARS (Navy Communication Processing and Routing System) (see Dunn, 1980).

JOINING THE NAVY

Ranks and Ratings

Consider briefly a new recruit's encounter with the U.S. Navy as he (she) walks into a blizzard of new language. He enlists at the AFEES (Armed Forces Examining and Entrance Station), otherwise known as his home town recruiting station. He then goes to a RTC (Recruit Training Command) at the nearest NTC (Naval Training Center). "The RTC puts you through the transition from civilian to military life with a very busy schedule of lectures and drills on the Navy's history, traditions, customs and regulations" (Wedertz, 1978, p. 64). Here he learns the first key words in his new (i.e., Navy) vocabulary, such as the CC (Company Commander), the POD (Plan of the Day), BI (Barracks Inspection), EPO (Educational Petty Officer), MD (Military Drill), TOD (Term of the Day), TAD (Temporary Additional Duty), etc.

The newly enlisted recruit is given three tests; the ASVAB (Armed Services Vocational Aptitude Battery), the NFQT (Nuclear Field Qualifications Test) and the FLAT (Foriegn Language Aptitude Test). The recruit is also given a four digit NEC code (Navy Enlisted Classification) which codifies the recruit's incoming skills, qualifications, and aptitudes. For example, a 3221 would be a Navy Broadcast Journalist.

As a result of the recruit training program, the recruit is assigned an occupational classification called a *rating*. There are some eleven broad occupational groups with a total of seventy different ratings, each identified by two letters. Group III, for example, is Electronics, comprised of the two ratings "Electronics Technician" (ET), and "Data Systems Technician" (DS). Our recruit also learns that each occupational rating has a common nickname that only Navy folk know: A Radioman (RM) is known as *sparks,* a Signalman (SM) is a *skivvy waver,* a Communications Technician (CT) is a *spook,* and so forth. He also finds out that the CT rating was recently changed; it now stands for cryptographic technician.

Every organization has its own payscale system which defines much of the organizational reality of the organization so specified. In the Navy there are paygrades for the enlisted ranks (i.e., *white hats*) designated E–1 through E–9. Men with grades E–1 through E–3 are called Strikers; E–4 through E–9 are called Petty Officers. There are Warrant Officers, designated W–1 through W–4, and Commissioned Officers, designated O–1 through O–6, and beyond to the various types of Admiral. Enlisted men who eventually become commissioned officers are known as *mustangs,* as every Navy man knows.

This classification system for rank and rating level has been further codified in the various badges, markings and insignia worn on the uniforms. The rating, rate, special qualifications, length of service, and good-conduct records of enlisted men and women are indicated by their sleeve and breast insignia. Additionally, there are over 150 possible awards that may be worn as decoration "ribbons" each signifying something about the wearer. A grade level system combines rank, pay, age, occupational ratings and experience history into career assignment patterns. The mention of E-8, W-2, O-5, or GS-13 (for civilian grades) conveys a whole universe of meaning to a Navy person, but very little to a non-Navy person.

There is, of course, much more to ratings. ranks, uniforms, and insignia than discussed here. The point, however, is this: there is a highly developed *language* of ratings/ranks/uniforms/insignia; it is *communicated* constantly as a natural part of the daily discourse, and it is systematically *learned* by the new recruit. As the *Blue Jackets' Manual* says, "The matter of ranks, rates and insignia will seem confusing at first, but once you learn the system you'll find it fairly simple. First, learn all the officers' rank marks and insignia, the rating badge chevrons that show the rate of enlisted personnel, the line insignia, and special identification marks" (Wedertz, 1978, p. 39). A Navy man recently said to me, "So much is communicated by the uniform and its markings that it's as if the man is wearing his resume—assuming, of course, that you're a Navy man." Non-Navy persons who do not know the language get very little information.

Rules and Regulations

To join an organization necessitates the learning of the *rules and regulations,* prescribed by and peculiar to that organization, that explicitly set out to govern the actions, behaviors, choices, and decisions of its members. The newcomer is required to learn this new language and to exhibit conduct that is congruent with this language. Eventually the proper kind of conduct (congruent with the rules and regulations) becomes a language in itself that is "read" by the other members. Members whose conduct is too deviant from the prescribed code are, in effect, speaking a different language and will eventually become out-group. Members who want "in" must learn the language of proper conduct set down in the rules and regulations and exhibited daily by those whose behaviors conform to these rules and regulations.

The Navy is a world of extensive codification of objects, events, situations, and appropriate conduct. The manuals of official regulations and standardized procedures are extremely voluminous and seemingly cover every imaginable contingency. Some of the principal regulatory documents that govern the Navy person's world are the following:

1. *Navy Regulations* (NAVREGS)
2. *Bureau of Naval Personnel Manual* (BUPERSMAN)
3. *Uniform Code of Military Justice* (UCMJ)
4. *U.S. Navy Uniform Regulations*
5. *Navy Pay and Personnel Procedures Manual* (PAYPERSMAN)
6. *Manual of Advancement*
7. *Standard Organization and Regulations Manual* (SORM)

There are additional manuals for a wide range of activities. The two-volume *Joint Travel Regulations* (JTR), for example, deals with the governance of travel, including the transportation of HHG's (Household Goods).

In addition, a number of offices within the Navy Department issue extensive *directives* which prescribe or establish policy, organization, conduct methods or procedures. These directives are issued either as "instructions" (INST), or "notices" (NOTE), implying either permanent guidance or temporary advise. The four most prolific sources of command directives at DOD (Department of Defense), SECNAV (Secretary of the Navy), OPNAV (Office of the Chief of Naval Operations), and *Bureau of Naval Personnel* (BUPERS), (which recently changed to Naval Military Personnel Command, (MILPERS) as every Navy man knows). Directives covering a very wide range of topics are typically labeled as follows:

Standard Organization and Regulations of the U.S. Navy,	OPNAVINST 3120.32A
Standards of Conduct	SECNAVINST 5370.2F

Retirement Ceremony BUPERSMAN, Art. 2810200
Disciplinary Control Boards BUPERSINST 1620.4B

Memos and correspondence in the Navy are typically laden with references to directives such as the above, presumably to validate the authority of the message. There are, however, so many directives that cover such a wide range of topics that directives can be found (as with the Bible and the works of Shakespeare) to support a broad spectrum of decisions and actions.

The content of OPNAVINST 3120.32A (above) is of particular interest to both organizational scientists and to the theme of this paper. It specifies in the form of a fiat how the Navy is to be organized, administered, and regulated. Familiar concepts are given a distinctly Navy flavor.

A Navy man works in a particular regulatory environment that is unique to the Navy. The codification of his world is, to a large extent, contained in the regulations manuals and directives. In a Whorfian sense, the particular set of rules and regulations of a man's organization significantly influences the way he views his world (Whorf, 1964). Data in this section are taken mainly from Agerton and Mack (1976) and Wedertz (1978).

Character and Style

A newcomer to the Navy (whether as an enlisted man, a junior officer or a civilian in the Navy) soon comes to appreciate that there is a unique flavor to "Navy" that distinguishes it from all other organizations. The particular culture called "Navy" is steadily transmitted to the newcomer. What are the characteristics of this culture and how are they symbolically communicated? My purpose here is to illustrate the notion of culture transmission through symbols rather than to describe exhaustively the Navy culture.

Consider briefly the more obvious character of Navy. Navy officers commonly convey a well-mannered, alert, competent professionalism. There are also qualities of "responsiveness to authority", "being ready", "can do", and "not fazed by sudden contingencies".

There are at least three ways that such values are transmitted.

1. Training programs. The desired qualities can be explicitly articulated and rewarded. For example, in *Naval Orientation* (a book "prepared mainly for use in officer training programs") we read the following:

> The terms 'officer' and 'gentleman' are synonymous. Some of the requisite traits of the true officer are integrity, loyalty, dependability, regard for the rights of others, tolerance, self-confidence, sense of humor, ability to treat all men as equals,

tact, and good manners. A careful study of the above characteristics will prove that these also are the traits of the genuine gentleman (US, BNP, 1970).

2. Ceremonies. The Navy has an abundance of customs and ceremonies by means of which the crucial values are actualized. They range from a hand salute to flag etiquette, boat etiquette, shipboard customs, gun salutes and passing honors, etc. (Lovette, 1959). Consider these two examples: a) The procedure for entering boats is—senior in last and out first (businessmen would call it a LIFO system). "The idea is that the captain should not have to wait in a boat for anyone. The senior gets out first because normally business is more important and pressing than that of the men under him" (Wedertz, 1978, p. 87). b) When a Vice-Admiral pays an official visit he is accorded the following honors—dress uniform, "Admiral's March" music, full guard, 17 gun salute on arrival, 15 on leaving, 3 ruffles and flourishes, 8 side boys. In contrast, a Rear Admiral is accorded—dress uniform, "Admiral's March" music, full guard, 17 gun salute on arrival, but only 13 on leaving, only 2 ruffles and flourishes, and only 6 side boys!

Each of these two seemingly trivial examples is selected almost randomly from the vast language of ceremonies and customs with which a Navy man becomes familiar. Change of command ceremonies present another excellent example. In part, they constitute some of the perquisite system of the Navy, but more importantly, they serve to make tangible the values of a naval officer—well-mannered, respecting authority and discipline, being ready. etc.

3. Historical models. In few organizations is the sense of historical tradition so much a part of its present as it is in the Navy. A visit to any of the Navy centers (for example, the Naval Academy at Annapolis) is exposure to naval traditions and a heritage of key values. We are exposed to John Paul Jones ("In time of peace it is necessary to prepare, and be always prepared, for war at sea"); Captain Truxton ("Care for your men; see that each understands his duties; exact instant obedience; superintend everything; practice daily with the guns"); Captain Perry ("Don't give up the ship!"); Commodore Dewey ("You may fire when you are ready, Gridley"—at a range of 2-½ miles); Admiral Farragut ("Damn the torpedoes—full steam ahead!"), etc., etc. All part of the value language that is symbolically transmitted within the organization.

Let me elaborate on the process for clarity. Many of the famous events of naval history and the famous statements uttered at those events have been "captured" by Navy painters, and copies of these paintings are available for framing and hanging in appropriate places—offices, lobbies, etc. At the Naval Postgraduate School in Monterey, for example, there is a small conference room in daily use. On the end wall is a beautiful, dramatic painting that captures the moment on May 4th, 1917, when the first U.S. destroyers met with the British fleet to join them in the war against Germany. The caption reads as follows:

> After a rough (transatlantic) passage, the first U.S. destroyer division, under Commander Joseph Taussig, reached Queenstown, Ireland, when America joined the Allies in World War I. When asked by the British Vice Admiral Sir Lewis Bayly how long it would be before the division would be ready to deploy an antisubmarine patrol, Taussig signaled, 'We are ready now.'

In these examples, history and art combine to transmit the critical language that conveys the valued qualities of Navy.

THE VOCABULARY OF SEAFARING

Craft Terms

Every craft, trade and technology generates its own vocabulary and specialized terminology. Those whose craft is concerned with the *sea* have been particularly fertile in generating specialized vocabulary. Dictionaries and glossaries of sailing, nautical knowledge, navigation and marine terms abound. (See for example McEwen & Lewis, 1953; US, NOO, 1969; Noel & Beach, 1971; Bradford, 1972; Rousmaniere, 1976; Kemp, 1976; Vandenberghe, 1978). During the 8 years 1966 to 1974, no fewer than 77 dictionaries on the general naval sciences (maritime/navigation/Navy) have been published (Brewer, 1975).

These dictionaries of seafaring or maritime vocabularies seem to be comprised of several categories of words.

1. English words whose primary meaning is maritime. They range in general intelligibility from easy words (e.g., anchor, rudder) to difficult words (e.g., martingales, catharpings, starbowlines, mizzen-futtock-shrouds, gilguys, royal stu'n's'ls, fore-topgallant-standing-backstay, etc.).
2. English words that have taken on a special meaning in a seafaring context (eg., port, fake, gypsy).
3. Technology words that developed in the general naval sciences (e.g., sidereal hour angle, calculated zenith distance, Mohn effect).
4. Customs and sea lore (e.g., Davy Jones' locker, splicing the mainbrace).
5. Acronyms and abbreviations (e.g., DESFLOT, NAVFAC, C^3).
6. Signal letters (e.g., P, NC, MAA).

7.   Slang (e.g., sandcrab = civilian worker in a Navy shipyard, jar-head = a marine).

The last three items—acronyms and abbreviations, signal letters, and slang—warrant further discussion in view of their distinctive use in the Navy.

It should be noted in passing, however, that some sea language has entered the common pool of everyday English (see Colcord, 1977). In most *non-Navy* organizations, for example, you are likely to hear a number of boating terms. When you join you will probably be "welcomed aboard". You will also hear managers talk about getting the project "under way", "taking a different tack", "keeping an even keel", and "seeing that everything is shipshape". You may be told that as long as you don't "make waves," or "go overboard," everything will be "smooth sailing." You will soon come to know which individuals in the organization are "fair weather friends", who "sails too close to the wind", and who "swings the lead". Your job is to see that the project doesn't "run aground". After work you may find yourself saying "down the hatch!" and then "going to the head"—hopefully when you are not "three sheets to the wind".

Paradoxically, when the language that characterizes an organization enters the common pool of everyday English, it no longer differentiates that organization.

Acronyms and Abbreviations

Even the most causal observer of the Navy cannot fail to notice the vast number of capitalized acronyms in common everyday use. It is often referred to as "alphabet soup".

Acronyms are, of course, not unique to the Navy. Acronyms were widely used by both the Greeks and the Romans. One example is the familiar SPQR (Senatus Populusque Romanus) standing for the "Senate and the People of Rome". World War II produced thousands of acronyms, such as ANZAC (Australian and New Zealand Army Corps), SEAC (South East Asia Command), DESFLOT (Destroyer Flotilla), and RADAR (Radio Detecting and Ranging). Government generally, and the military in particular, are acronym prone, for some reason.

There are by now a number of dictionaries of acronyms and military abbreviations which list abbreviations in common use and/or officially approved (see for example Crowley, 1976; and US, DOD, 1979) and the Navy has regularly published its "approved" list of abbreviations for use in official communications and messages.

Acronym dictionaries come in various forms. Many are Xerox copies of privately assembled abbreviations used by a particular organizational unit within the Navy. Some are privately published as books, such as DICNAVAB, WASH-MIC, and OCECODE (Wedertz, 1977; Honour & Kossan, 1973; and Aalberts, 1962, respectively), and some are official reports issued as directives, such as VS, JCS, 1979; US, DDC, 1977; and US, DDC, 1979.

The Navy (and most military organizations) uses acronyms extensively for organizational groups, for projects and for technological devices. Some of these acronyms may be recognized outside the Navy, such as DOD (Department of Defense), SECDEF (Secretary of Defense), and CNO (Chief of Naval Operations). Other acronyms are easily decipherable, such as NAVSUPSYSCOM (Navy Supply Systems Command), CHNAVPERS (Chief, Bureau of Naval Personnel), and CINCLANFLT (Commander in Chief, Atlantic Fleet). All organizational units within the Navy have official acronym designations. Thus, OP-10 signifies the Office of Military Manpower Planning and Programming Division of the Deputy Chief of Naval Operations (Manpower), and NMAT-08 designates the Office of the Deputy Chief of Naval Management for Acquisition at the Headquarters, Naval Material Command, and so forth.

The Navy also uses its own abbreviation language to designate all its hardware assets (see U.S., DOD, 1976). Every Navy ship and service craft is given a name and a letter designation that broadly classifies it as to function, major capability and specific use. Thus, the USS Enterprise is designated CVN-65. Similar, but more complex, designation systems are used for aircraft, missiles and equipment packages. A Navy man would immediately know that an aircraft designated YRF-4B is a prototype version of a Phantom-II fighter (the F-4) fitted with photo-reconnaisance. Likewise, he would immediately know that a missle designated as AIM-9E is an air-launched, intercept, guided missile, model 9, design E—also known as Sidewinder. And a piece of equipment labeled AN/APB-2D instantly indicates that its use is as follows: AN = electronics type, A = aircraft use, P = radar, B = bombing, 2 = model number, D = modification D, model 2. All very obvious to a Navy person—at least to persons in the "jet jockey" subcommunity of the Navy (i.e., Navy jet pilots).

Probably all fields now have their own particular acronyms; biochemistry has DNA and LSD, medicine has EKG and ENT, computer science has COBOL, APL, and PL1, government has DOD, HEW and HUD (which use GNP, CPI, and COLA) and business has IBM, BMW and NBC. And, at schools of management we teach OR, OB, OD, and MIS to BS, MBA or MS students (who have the proper SAT scores), and we write articles for ASQ, JAP, and AMR. But surely no field has so many acronyms as the Navy has.

The International Code of Signals

The U.S. Navy shares with other navies and mariners an International Code of Signals that constitutes a language system in its own right (US, NOO, 1969). The Code enables communication in situations related essentially to safety of navigations and persons. It transcends problems associated with different spoken languages (English, French, etc.), and allows for several different methods of signaling.

The core of the Code is a vocabulary of letters and digits that stand for lengthier message phrases. The signals consist of

  a) Single-letter signals allocated to messages that are very urgent,
     important, or of very common usage.
     Example: (i) F, code word "Foxtrot", signifies "I am disabled;
                   communicate with me."

  b) Two-letter signals for general signals.
     Example: (i) CJ signifies "Do you require assistance?"

  c) Three-letter signals beginning with "M" for medical signals.
     Example: (i) MRL signifies "Commence artificial respiration
                   immediately."

The meaning of these letter signals is amplified by the use of numerical complements. For example:

> QG signifies 'You should go ahead.'
> QG2 signifies 'You should go full speed ahead.'

Further conventions enable the signaling of such information as location, speed, distance, bearing, identity, etc. Thus, the signal "BH T1045 L2015N G3840W C125" would be seen by a Navy officer to say "I sighted an aircraft at local time 10:45 in latitude 20°15′ North, Longitude 38°40′ West flying on course 125°." Easy, when you know the language.

Moreover, such messages as these can be exchanged by flag hoist, by flashing light signaling, by Morse sound, by Morse radiotelegraphy, by semaphore, by radiotelephony or by voice over a loud hailer.

Of special importance to seafarers, are the twelve internationally accepted ways of signaling distress. Everyone in the Navy knows them, but few outside the Navy would recognize more than the SOS and MAY-DAY signals. The International Code Signal for distress is NC (November Charlie). Other accepted distress signals include a gun fired every minute, the continuous sounding with a fog horn, red rockets fired at regular intervals, an orange smoke signal, a red hand-flare, a square flag with a ball above or below it and the slow raising and lowering of out-stretched arms (US, NOO, 1969, pp. 133–139). The language of distress is both well developed and familiar to Navy people.

Slang

All organizations develop their own informal lexicons that help characterize and give meaning to their particular circumstance (see Partridge, 1960; and Wentworth & Flexner, 1975). The slang, jargon and cant of a group provide the connective idioms that significantly define the group's reality and differentiate it from that of other groups.

In terms of slang the Navy is extremely rich. (See, for example, Granville, 1962). Terms range from the commonly used terms that are almost official (e.g., "fish" = torpedo) through the jocular and colloquial (e.g., "airdale" = aviator), to the unequivocally obscene (I'll refrain from an example here; any Navy man can tell you at least one). Slang terms help define the reality of an organization as much as the craft and technology terms do.

Slang words are highly differentiating as to group membership and organizational structure. There are literally thousands of slang words used in the Navy that have little meaning outside the Navy, such as "dirtbags", "two-wires", "blackshoes", "seals", and "group 9 personnel". The three primary communities in the Navy-surface, aviation and submariners—have each evolved their own slang terms within the Navy. Further slang inventions differentiate subgroups within these communities; thus, the nuclear submariners use a different slang from diesel submariners; the Navy supply people use different slang from the operating fleet people; and aircraft carrier language has evolved differently from destroyer language.

Slang terms also change rapidly. The lexicon expands, words transform, pronunciation shifts. Thus, an aviator is now commonly called an "airedale" in preference to the term "jet jockey" (to distinguish him from "prop pukes" and "rotor heads"). Earlier yet, an aviator was called a "zoomie," though this term is now more commonly used to refer to those who favor Admiral Zumwalt's style of leadership, particularly his famous "Z-grams."

In many ways slang is one of the major reality-setters in organizations. Hence slang-generating becomes a core reality-generating process. New slang words mark the specialness and belongingness of members. They provide the passwords and shibboleths that indicate who is "in" the group and who is "out". They provide the critical ingredient for acceptance and the exercise of social power, to counterbalance the legitimate power.

DISCUSSION AND SUMMARY

On the surface this is a paper about the Navy. More fundamentally, however, it is about *language and the role it plays in generating and maintaining organization*. I have explored some ways in which one particular organization (the U.S. Navy) uses language that is unique to that organization. There are words, symbols and modes of discourse that characterize this organization and which are unintelligible outside the organization.

The thesis is that every organization, task/activity and social group has its own language (lexicon, sign system, mode of discourse). The facts of linguistic differentiation are apparent, but the determinants of, reasons for, and functions of this fact remain obscure.

There are well over a million words in the English language, which includes about 100,000 slang words (Pei, 1966; Partridge, 1960; and Matthews, 1956). The average person who has been to college can recognize about 20,000 words (including about 2000 slang words), but uses only about 3000 words regularly. Several studies of spoken English (e.g., telephone conversations, etc.) indicate that 25% of the words in a conversation is comprised of only 9 words (a, and, I, it, etc.) and 50% of the words is comprised of only 43 words! (McKnight, 1923) As few as a thousand words constitute the common pool of words that make up 99% of our communication. Why then the discrepancy?

> The principal reason for this startling discrepancy between what we have at our disposal and what we know and use lies in the highly specialized vocabularies of the various and numerous branches of activity to which modern man devotes himself. As these forms of activity increase and multiply, so does the vocabulary. Each field finds it necessary to borrow, adapt, combine, coin, or otherwise create the nouns, adjectives, and verbs that describe its objects and concepts, its qualities, its forms of action (Pei, 1966, p. ix).

Every specialized activity forms a subcommunity for two reasons: a) because those engaged in an activity tend to communicate with each other more than with those in other activity fields, and b) because those engaged in an activity tend to organize themselves into more cohesive units in the interests of efficiency, productivity, protection, etc. The language of many subcommunity activities have indeed been recorded (see, for example, Safire, 1968; Partridge, 1961).

In addition to task/activity reasons, specialized language is generated for social/behavioral reasons. Every group creates its own secret "in" words that differentiate that group from other groups. "In" language marks both belongingness to a group as well as the world view of the group. Words are markers of the class/caste/status/role of the members of the group. Perhaps more than anything else, it is this particularization of group language that differentiates and structures a social system.

The language used by the members of a particular organization characterizes that organization in terms of a) its similarities to and differences from other organizations, b) its societal role, and c) the world view and "reality" definition of its members. Language variations occur both *between* different organizations and *within* organizations, partly from task/activity reasons and partly from social/behavioral reasons.

One of the exciting corollaries of studying the relationship between organizations and language is the realization that *organizational change necessitates a language change*. Organizations only really change when there are concomitant changes in the words, symbols and metaphors of an organization. It also follows that organizational development consultants must give more attention to the reality-defining words, symbols and metaphors if they hope to facilitate any real organization change. Organizational linguistics offer a new research approach to the study of organizations. It is an approach that avoids the pitfalls of buying into positivistic assumptions—with all its attendant deficiencies. The study of organizational language offers a research approach that is both data-rich and grounded (i.e., experientially rooted) in the reality of the participants in organizational life.

REFERENCES

Aalberts, R. J. *Navigation-electronics OCECODE*. Hilversom, Holland. Oceco Technical Publishers, 1962.

Agerton, A. A., & Mack, W. P. *The naval officer's guide*. Annapolis, Md.: U.S. Naval Institute, 1976.

Berger, P., & Luckman, T. *The social construction of reality*. New York: Doubleday, 1966.

Bernstein, B. *Class, codes and control: Theoretical studies towards a sociology of language*. New York: Schocken, 1974.

Blumer, H. *Symbolic interactionism: Perspective and method*. Englewood Cliffs, N.J.: Prentice-Hall, 1969.

Bradford, G. *The mariner's dictionary*. Barre, Mass.: Barre, 1972.

Brewer, A. M. *Dictionaries, encyclopedias and other word-related books: 1966–1974*. Detroit: Gale Research Co., 1975.

Butler, P. The tap code: Ascribed meanings in prisoner of war communications. *Urban Life*, 1977, *5*, 399–416.

Colcord, J. C. *Sea language comes ashore*. New York: Arno Press, 1977.

Crowly, E. T. (Ed.). *Acronyms, initialisms and abbreviations dictionary* (5th ed.). Detroit: Gale Research Co., 1976.

Dewey, G. Relative frequency of English speech sounds. *Harvard Studies in Education*, 1923, *4*.

Dunn, J. F. *Defense telecommunications and the management environment*. Unpublished MS thesis. Naval Postgraduate School, Monterey, California, March 1980.

Gadamer, H. G. *Truth and method*. New York: Seabury, 1975.

Granville, W. *A dictionary of sailors' slang*. London: Andre Deutsch, 1962.

Habermas, J. *Communication and the evolution of society*. Boston: Beacon, 1979.

Honour, W., & Kossan, R. (Eds.). *WASH-MIC*. McLean, Virginia: Rany Co., 1973.

Kemp, P. (Ed.). *The Oxford companion to ships and the sea*. Oxford: Oxford University Press, 1976.

Louis, M. R. Surprise and sense making: Newcomers' experiences in entering unfamiliar organizational settings. *Administrative Science Quarterly*, 1980, *25*, 226–251.

Lovette, L. D. *Naval customs, traditions and usage*. Annapolis, Md.: U.S. Naval Institute, 1959.

Matthews, M. N. *A dictionary of Americanisms*. Chicago: University of Chicago Press, 1956.

McEwen, W. A., & Lewis, A. H. *Encyclopedia of nautical knowledge*. Cambridge, Md.: Cornell Maritime Press, 1953.

McKnight, G. H. *English words and their background*. New York: Appleton-Century-Crofts, 1923.

Mead, G. H. *Mind, self and society*. Chicago: University of Chicago Press, 1943.

Noel, J. V. & Beach, E. L. *Naval terms dictionary*. Annapolis, Md.: U.S. Naval Institute, 1971.

Partridge, E. *A dictionary of the underworld*. London: Routledge & Kegan Paul, 1961.

Partridge, E. *A dictionary of slang and unconventional English* (7th ed.). New York: Macmillan, 1960.

Pei, M. *Invitation to linguistics*. South Bend, Ind.: Henry Regnery, 1971.

Pei, M. *The language of the specialists*. New York: Funk and Wagnalls, 1966.

Pei, M. *The story of language*. New York: New American Library, 1965.

Rousmaniere, J. *A glossary of modern sailing terms*. New York: Dodd, Mead & Co., 1976.

Safire, W. *The new language of politics*. New York: Random House, 1968.

Sapir, E. *Selected writings of Edward Sapir in language, culture and personality*. Berkeley: University of California Press, 1949.

Schutz, A., & Luckmann, T. *The structure of the life-world*. Evanston, Ill.: Northwestern University Press, 1973.

U.S. Bureau of Naval Personnel. *Naval orientation*. NAVPERS 16138, 1970.

U.S. Chief of Naval Operations. *CNO report*. Washington, D.C.: Office of Naval Operations, March 1979.

U.S. Defense Documentation Center. *Government acronyms and alphabetic organizational designations used in the defense documentation center*, Report number DDC/TR-77/3, August 1977.

U.S. Defense Documentation Center. *DDC retrieval and indexing terminology—DRIT*, Report number DDCH 4185.7, May 1979.

U.S. Department of Defense. *Department of Defense dictionary of military and associated terms*, Report number JCS-PUB 1, 1 June 1979.

U.S. Department of Defense. *Model designation of military aircraft, rockets and guided missiles*, Report number DOD 4120.15-L, 1976.

U.S. Naval Oceanographic Office. *Navigational dictionary* (HM 220). Washington, D.C.: U.S. Government Printing Office, 1969.

U.S. Naval Oceanographic Office. *International code of signals* (HM 102). Washington, D.C.: U.S. Government Printing Office, 1968.

U.S. Office of Management and Budget. *The budget of the U.S. government: FY 1980.* Washington, D.C.: U.S. Government Printing Office, 1979.

U.S. Office of the Federal Register. *U.S. Government Manual: 1979–80.* Washington, D.C.: U.S. Government Printing Office, 1979.

Vandenbeghe, J. P. (Ed.) *Elsevier's nautical dictionary.* Amsterdam: Elsevier Scientific, 1978.

Wedertz, B. (Ed.) *The bluejackets' manual* (20th ed.). Annapolis, Md.: U.S. Naval Institute, 1978.

Wedertz, B. (Ed.) *Dictionary of naval abbreviations (DICNAVAB).* Annapolis, Md.: U.S. Naval Institute, 1977.

Wentworth, H., & Flexner, S. *Dictionary of American slang.* New York: Thomas Crowell, 1975.

Wittgenstein, L. *Tractatus.* London: Routledge & Kegan Paul, 1922.

Whorf, B. L. *Language, thought and reality.* Cambridge, Mass.: MIT Press, 1964.

AMBUSHES, SHOOTOUTS, AND KNIGHTS OF THE ROUNDTABLE:
THE LANGUAGE OF CORPORATE TAKEOVERS

Paul M. Hirsch and John A. Y. Andrews

'It's the closest thing to combat I've seen since World War II,' says R. Eberstadt, Jr., who found out one evening last December that his Microdot, Inc. was the target of a . . . raider called General Cable Corporation. 'There's especially a lot of emotion in it when you're the one under attack,' adds John Grady, former vice president for finance at Garlock. 'It's as if you've just found out that someone's made a more attractive offer to your wife.'

The first time I called, he (Arthur Long, president of D. F. King [stock solicitors]) explained giddily that he couldn't see me for two days because 'I'm raping someone today and defending someone tomorrow.'

Quotations from "Two Tough Lawyers in the Tender-Offer Game," by Stephen Brill. *New York*, June 21, 1976, pp. 54 and 58 respectively.

INTRODUCTION: ENVIRONMENTAL SETTING

If accounting is the language of business, the frameworks and terms in which mergers and acquisitions are now discussed in the business world constitute a clear anomaly. In this paper, we set forth the categories into which the imagery used most often clusters, propose several interpretations to explain its emergence and widespread usage, and suggest implications for the study of big business by social scientists.

The "takeover" of one large business firm by another differs from those of earlier times on two major dimensions. First, the product lines or lines of business each firm is engaged in are unrelated horizontally or vertically. This sets them off from the formation of trusts prior to the passage of anti-trust laws which, in turn, channeled mergers into the "conglomerate" or "portfolio" variety. Second, the manner in which firms are acquired today includes (friendly or hostile) buying of the acquiree's stock in the public market, supplemented by a tender offer for enough other shares to effect transfer of ownership. The diffusion of stock ownership characteristic of most publicly held firms, combined with the typically small percent of stock owned by most big firms' managements, makes it a simple matter for "outsiders" to come in and take over what managers usually are encouraged to think of as "their" company.

The environmental setting facilitating today's forms of merger and acquisition thus includes (1) anti-trust laws channeling acquisitions into the form of investments in other lines of business activity, and (2) the separation of owners from managers, enabling "control" of the corporation to fall outside the purview of its own executives.

THE DIFFUSION OF HOSTILE TAKEOVERS AS AN INNOVATION

Hostile takeovers, in the form of tender offers, began about 15 years ago. They were a "deviant" innovation whose earliest adopters were located in the southwest (e.g., James Ling of LTV). Their promulgators, referred to on Wall Street at the time as "big hat boys", were largely "outsiders" whose behavior was gradually emulated by others and incorporated into more widely accepted business practice. Acquisition committees are not unusual today in large corporations. As the innovation has gained in respectability, the roles assigned and imagery employed have also changed. Because normative consensus is still lacking, we shall see that the frames and imagery employed still reflect substantial ambivalence, bordering on the derogatory.

NORMATIVE AMBIVALENCE AND ITS SYMBOLIC REPRESENTATION

Conglomerate takeovers are surrounded by an aura of normative ambivalence for several reasons:

1. Many economists see market valuation as "true" value—so the premiums paid over share price constitute windfalls to the owners of the target firm. Under this argument, it is foolish to offer but even more foolish to refuse.

2. Absenting clear gains on economic grounds (like efficiency and productivity), unbridled growth is inherently suspect in the broader context of American culture. Here, big is not considered necessarily better (for example, Senator Kennedy's recent bill(s) to prevent firms of large size and scale from making further acquisitions).

3. There is a frequent attribution to promulgators, depending on time and place, of being egomaniacs or stock price operators, or, more interestingly, non-legitimate people with no real interest in the firm's "substance" (e.g., will "loot," abuse cash flows, or "milk").

The conflicts generated by acquisitions, and by hostile takeovers in particular, generate substantial discussion in not only the public arenas of government policy-making, speculative investing, and observations of the process as a spectator sport; takeovers—as one might expect—also are a subject of considerable discussion among their insiders, participants, targets as well. The potential heroes and villains, victors or victims, or winners and losers include most corporate executives, managers, and owners. Nearly all are familiar, from personal experience or those of friends and associates, with examples of takeovers; and discussions of mergers are laced with drama, uncertainty, exhilaration, conflicts, and resentment. The potential range of frameworks for such discussions and interpretations is very large; it is made even larger by the normative ambiguity surrounding the legitimacy of the events in the minds of both observers and participants. That the drama of the events captures the public's imagination is a plausible inference from the disproportionate amount of coverage accorded "takeover artists" (e.g., H. Geneen, C. Bluhdorn), the success of "Dallas", and the spate of cartoons (e.g., in the *New Yorker*) which have appeared consistently over the last decade.

More interesting are the ways in which the business community (both press and participants) have turned to genres from common culture to frame and discuss the takeover process. It is to these, and their role in articulating and expressing the normative ambivalence felt in the business world, that we now turn.

LANGUAGE AS AN INDICATOR OF ORGANIZATIONAL RELATIONSHIPS: THE FUNCTIONS OF FRAMING TAKEOVERS IN TERMS OF POPULAR GENRES

The takeover event in itself clearly conforms to a predictable set of scenarios or scripts. In the most neutral terms, this boils down to: Offer → decisions/actions taken → outcome. In the business world, this relatively simple diagram has taken on the far more colorful forms available from such well known popular genres as the western (ambush and shootout replace offer and actions taken), the love affair and/or marriage, warfare (replete with sieges, barricades, flak, and soldierly honor), mystery, and piracy on the high seas (with raiders and safe harbors). Generic formulations also entail the frequent appearance of mercenaries or hired guns (investment houses to whom most of the negotiating is delegated), and black and white knights (culled from tales of chivalry in which the distressed damsel is either undone or rescued). In virtually all formulations, the acquiring executive is macho and the target company is accorded the female gender ("sleeping beauty" or a bride brought to the altar; reference to rape also is not uncommon).

Appendix I provides a list of the terms we have found in frequent use, sorted into genre clusters. A glossary of meanings of the terms is given in Appendix 2.

Which genre is used accords most often with the degree of "friendliness" perceived between the parties. For example, the efforts of American Express to acquire McGraw Hill were said by many to test the limits of the normative boundaries for legitimate acquisition tactics: the appropriate genre here, for coding purposes, became all-out warfare. The recent, "friendly" merger of GE and Utah International, in contrast, conforms more to entries within the Courtship cluster. In between fall the majority of publicized "fights", wherein the parties and their posses each wage a good fight, in terms closely approximating (and often described in the business press as) a western.

Mencken, in his study of language, proposed that such a public use of common slang and genres by any group contains a healthy component of self-criticism, beyond playfulness. This observation accords with the above-stated observations concerning the aura of normative ambiguity surrounding takeovers. In what ways might such extensive referencing of popular genres serve to reduce such ambiguity? Or, rephrased, why borrow images from these fictional genres instead of slugging it out with adjectives and adverbs?

Four Functions

We propose four functions of the "pretend" which makes it particularly suitable for waging this battle over situational definition. The first of these is distancing from the action. By transposing the conflict to a fictional basis, judgments about the propriety of particular actions can be made implicitly and indirectly with a significant degree of detachment and abstraction from the particular situation. This function is somewhat analogous to the use of hypothetical examples in pedagogy, but there is a bit more to it than that. Rather than serving to protect anonymity and confidentiality, the distancing here serves to drain off extraneous affectivity surrounding the particular conflict (such as loose friendship bonds with the principals and established respect for particular individuals and companies), so that the interaction may be judged under the criteria of the general normative category of takeovers.

The second function is specification of the relation between the actors. Roles are assigned and the relations between them are defined by these images, with the result that extraneous detail is eliminated and the abstracted ideas are made available for interpretation.

The third function, evaluation of the action, is dependent on the abstracted specification of roles and relations produced by the second function, and is made allowable by the distancing produced by the first. Most of these genre images come from fictional formulae so familiar that once the roles and relations are assigned, proper procedures and/or proper outcomes can be readily deduced. Sleeping Beauty must be liberated and wed; the shark must be annihilated; the black-hat brought to justice; the honorable soldier must fight doggedly, and so on. In fact, if these procedures and outcomes do not occur, the story is presumed to be incomplete. George Bush's comment that "the opera isn't over until the last fat lady sings", which doubtless won him no votes among sopranos, is equally applicable here. The episode isn't over until the bad guy gets his or the shark gets its (or devours the victim): otherwise, the system remains in a state of instability, irresolution and normative chaos. Even partial resolutions may produce temporary stability, however, provided that the formula includes ultimate justice for the villain. The genial felon may win quite a few rounds, and his flamboyance may elicit admiration or at least amusement, but we know that ultimately he will go too far and will have to face the music. The major result of this third function is therefore to reestablish at least the presumption of sanctions for violations of business norms, based on the specification of roles and relationships already made. This result is entirely similar to that of the use of fables in common discourse.

The final function is that of appeal. If the normative order of business is challenged and forced to reconstruct itself, the basis for this reconstruction must be found in a set of value definitions which both transcends the business community and is known to and observed by its members. Positions in the conflict are thus justified by reference to established and favored values at the more generalized level of common culture, in the same way that issues of civil disobedience to particular laws are debated with reference to more general common values, for example. To the degree that reputational criteria influence business relationships, such as appeal is not wholly in vain, though the strength of its impact is very unclear.

IMPLICATIONS FOR THE TREATMENT OF BIG BUSINESS BY SOCIAL SCIENTISTS: CONCLUSION

We have proposed here that the language of takeovers serves as an indicator of normative confusion, and functions to distance both participants and observers from the stress and fast pace involved in an organizational sequence amply spiced with drama, pain (for many), and uncertainty over legitimacy and final outcome. The language also encompasses the likely possibility that the same actors, over time, can be accorded different parts in the same morality play. (Most large acquired firms have also engaged in their share of acquiring others previously.)

More generally the study of the language and frameworks employed by participants and close observers is a useful supplement to much of the literature which analyzes motives, actions, functions and consequences from a far more abstract theoretical standpoint. For example, unless one codes fights over tender offers as an instance of friendly business activity, or as a mere family quarrel, it is difficult to write blithely about the hegemony of the capitalist class and its common formulation of class interests. At least, from the standpoint of participants in that class, their day-to-day activities (including strategies towards mergers and acquisitions) take up a far greater amount of time and interest than considerations about how well their institution (the business sector) is doing in the aggregate.[1] A related implication is that from a cursory look at the roster of acquirers and acquirees over the last decade, it does not appear that having a more interlocked board provides any more insurance against being taken over than does a firm's having fewer board members with wide connections. Studies of such networks and functionalist theories of what businessmen do might do well to take such possibilities into better account.

In short, we have found the study of language and symbols, used by the observers and participants in organizations' activities, to yield suggestive and testable insights and propositions about the nature of these organizations and their relations with one another.

APPENDIX I. IMAGE CLUSTERS AND GENRES

Courtship

studs	matchmakers
preferred suitors	sleeping beauties
pigeons	Racquel
Don Giovanni	Faye
dancing	wooing
bringing to the altar	marrying
playing Cupid	confetti
takeover by rape	sex without marriage
afterglow	pursuit
on the rocks	

Warfare

wounded list	cyanide pill
running into flak	hot pursuit
throwing up barricades	siege
summer soldier	

Western

hired guns	ambush
shootout	tombstones
surviving company	

Chivalry

white knights	black knights

Macho

Faye as Bonnie in "Bonnie & Clyde"	Saturday Night Special
hired guns	

Nautical

on the rocks	safe harbor
pirates	raiders

(continued)

(Appendix I. Continued)

Games

chess	Monopoly
marbles	

"Jaws"

sharks	shark repellant

Sport

big game hunting	target companies

Miscellaneous

bearhug	Age of Acquireus
Russian rubles	Mad Austrian
Mankiller	headhunters
LIDO's	big-hat boys
shopping center	mushroom treatment

APPENDIX II.   GLOSSARY OF IMAGES*

---

afterglow	postmerger euphoria of acquirer and/or acquiree, usually soon lost
Age of Acquireus	post-1967 to date
ambush	a clever, premeditated and swift takeover attempt
Austrian, Mad	see Mad Austrian
bank robber	see Faye
barricades	impediments to a takeover (e.g. suits) raised by acquiree ("throwing up barricades")
battle	see warfare
bearhug	a hostile tender offer, usually with considerable muscle behind it
beauties, sleeping	see sleeping beauties
big game hunting	plotting and executing takeovers against Fortune-500 level firms
big-hat boys	Texan executives esp. those working for Ling of Ling Temco Vought, a major takeover artist who fell on hard times in the early 1970's
black knights	unfriendly acquirers drawn to a target by news that the target is under consideration by other potential acquirers
bring to the altar	consummate a merger, usually friendly
chess	metaphor for takeover activity in general, used by investment bankers

---

*In addition to numerous periodical articles on corporate takeovers, the sources consulted in compiling this glossary include the following work: Isadore Barmash, *Welcome to Our Conglomerate: You're Fired!* New York: Delacourte Press, 1971.

(Appendix II. Continued)

chivalry	see black and white knights
company, surviving	see surviving company
company, target	see target company
confetti	stock traded by acquirer for that of acquiree, particularly if thought of little value; see also Russian rubles
courtship	metaphor for specific mergers, usually more or less friendly
Cupid	see also matchmaker; role played by merger brokers
cyanide pill	image used by a judge to criticize one target's antitakeover finance strategy: the company borrowed a large amount of money in long term debt on the condition that if the company were acquired, the debt would immediately fall due in full
dancing	negotiations and preliminary talks in a more or less friendly merger
Don Giovanni	description of Bluhdohrn (c.f. Mad Austrian) in his solicitation of many target companies
Faye	code name used by Leasco in Chemical Bank takeover planning, used because of Faye Dunaway's role of bank robber in "Bonnie & Clyde"
flak	impediments raised against a takeover leading to trouble for acquirer
games	metaphor for takeover activity in general, used by investment bankers
harbor, safe	see safe harbor
headhunters	executive search firms and consultants
hired guns	lawyers, merger & acquisition specialists and other investment bankers employed by either side in a contested takeover
hot pursuit	see pursuit
hunting, big game	see big game hunting
Jaws	1) a genre of hostile takeover images 2) a predatory takeover artist, specifically applied to Evans of Crane who is known for punishing white knights who come into a deal against him
knights	see black and white knights
LIDO's	Litton Industries Dropouts: executives displaced by the merger-induced confusion in Litton's personnel policies
macho	a genre of imagery relating to contested takeover activity

(continued)

(Appendix II. Continued)

Mad Austrian	Bluhdohrn of Gulf & Western: a hard-driving takeover artist not well-liked in the business community
mankiller	Geneen of ITT: known for placing extraordinary demands on his executives, whether hired or acquired
marbles	sometimes used to refer to the payout of five year contracts for acquired executives to stay on with the conglomerate (hence a part of the sweetener for the original deal)
marrying	accomplishing a merger
matchmaking	scouting for possible deals and helping bring them off as an outsider, e.g. the main activity of merger and acquisition staffs at investment banking houses
merger shopping center	see shopping center
Monopoly	another games image used by outsiders dealing with takeover activity as a whole
mushroom treatment	description of post-merger problems by an acquired executive: "first they buried us in manure, then they left us in the dark awhile. then they let us stew, and finally they canned us"
nautical	a cluster of adventure images used in contested merger situations: comes from longstanding image of the firm as a ship
pigeons	highly vulnerable targets
pirates	like raiders, hostile acquirers
playing Cupid	see Cupid, matchmaker
preferred suitor	see white knight: possibly a less conflictual view of same
pursuit	Hot: a warfare image referring to an aggressive hostile acquirer Otherwise: a courtship image referring to strenuous wooing
Racquel	code name used by Leasco in Reliance takeover: coined for the voluptuousness of Reliance's surplus capital amounts and vulnerability to a takeover
raiders	see pirates
rape	takeover by rape: forcible, unresisted hostile takeover, sometimes accompanied by looting of the acquiree's profitability
repellant, shark	see shark repellant
rocks, on the	state of a failed, incompatible merger
Russian rubles	like confetti, worthless paper (used also outside of the merger arena): originates in the fact that Soviet currency is controlled at an inflated exchange rate and is not honored outside of the Warsaw Pact countries
safe harbor	refers to the various ways of protecting a company against the threat of takeover; e.g., buying small firms in a heavily regulated industry like radio stations and interstate trucking lines, where the federal paperwork makes

(Appendix II. Continued)

---

	acquisition by another company an interminably long and arduous process
Saturday Night Special	coined to refer to Colt's swift takeover of Garlock, sometimes used of swift and somewhat predatory mergers in general (c.f., ambushes)
sex without marriage	extended negotiations for a friendly merger which doesn't come off
sharks	extremely predatory takeover artists
shark repellant	protective strategies for preventing or combatting the tender offer of a shark
shootout	the climax of a takeover battle, usually conducted by the hired guns
shopping center	a mass matchmaking fest sponsored by a group of merger finders in New Jersey in the early 1970's: executives from dozens of firms met in carefully arranged interviews to discuss the possibilities of negotiating acquisitions between their companies
siege	undertaking a hostile takeover against a target
sleeping beauties	like pigeons, vulnerable targets (though perhaps more desirable than pigeons)
sport genre	includes big game hunting and target images
studs	aggressive suitors
suitors, preferred	see preferred suitors, white knights
summer soldier	an executive offering only token resistance against a takeover that could and should be strenuously resisted
surviving company	the winner, or at least the nonloser of a shootout
target companies	those firms against which a takeover is planned and/or executed
tombstones	of older vintage than the takeover movement: the advertisements of stock offerings, mergers and corporate liquidations in papers like the Wall Street Journal
warfare	a genre of hostile takeover imagery: note that this cluster should be seen as warfare, not as a war *per se*—it is battles, not wars that are fought in the takeover arena
western	a genre of contested takeover imagery
white knights	friendly acquirers sought out by a potential acquiree to forestall unfriendly acquirers
wooing	negotiation for a friendly or uncontested merger
wounded list	executives of an acquired firm who develop health or career problems from the deal and its anxieties

---

NOTE

1. As one investment banker put it, answering a question on a visit to the University of Chicago, "What we are doing may not be in the public interest, but so long as it is legal, I plan to be better at mergers and acquisitions than anyone else in the field."

THE ROLE OF METAPHORS AND MYTHS IN ORGANIZATION AND IN THE FACILITATION OF CHANGE

Louis R. Pondy

PURPOSE

My purpose in this paper is to explore the possible relationship of myths and other "extended metaphors" to organization and organizing, and especially the facilitation of organizational change. The central hypothesis is that the use of metaphors in organizational dialog plays a necessary role in helping organization participants to in-fuse their organizational experiences with meaning and to resolve apparent paradoxes and contradictions, and that this infusion of meaning or resolution of paradox is a form of organizing. In this sense, the use of metaphors helps to couple the organization, to tie its parts together into some kind of meaningful whole; that is, metaphors help to organize the objective facts of the situation in the minds of the participants. An alternative hypothesis is that the very creation of the objective facts of the organization is guided by underlying root metaphors. That is, metaphors serve both as models *of* the situation and models *for* the situation. (Geertz, 1973, p. 93).

I shall introduce two extended examples of the use of metaphor and myth in organization, which will serve to ground our theoretical exploration. One example is definitely drawn, and the other is marginally drawn, from outside of what is normally thought of as the class of formal organizations. Instead the examples more nearly illustrate cultural or social organization than formal organization. There are two reasons for this choice:

First, despite a small, but growing, amount of work by formal organization theorists (e.g., Mitroff & Kilmann, 1975; Meyer & Rowan, 1977; S. Turner, 1977; Boje & Rowland, 1977; Feldman & March, 1981; Huff, 1980; and the various papers in this volume), the rational bias of the formal organization paradigm has for the most part precluded the investigation of myths and metaphors in formal organizations. On the other hand, the role of myths and metaphors in society outside of formal organizations is more visible and has been the object of more inquiry, primarily by social anthropologists. (See, for example, V. Turner, 1974; Levi-Strauss, 1963; Geertz, 1973.)

Second, the analytical distinction between social organization and formal organization (Blau & Scott, 1962, pp. 2–5) has tended to reify the difference between them to the point that social organization and formal organization have come to be treated within the field of organization theory as distinct phenomena subject to different laws, with social organization being conceptualized as naturally occurring and formal organization as being the artifact of conscious design. Ouchi and Johnson (1978) have recognized the theoretical limitation of this social-formal distinction in their attempt to understand Type Z organizations. Instead, if we treat formal organizations as just one type of social organization that obeys many of the same laws as other types of social organization, they by studying myths and metaphors in societies that are not "formally" organized, we can more easily develop an understanding of the role that myths and metaphors play in social systems intendedly designed in accord with the rational model. In other words, by treating formal organizations as if they were members of the same family of social phenomena as kinship structures and religious belief systems and therefore subject to the same set of underlying laws, we can achieve new insights into the role that metaphors and myths play in their structure and operation.

A WORKING DEFINITION OF METAPHOR AND MYTH

Philosophers, linguists, psychologists, and literary critics do not agree even within their own disciplines on what metaphor is, how it works, or why it seems to be such a powerful device, despite the fact that the concept has been discussed since Aristotle (Ortony, 1979). Most analysts seem to agree that it has something to do with calling one entity by the name of another (e.g., "man is a wolf") or describing one event in terms appropriate to another (e.g.,, "she wore a cloak of sadness"). Turbayne (1962) expands Ryle's (1949) concept of a "category mistake," and defines metaphor as substituting part for whole (e.g., referring to a star athlete as "the franchise"), whole for part (e.g., "Notre Dame beat Pitt," when referring to their football teams), or the more common, one thing for another (e.g., "Sally is a block of ice.")

Let us mean by a metaphor the assertion, perhaps made indirectly and surreptitiously, that "A is B", where A and B belong manifestly to two different categories (e.g., individual human beings and baseball teams). All of the above examples are simple metaphors—one sentence assertions of relationship. But sometimes two things or events are identified over and over in different ways over long periods of time. Let us refer to these uses as "extended metaphors". Both of our examples will be extended metaphors, in this sense.

Myths can now be seen to be a type of extended metaphor, with the implicit assertion that the story told in the myth stands in a metaphoric relationship to real events. Sagan (1977, p. 8), defines myth as "a metaphor of some subtlety difficult to describe in any other way," and quotes Salustius' characterization of myth as "things which never happened but always are" (p. 7). Levi-Strauss (1963, pp. 208–209) observes that "myth always refers to events alleged to have taken place long ago" with a timeless pattern that "explains the present and the past as well as the future," and which has a universal character whose substance lies in "the *story* which it tells" (italics in original). Thus, myth establishes an extended metaphorical relationship between events separated in time and space. It will be seen to be important for our purposes that myth frequently involves fantastical elements (e.g., man-eating ogres) subject to neither the constraints of logic nor empirical falsifiability.

Metaphors, including the special case of myths, belong to the level of symbolic reality in organizations. "Symbolic reality" is contrasted with the level of "objective reality," or the set of empirical objects and events that constitute organizational action. An objectivist analysis of organization would assign only peripheral significance to organizational myths and metaphors, and would argue that a given situation admits only one objective reality and pattern of organization. But symbolic reality constitutes a patterned set of meanings, and is socially constructed by the actors in the situation (including as one of the actors the scientist who attempts to understand the phenomena being studied). A given objective reality can support a number of symbolic realities. The distinction is important because I shall argue that "organization" inhers in these symbolic realities as well as in the objective facts of the situation. And organizational metaphors and myths are prime devices by which symbolic realities are created and transmitted.

These abstract generalizations about metaphor and myth will take on more meaning in the context of the two examples, which are described below.

The First Example: Military Metaphors in Chinese Communes

Hsia (1961) has described the use of an extended military metaphor in organizing Chinese communes. I have listed below a number of specific examples that Hsia has drawn from government documents. In each case, both the literal translation of the Chinese phrase and its intended "meaning in context" are given.

Literal Translation	Meaning in Context
to fight a battle	to exert for production
a fighter	a production worker
a battle-line	areas where effort at mass production is made
a large army	a large body of persons drafted and organized to serve a definite function in socialist revolution and reconstruction
to declare war against heaven	to overcome natural handicaps in production
to get hold of information about the enemy	to understand, through chemical analysis or otherwise, the difficulty faced in production
to stage a march	to advance toward a certain goal
mobile warfare on a small scale	subsidiary work which can be done in spare time and requires only a fraction of the body of laborers engaged in a major project
a battle of annihilation	a production project which, because of careful planning and the employment of an overwhelming

	number of laborers, is assured of complete success
a major battle	a production project that requires thousands of laborers and several months to complete
to storm attack	concentrated effort in a production project
the whole nation is a game of chess	emphasis on overall strategy in production
battle positions	methods and procedures

Sometimes the military metaphor is invoked explicitly and fairly completely:

> We have won the victory for the Revolutionary War under the direction of the brilliant strategic thinking of Chairman Mao. Production is another kind of war, and the 'enemy' to be engaged in production is the contradictions, difficulties and other unfavorable factors (quoted in Hsia, 1961, p. 4).

But sometimes it is evoked implicitly through the partial use of the metaphor, as the following two examples:

> Literary workers are sentinels on the revolution-battleline. . . I am a new soldier (a recruit) on the literature-battleline (Hsia, 1961, p. 7, quoting a dramatist).

> The tailors who have learned new designs and cutting methods are said to have 'changed their old chen-ti (battle positions) which they have held for more than one thousand years' (Hsia, 1961, p. 10).

My intent in this section is not to analyze the metaphorical use of military images and language, but only to establish it as one of our two examples of extended metaphor. The analysis will be undertaken after we establish the second metaphor in the next section.

The Second Example

In his ethnography of the Nuer of East Africa, Evans-Pritchard (1940) relates the following myth:

> Denac was said to have had . . . four sons, named Yin, Dak, Bal, and Bany, by one wife (Nyagun), and Nyang and two nameless brothers by a second wife (Nyamor) . . . Nyang's two brothers were eaten by an ogre. When, afterwards, the sons of Denac went fishing, the four sons of one mother went by themselves and

Nyang by himself, for he would not accompany his half-brothers, but pined for the sons of his mother. When he caught a fish someone would come and steal it from him, for he was all by himself and only a boy. When he came home he would not sit with the other boys facing his father, but sat apart with his back to him, and when his father asked him why he was troubled he replied that he was thinking of his brothers whom the ogre had eaten. His father said to him, 'Never mind, take your two sisters and let them be your brothers.' So when Nyang went fishing he was accompanied by his sisters Nyabil and Fadwai (Evans-Pritchard, 1940, pp. 229–230).

In order to appreciate the significance of this myth, one must understand that the Nuer are organized politically into tribes, and the tribes in turn into primary and secondary sections. The political structure closely, *but not perfectly,* parallels the lineage structure of kinship relationships. Some sections take the name of a dominant clan or lineage structure, but comprise other lineages as well, and some sections are composed of foreigners from the neighboring Dinka. The founder of the Jinaca clan that dominates the Lou tribe was named Denac, as in the myth, and the names of the two primary sections are Gun and Mor (as in Nya*gun* and Nya*mor,* from the myth). Bal and Dak, two of the mythical sons of Nyagun, were names of the founders of the lineages that make up the two secondary sections of the Gun primary section. Nyang was the name of the founder of the Gaaliek secondary section, but there are two other secondary sections that make up the Mor primary section that are not accounted for by the genealogical tree because they have clan nuclei of foreign origin. Since among the patrilineal Nuer only males can found clans, one way of accounting for the special status of the two sections of foreign origin is, within the myth, to have them founded by the *sisters* of Nyang. The myth thus explains the association of the three Mor secondary sections. The possession of a common mythological parent gives the two foreign sections equal status with the "diel" or aristocrats of the Gaaliek, except for questions of ritual, and intermarriage with the Gaaliek lineage.

ANALYSIS AND THE SKETCH OF A THEORY

The key question we must face up to is: Why are metaphors and myths, as in our two examples, used at all? In the Chinese commune example, why couldn't the authorities just as well have spoken literally of industrial production and work forces instead of metaphorically of battles and armies? In the Nuer example, what, if anything, does the myth add to the reconstructed political and kinship structure of tribes and lineages?

Obviously, we cannot hope for a definitive answer to this central question on the basis of two cases. But, as I have argued elsewhere (Pondy &

Olson, 1977), an effective theory-building strategy is to ground theory in a detailed understanding of individual cases, especially extreme cases. For this purpose, an analysis of two cases is sufficient.

One function of metaphor/myth that our two examples seem to share is that they place explanation beyond doubt and argumentation. In the Chinese commune case, one might expect that the recent success of the revolution and the heroics of the long march make the military metaphor an especially powerful and persuasive device in three ways. First, it evokes rich and emotional detail that bypasses logic. Second, because of the very success of the revolution, it is difficult to question the validity of the metaphor. Third, the theme of a long struggle against difficult odds has been a dominant motif in Chinese thought for centuries.[1] The military metaphor capitalizes on recency, familiarity, association with success, and association with long-standing themes central to cultural values. In the Nuer case, the explanation is placed beyond doubt by resort to fantasy. Since a man-eating ogre is not to be found, the explanation is not empirically falsifiable. Furthermore, since, in myth, the ordinary rules of logic are suspended, anomaly and contradiction (as in the lack of fit between lineage and political structures) can be resolved within the mythical explanation. Both metaphor and myth provide a convincing stopping place in the chain of explanation. One need *not* frame an additional "why"—e.g., Why is struggling against odds to be valued; it simply is. Why are there ogres; there simply are. If explanation is thus placed beyond doubt and argumentation, the social system can get on with its activities, rather than continuing to question its origins and legitimacy.

A second function of metaphor suggested by the Chinese example is that of bridging from the familiar to the strange, of facilitating change. The shift to industrialization and communization are made familiar by casting them as having the same structure as military operations and traditional values; the metaphor provides a road map in strange territory. This is a separate function from persuasion and placing beyond doubt, and it requires that the metaphor be as rich in detail as the new situation that it attempts to organize or to provide an organization for.

At first glance, the myth in the Nuer example does not seem to play the role of facilitating change; what seems to be at issue there is not change but continuity. However, there is a mapping within the myth from the kinship structure into the political structure. That is, the political structure of the tribe is made familiar by re-presenting it as a structure of kinship relations. Kinship forms a core set of values for the Nuer, and most Nuer tribesmen can recount their lineage back through six generations. The political structure may change, but the kinship structure is the source of continuity and is the more important to the Nuer.

Let me suggest an abstract generalization that emerges from considering this second function in the context of two apparently conflicting examples. In one case, metaphor appears to facilitate change, but in the other it (as myth) appears to foster continuity. Note that in the Chinese case, even though change was taking place to industrialization and communization, something is being conserved, something was invariant. What was conserved was the traditional concept of struggle. The metaphor not only facilitates change, but it *shapes* it. One might argue that by metaphorically extending the concept of struggle from the military to the factory and commune one not only structures the factory or commune in a certain way, but one also reinforces the values common to both ends of the metaphor. Similarly, in the case of the Nuer myth, the underlying value of kinship ties are reinforced by using them as the basis in the myth that justifies the political organization.

These considerations suggest a direction that a theory of organizational metaphor should take. The basic insight is this: In organizing, the use of metaphor *simultaneously* facilitates change *and* reinforces traditional values. Continued development and adaptation on a deepening foundation of values is, in this context, what we might mean by being "more organized." Metaphor facilitates change by making the strange familiar, but in that very process it deepens the meaning or values of the organization by giving them expression in novel situations. Change without the recognition of a continuity in meaning does not increase organization but only modifies it. Similarly, a mere repetition of meaning in the same narrow class of settings or activities does not increase the level of organization. Because of its inherent ambivalence of meaning, metaphor can fulfill the dual function of enabling change and preserving continuity.

Most organization theorists who have written about metaphor seem not to have recognized this dual function. For example, Huff (1977) examines the role of metaphorical expressions in "understanding the unfamiliar," but does not attend to the value-reinforcement process. Weick (1976, p. 13) suggests that myths play a sense-making or meaning-creating role in loosely coupled systems, but does not connect the use of myths to deepening *existing* systems of meaning. Clark's (1972) concept of an "organizational saga" functions to express deeply held values, but does not seem to serve as a bridge to the unfamiliar. Boje and Rowland (1977) recognize that myths function both to legitimize actions and to make complexity manageable, but they treat these as separate, rather than intimately related, functions. Mitroff and Kilmann's (1975) analysis of "stories" in organizations comes very close to our conception of simultaneous function. They argue that the story or corporate myth "establishes and perpetuates corporate traditions . . . it gives basic meaning to the corporation" (p. 18). They go on to study how sharing organizational stories "sensitizes managers to other realities . . . other ways of perceiving and analyzing organizational disturbances and problems" (p. 25). But they stop short of stating that myths, stories and metaphors carry out both functions simultaneously. Meyer and Rowan (1977) take a position which is precisely counter to the one developing here, that structure is a myth that legitimizes the organization, but works exactly because it is *not* coupled to the actual functioning of the organization.

A commonly noted feature of metaphors is that they operate at two different levels at the same time. They assert a coincidence, but they assert it playfully: man both *is* a wolf and is *not* a wolf. This capacity of metaphor to carry several meanings at once suits it ideally to express the simultaneous facilitation of change and continuity that forms the core of our theory of organizational metaphor. And that provides a tentative answer to the question that began this section: Why are metaphors and myths used at all? The answer that we have arrived at is that literal (i.e., non-metaphorical) attempts to talk about change sacrifice tradition, and literal attempts to preserve tradition block change, but metaphor can express both change and tradition, both novelty and familiarity.

This conclusion further reinforces the point made throughout this volume that attention to symbolic aspects is necessary for the effective management of organizations.

ACKNOWLEDGMENT

The assistance of Mary Linda Olson in the preparation of this paper is gratefully acknowledged.

NOTE

1. I am indebted to Paul Wilson for this information and insight.

REFERENCES

Blau, P., & Scott, W. R. *Formal organizations.* San Francisco: Chandler, 1962.

Boje, D. M., & Rowland, K. M. *A dialectical approach to reification in myth making and other social reality constructions. The 1-A-C-E model and OD.* (Working Paper No. 435). Urbana: University of Illinois, 1972.

Clark, B. R. The organization saga in higher education. *Administrative Science Quarterly,* 1972, *17,* 178–184.

Evans-Pritchard, E. E. *The Nuer.* New York: Oxford University Press, 1940.

Feldman, M. S., & March, J. G. Information in organizations as signal and symbol. *Administrative Science Quarterly,* 1981, *26,* 171–186.

Geertz, C. *The interpretation of cultures.* New York: Basic Books, 1973.

Hsia, T. A. *Metaphor, myth, ritual and the people's commune.* Berkeley: Center for Chinese Studies, University of California, 1961.

Huff, A. S. Evocative metaphors. *Human Systems Management,* 1980, *1,* 219–228.

Levi-Strauss, C. *Structural anthropology.* New York: Basic Books, 1963.

March, J. G., & Olsen, J. P. *Ambiguity and choice in organizations.* Bergen, Norway: Universitetsforlaget, 1976.

Meyer, J. W., & Rowan, B. Institutionalized organizations: Formal structure as myth and ceremony. *American Journal of Sociology,* 1977, *83,* 340–363.

Mitroff, I. I., & Kilmann, R. H. Stories managers tell: A new tool for organizational problem solving. *Management Review,* 1975, *July,* 18–28.

Ortony, A. *Metaphor and thought.* Cambridge: Cambridge University Press, 1979.

Ouchi, W., & Johnson, J. Types of organizational control and their relationship to emotional well being. *Administrative Science Quarterly,* 1978, *23,* 293–317.

Pondy, L. R., & Olson, M. L. *Theories of extreme cases.* (Working Paper No. 878). Urbana: University of Illinois, 1977.

Ryle, G. *The concept of mind.* New York: Barnes & Noble, 1949.

Sagan, C. *The dragons of Eden.* New York: Random House, 1977.

Turbayne, Colin M. *The myth of metaphor.* New Haven, Conn.: Yale University Press, 1962.

Turner, S. P. Complex organizations as savage tribes. *Journal for the Theory of Social Behaviour,* 1977, *7,* 99–125.

Turner, V. *Dramas, fields and metaphors: Symbolic action in human society.* Ithaca, N.Y.: Cornell University Press, 1974.

Weick, K. E. Educational organizations as loosely coupled systems. *Administrative Science Quarterly,* 1976, *21,* 1–19.

A RHETORICAL EXAMINATION OF STRATEGIC CHANGE

Anne Sigismund Huff

The strategy of an organization is rarely, if ever, non-controversial. Organizations embrace too many viewpoints and interests for complete accord. When disagreement over strategy arises, as is quite likely among those whose interests are less compatible with the current way of doing things, the disagreement is not just analytic. It has the strong symbolic content and rich subjective meanings which rise out of different world views and experience.

This paper suggests that rhetorical analysis of documents provides one method for reconstructing and understanding the gradual development of ideas which "frame" and "reframe" the nature of the organization and its mission for organization participants. The rhetorical approach used, although simple, provides a useful tool for broadly identifying the nature of the ongoing internal "conversation" about what an organization should be doing.

A METHOD FOR TRACING THE DEVELOPMENT OF STRATEGIC ARGUMENT

The study of disagreement's impact on strategy implies the study of language and argument. This is almost untouched territory in management, though a start has been made. Churchman's book *The Design of Inquiring Systems* (1971), for example, draws on philosophical sources to suggest alternative modes of inquiry. His description of dialectical inquiry is argumentative in spirit and has been used in policy-making settings (e.g., Mason, 1969). More recently, Mason and Mitroff (1979) have used Toulmin's *The Uses of Argument* (1958) to help policy makers clarify their reasoning. In political science, Axelrod (1976) has tried to identify and compare the "cognitive maps" of political policy makers.

None of these approaches, however, stresses an important aspect of naturally occurring argument between organization members. Talk in organizations is often meant to persuade or convince someone that a specific action is appropriate. The discipline of literary criticism, which has looked at the use of language from a broad communicative perspective, seems a useful guide here. The *rhetorical* approach to literary analysis pays particular attention to the way language links author and audience (Corbett, 1969).

This perspective has much to offer those interested in how groups of individuals come to see strategic alternatives in ways compatible enough to allow collective action. It offers categories to understand how arguments are constructed, and it offers many insights for document-based analysis (e.g., Smith, 1969). The focus on documents is particularly important for the study of changing strategy since organizational policies often develop over long periods. It is rarely possible to have the insiders' field notes as new developments occur in the environment or organization capacity changes over a period of years. What we have instead are incomplete documents: letters, texts of more important speeches, the minutes of meetings, final directives. These documents can be analyzed in ways similar to those used to understand how a poem or novel affects its audience.

Yet this is not the only reason to explore the study of argument and persuasion. Rhetoric stakes out as its territory the study of the debatable:

> . . . The very nature of deliberation and argumentation is opposed to necessity and self-evidence, since no one deliberates where the solution is necessary or argues against what is self-evident. The domain of argumentation is that of the credible, the plausible, the probable . . . (Perelman & Olbrechts-Tyteca, 1969, p. 1)

This focus of rhetoric is very similar that of the strategist—each pays closest attention to uncertainty. Rhetorical analysis may shed light on the way in which policy makers construct and come to accept some arguments as strong *enough* to warrant action.

DATA AND SETTING

This study examined a series of documents produced over an eight year time span in one organization, with special emphasis on six lengthy and widely distributed statements. Each document was taken as a purposeful attempt to state the author's perspective, and to persuade others to accept it. The first document studied, by the formal leader of the organization, outlines a view of the organization and its situation, and then specifies a series of actions to improve the position of the organization. Four of the other documents examined in detail were written by a branch of the organization whose interests were de-emphasized by this general statement of strategic direction. The final statement was written at the end of the period studied by the person who replaced the head of the organization when he accepted another position.

The purpose of the study was to try and understand the rhetorical devices used in the first leader's statement (if any) which contribute to the document's persuasiveness and make dissent difficult. Second, rhetorical devices were sought in the writings of those whose interests were not well represented which similarly might be expected to affect others' perception of their position. Finally, an attempt was made to relate the new statement of strategy developed at the end of the study period to concerns demonstrated in the previous documents.

Analysis of these documents focused on four topics:

1. the extent to which the *arrangement* of the work as a whole indicates the author's purpose and supports more specific arguments.
2. the contribution of *style,* or grammatical structure, to the impression of the whole.
3. the construction and content of the *arguments* themselves.

In addition, separate attention was given to another aspect of style, word choice. In each of the documents the authors use certain words repeatedly. And, interestingly enough, some of these key words appear in all of the documents. The use of the same word, and its synonyms, in various arguments is called a "theme," and each document is examined for

4. the contribution of *theme* to the development of more than one argument.

The setting for the study is a state university school of business. Founded as a graduate school in the early 1950s, the school made a major shift in programmatic emphasis in the early 1970s toward professional versus academic preparation. A new Dean, appointed in 1970 and the first Dean in the history of the graduate school without prior academic experience, played a key part in developing the new emphasis. Under his administration major changes in organization structure, program design and relations with the business community were accomplished. The size of the faculty and the number of students graduating at the masters level increased significantly. Additional resources were secured from the university and business community. The success of the School was further marked by a significant improvement in national rankings.

The Dean's arrival coincided with and encouraged a period of intense effort by the faculty to articulate the direction of School programs, and the rationale behind a variety of other policies. Formal documents were frequently distributed for faculty information and discussion. The Dean himself for the first five years of his administration prepared an extensive "State of the School" message at the end of the academic year. The documents chosen for intensive study are thus summarizing reports, a few of the many available, especially from the first several years after the Dean's arrival in 1970.

THE DEAN'S STATEMENT

In 1972, two year's after his arrival, the Dean of the School published a formal statement of "Philosophy and Thrust" for the School. This document is the most complete single statement of his organizational strategy available. Although it is clearly an attempt to phrase his leadership in the most persuasive terms possible, it can be safely assumed that the basic ideas included were not novel to the faculty, but had been expressed less formally in a variety of previous settings. Indeed, several faculty committees played a key part in developing a new orientation for the School. The Dean's document attempted to codify this orientation more formally.

Arrangement

The Dean's statement consists of 51 double spaced pages, or 916 lines of text.[1] Rhetorically, the document has four main parts: an initial introduction (30 lines or 3% of the total),[2] an extensive overview of the future needs of management and the appropriate response by schools of professional management education (30%), the "body" of the paper which outlines an overall philosophy for the School and specifies some programmatic implications (59%), followed by a concluding section which summarizes key points, introduces the need for additional faculty, and ties the discussion back to the introduction (8%).

This arrangement, which moves from a broad environmental overview inward, has the practical effect of delaying discussion of the School itself to page 17, while programmatic concerns are not broached directly until page 37. Those who agree thus have a framework within which to place their agreement. Those who do not agree are put in the position of having to argue with an overarching view of the world as well as a specific account of what the School should do.

Style

The tone of the document is almost uniformly declarative, but not phrased as a single person's opinion. Rather, the approach is one of "describing" or "articulating." The implication is that evident facts and widely held opinion are being codified into a strategic statement for general use, as established in the first two sentences of the introduction:

> This document describes a thrust for the School. Its objective is to articulate a unifying principle, one which will require commitment on the part of us all, and will give purpose and direction to our efforts individually and collectively.

The use of "us all" and "our efforts" underscores the impression that the writer is—at least in part—a scribe rather than creator, an approach which might be considered particularly appropriate for a professional organization which stressed faculty-level decision making.

The confident tone of the document is created primarily through the straightforward use of simple declarative verbs, as illustrated in these examples among many in the opening pages of the statement:[3]

> the professional school . . . *has* a unique contribution
>   to make
> the climate that compels changes . . . *is* . . . *critical*
> our School *aspires* to play a significant role . . . and to
>   rank indisputably among the nation's best

There is room for argument, as acknowledged in the second paragraph of the introduction:

> [This document] should serve as a basis for further deliberation and discussion within the School, and with the relevant external communities, from which a continuing consensus as to direction can emerge. It is not the purpose of the document to establish a set of "marching orders" or to dictate a direction.

But the word "basis" is critical here. The document is intended as the framework *within which* discussion is to take place. Choices remain to be made, but there is no hint of doubt or haziness in the overall vision expressed.

Argument

In a document of this length, many arguments are made. For the subsequent discussion the most critical of these are found in the introduction and background sections of the document. The Dean suggests in these pages that a new plan for the school is needed and that fundamental disagreement within the school would make "moving ahead" difficult. More broadly, he argues that management is the highest calling in a society with pressing social problems. Professional management education is described as requiring a synthesis of research, teaching and practice. In fact, the argument that "both faculty and students [must] relate theory with reality as integral parts of their professional development activities," appears to be the overriding concern of the document and is reiterated in many ways:

> "In a professional school, then, the functions of research, teaching and service are *not alternatives* from which to derive priorities. They are *closely inter-related* functions which contribute to each other in unique, quality ways. None is dispensable."

Underlying Themes

There are a number of concepts, frequently expressed in the same words, which appear as the "building blocks" of more than one argument. "Commitment," for example, is a key concept in this long document. The Dean sought "to articulate a unifying principle . . . which will require *commitment* on the part of us all." He also felt "business firms increasingly combine . . . *commitments* to produce with participation in solving public problems." Faculty have a "*commitment* to a given set of interests." Similarly, the School is "*committed* to attracting a greater number of women students," and has a "*commitment* to assure the reward structure in order to promote activities which are institutionally compatible."

Whereas earlier it was suggested that those in disagreement with the Dean's statement were put in the position of having to argue with the broad view of management and management education the Dean articulated, and would have to be concerned with having their counter proposals seem to argue for a less unique and exalted view of the School, it is now suggested that the more subtle requirement for effective argument involves addressing the underlying "themes" in the Dean's strategic vision. Four clusters of such themes are particularly apparent.

Unity and participation. The Dean wanted to "[identify] a *unifying principle* which can enable each individual within the School to determine whether and how he becomes a participant and beneficiary in the development and continued growth of the School." This concern with unity and participation remains important. The Dean suggests, for example, that "*collaborative relationships* between a professional school and practicing professionals can be established *without conflict or compromise.*" And he called for a new kind of research that would involve "*joint* efforts among combinations of faculty, students and practitioners and *cross many traditional boundaries.*" Perhaps this insistence on unity grew out of the Dean's managerial experience. He suggests that "the training of the manager is complicated by the fact that management is a *collective* function—a heterogeneous *collection* representing persons who are highly specialized in different fields of study."

Relevance. The Dean's view of research and teaching, or what he sometimes called "multi-professional scholarship," is closely tied to the view that "management is universally needed as a discipline for solving social problems." The words "social" and "societal" appear at least fifteen times in the text, and are supplemented with other references to the public sector, government and other non-profit organizations. Here again it is interesting to speculate on the importance of the Dean's own practical experience in shaping his concept of relevance. The statement that "most advances are made in the world of practice and not in education," underscores the importance of professional school attention to the "real" world of organizations.

Creativity and learning. A third set of themes which appear throughout the text have to do with the imaginative, creative, innovative, new or unique. The document declares, for example, that:

> . . . preparing graduates for *creative* careers in managing the diverse institutions of society, and designing *new* institutions to improve society, requires fundamental *changes* in our schools of management.

This emphasis on the new, creative and innovative is linked to another theme appearing throughout the text, the importance of learning. There is considerable attention to the necessity of creating an appropriate learning environment for students, one that grows out of "situations where the student must apply his acquired skills and knowledge to making decisions." But the faculty too are expected to "be involved in a continuous process of learning, sharpening their tools of observation and analysis."

Effectiveness and excellence. CEO's, as Bower (1972) observes, communicate to others in the organization the kinds of activities which will be rewarded. The Dean's statement is quite straightforward about this responsibility. The introduction indicates that the document "will . . . provide individual faculty with a basis for making priority judgments which are institutionally compatible and supportable." In addition to the arguments which point to the importance of socially and organizationally *relevant* activities as likely to generate such rewards, a number of other words are potential signs of what will be rewarded. "Effective" is the word of approval which appears most often. For example, "professional management education" is described as "education for *effectiveness* in today's society." Six instances of the use of "excellent" supplement this concern with effectiveness, including a call for "research that meets the test of academic *excellence* while addressing real problems." The themes of *competence* and *efficient* also appear at several points.

IMPLICATIONS FOR THE DOCTORAL PROGRAM

There are only two direct references to the doctoral program in the Dean's statement. In the first, doctoral education is indirectly described as losing a central place in the School:

> . . . We need increasingly to acknowledge, participate in and manage a variety of activities which are central to the School in its new context, but which previously have been viewed by faculty as a tax to be paid in return for doing what *was perceived* as centrally important, i.e., research and doctoral study.

In the second, much later, reference, it is asserted that "a quality doctoral program is central to the mission of the school," but the following text indicates that:

> The marketplace criterion must be applied to our output of doctoral candidates, both in terms of total numbers and the areas of specialization they represent. Quality should be stressed over quantity, and placement will continue to be a basis for assessing the effectiveness of our efforts.

Given a history of faculty autonomy over doctoral education, this paragraph can hardly have been viewed with equinamity by all members of the School. In fact, the new Dean represented a radical departure from a history of academically trained Deans and programmatic emphasis on doctoral education. The two years preceding the distribution of the statement just analyzed had been primarily devoted to the design and implementation of a new masters level program, which also was seen as a signal of the Dean's priorities. The Dean's statement indirectly indicates in many places a preoccupation with this master's level professional program. For example, "our primary student body" is described as "the young graduate . . . who still has to be trained . . . for entry into *management*." Research is almost always given a second place in the Dean's strategy:

> . . . the essential thrust of the School, and the focus of its identity, and its existence as a professional School within the University, call for a primary emphasis on *learning and research* programs which are defined and perceived in the context of having a worthwhile impact upon *professional* practice and perspective.

Thus, direct references to the doctoral program, references to the student body, and references to research, combine to suggest relatively little interest in doctoral level work within the School. The Dean's statement of strategy rests upon a view of the work of the school quite different from previous administrations' emphasis on doctoral education. The question now of interest is how those responsible for doctoral education presented themselves in such a climate. This question was pursued by examining a series of documents prepared for the faculty by the Associate Dean of the Doctoral Program.

RESPONSE FROM THE
DOCTORAL PROGRAM—1972

In 1972—the same year the Dean published his statement—the Associate Dean of the Doctoral Program distributed a thirty-two page document entitled "Doctoral Program: Past, Present and Future—A report prepared for the Faculty." The historical arrangement of the report serves a function not unlike that served by the broad overview used in the Dean's statement. Both authors couch their arguments about what should be done in the School in a broader context which supports their primary arguments and make them more difficult to counter individually. The historical perspective, and an appendix listing all graduates and faculty advisors of the program since its inception, recalls the period in which the doctoral program captured the primary programmatic concern of the faculty. Description of the present program is further buffered by extensive consideration of future improvements. Those who might not agree with the present nature of the program are thus forced to also consider what was and will be.

The overall tone, or style, of the Doctoral Report is informative. It often presents the complete set of data available in the form of tables—noting, for example, the current ratio of applications to admissions and acceptances. Occassionally the Report draws conclusions from this material, but in general it presents it as "interesting" or "informative" and leaves the conclusion to the reader.

The choice of verbs in the Doctoral Report is often more hesitant than in the Dean's statement: "It would *seem* an appropriate time to review . . . the Program," "I *believe* that our Doctoral graduates *typically* are well trained," and so on. Nevertheless, there are declarative statements in the Report with a tone of conviction equal to those found in the Dean's statement. In each case these stronger statements have to do with the basic value of the doctoral program. For example:

> "an important aspect of planning by . . . the School *must* be the long-range goals of the Doctoral Program"

> "it is clear that such a task *must be* a primary assignment of . . . our faculty"

As in the Dean's statement, such broad declarative observations indicate a basic conviction within which discussion is to take place.

Familiar Themes in New Arguments

The Doctoral Report includes several references which reveal an overlap with the Dean's concerns. The idea of unity is found in several places, for example, and the report emphasizes "involved," and "interested" faculty.

"Relevance," the second major theme from the Dean's statement, appears but once in the Doctoral Report, but in a key argument about program identity. Here, the Associate dean for the Doctoral Program argues that "our Doctoral graduates end up with a useful blend of theoretical and *applied* interests" and that dissertations "[place] value on *relevance*." Finally, the Dean's third theme of creativity and learning also appears in the Doctoral Report. Doctoral study "should satisfy the important criteria or *original* research," several required papers "exhibited research *creativity*," and many dissertations "[probe] at the *frontiers*."

While these examples indicate considerable overlap in 1972 between the Dean and the Associate Dean responsible for the Doctoral Program, it is interesting to note the extent to which the arguments involved are different in intent. For example, "collaboration" has to do with student *evaluation*, a topic which does not appear at all in the Dean's statement.

Similarly, creativity and originality are linked only to research, and not to teaching and consulting as they are in the Dean's statement.

This use of vocabulary made familiar by the Dean to convey unfamiliar arguments is prominent in the Doctoral Report. The Associate Dean argues, for example, that the identity of the Doctoral Program rests first on research, but this point neglected by the Dean is surrounded by vocabulary which the Dean made familiar. Before mentioning research, the Report talks about the need for the program to be *consistent* with the School's identity, the importance of *efficient* use of resources, and the *collective* contribution of three elements to the Doctoral Program. Then, the introduction of research is followed by references to the *interdisciplinary* focus of graduates, the extent to which theoretical interests blend with *applied* interests and the fact that their research places value on *"relevance, implementation* and *usability."*

Themes Not Found in the Dean's Statement

Two themes stand out in the Doctoral Report as being unique from those found in the Dean's statement.

Review. The introductory statement suggests that it is "an appropriate time to *review* development and growth of . . . [the Doctoral] Program." The conclusion indicates that "it is important for the . . . faculty to continue to *evaluate* the Doctoral Program" in terms of long range goals. Discussion of monitoring (the word and its derivatives appear eight times), reviewing (seven occurences), and evaluating (five occurences) occur throughout the report. These ideas are not tied to the words of approval used in the Dean's statement. "Effective," the word used most often by the Dean, does not appear at all in the Doctoral Report. "Excellent" is used only in the context of "excellent computer capability;" "efficient" occurs only once.

Quality. The word of approval used most often by the Associate Dean of the Doctoral Program, is "quality." The *"quality* of the research papers" prepared by students is of concern, for example, as is the *"quality* of output" from "doctoral level seminars and faculty," and the *"quality* of opportunity afforded the graduate by association with a particular company or university."

DOCTORAL REPORTS IN 1973 AND 1974

The Associate Dean for the Doctoral Program held his position for three years. At the end of 1973 and 1974 he again distributed short (144 and

223 lines, respectively) formal reports on the program. The arrangement of these reports follows the formula established in 1972. Each report reviews the activities of the present year by looking at the work of four committees, updates statistics on current students, the list of participating faculty, and the table of graduates. Each then looks ahead to important topics for future consideration. The tone is informative again, with words like "hopefully", "it seems to me", "I would suspect" and "I believe" a reminder of the more tentative and personal voice of the author when compared with the Dean's statement. The reports continue to develop, however, an independent vocabulary and broader and more declarative arguments about the future of the program and indeed the future of the School as a whole.

Three developments are especially worth noting in these documents. First, there is some expression of *dissatisfaction with* the *quality* of the doctoral program. Second, the Associate dean introduces the idea that *confrontation* among those with "mixed feelings . . . concerning the nature of our Doctoral program" should not be avoided. This idea directly counters the Dean's emphasis on unity and consensus. Third, the concluding statement of the '74 report goes beyond discussion of the Doctoral Program to call for *"quality control"* and evaluation of the School as a whole, and goes on to suggest that evaluation might lead to a reallocation of School resources to the benefit of the Doctoral Program.

PROPOSED REVISIONS TO THE DOCTORAL PROGRAM—1977

The Associate Deans of the Doctoral Program from 1974 through 1978 did not publish end year reports similar to the documents just analyzed, but the effort to revise the curriculum came to a head in 1977, with a "stimulus" document and questionnaire distributed to both doctoral students and faculty. The results were analyzed and reported in a second document that suggested a new doctoral program. The revisions involved not only curriculum, but change in emphasis on teaching, recruiting, admissions and financial support. This second document, prepared by a faculty committee and reflecting broad faculty input, provides an interesting end-point to the above analysis.

There is an echo of the Dean's original philosophy in one aspect of the proposed program:

> The program should create opportunities for the development of a stronger *community* of scholars among the Ph.D. students. We have accomplished this quite well in the MBA program; the same needs to be done for the Ph.Ds.

A stronger link to the Associate Dean's concern with "competence" and "quality" is found, among other places, in the goal of "only turn[ing] out graduates who are *qualified* for appointments at top academic institutions (authors' emphasis)." The most interesting development in this document, however, is found in a statement that directly challenges the overall strategic vision found in the Dean's statement of 1972.

The Dean originally suggested that professional schools must be oriented toward social problems and the needs of managers. They had the unique responsibility of integrating teaching, consulting and research, and this synthesis accounted for their unique mission. The doctoral program revision has another view of the school's setting and the framework within which doctoral education should be carried out. This view emphasizes specialization.

> Organizations gain their energy and vitality by offering something of value to the larger society of which they are a part. Furthermore, the more specialized the role of the organization and the more its distinctive competence matches the demands of its role, the more effective it will be. Universities are no different. The special role of the university is the creation and dissemination of knowledge and the people who do this typically have Ph.D. degrees and to a lesser extent other doctoral degrees. Since other schools and colleges share in the dissemination of knowledge, the burden of creating its falls more heavily on universities. So it comes to be that the singular responsibility of universities is the creation of knowledge, with dissemination a responsibility they share with other institutions.

Thus by 1977 those most involved with the doctoral program have come full circle, with the development of a new "world view", more briefly stated than the Dean's, but almost as encompassing. This view abandons the socially oriented notion of "relevance", and suggests that teaching and contact with practitioners are not co-equal with research as the Dean claimed, but secondary. The emphasis on specialization conceptually returns the Doctoral Program to programmatic prominence.

DISCUSSION: HOW THE LANGUAGE OF STRATEGY MAY CHANGE

The Dean's statement of philosophy is taken to be both a powerful stimulus toward agreement (and reward) among organization members and the reflection of agreement already extant among many organization members, who participated in the selection of this new leader. Nevertheless, no one strategy can equally encompass all interests, and the paper follows statements from one less well represented group for a period of six years. The series of documents used to trace opinion within this group give some preliminary evidence for part of what might be called a theory of "policy-level discourse". Three phenomena evident in this material can be stated more generally:

1. *Use of the leader's vocabulary.* There is considerable use of the Dean's vocabulary in early documents prepared by the Doctoral Program. Such initial indications of "loyalty" might be predicted from disparate interests in the organization as a strong leader takes office. Organization members are motivated to make similar and compatible arguments to those expressed by the CEO. They are likely to use the same concepts and even very same words used by the leader.

2. *"Insulating" new ideas with accepted vocabulary.* First attempts to present interests which are not covered or which are expressed disadvantageously by the new leader, will tend to be expressed as compatibly as possible with the language and arguments used by the CEO. New ideas which cannot be well expressed as extensions of arguments made by the CEO require new language. But these new ideas will tend to be expressed in *conjunction* with more familiar argument and language, as illustrated in this study by emphasis on the *relevance* of doctoral student research.

3. *Negation of accepted vocabulary.* If the reexpression of a particular interest group's perspective in the language of the leader does not receive adequate response, more and more "new language" will appear in their statements. When discourse has not brought reconciliation, it is likely that these statements will be justified by new expressions of what the organization as a whole is facing, and should be doing, and decreased use of argument and language used by the leader. By the end of the period covered in this study, for example, only one statement might be described as still reflecting the Dean's original philosophy, and several key statements directly challenge the arguments which the Dean set down in 1972 as guiding principles.

These ideas about policy-level discourse might be reexpressed in the following way. What leaders so, at least sometimes, and often early in their appointments, is express what is important—their strategy—in a series of consistent terms which are grouped into arguments. The favored terms might be identified with the following notation:

$$\text{Leader at } t_0: a, b, c, d, e, f, g, h, i$$

To be recognized by strong leaders, every actor or department is highly motivated to choose among these terms to report their efforts, and thus gain the rewards which strong leaders are able to bestow. However, each department has experience and interests that make it likely they will not need to reference some terms, and that they will give some of the remaining terms special emphasis. Thus,

Program 1 at t_1: $\underline{c}$, d, f, $\underline{i}$

The more a group's tasks and interests do not coincide with the expressions of the leader (or dominant coalition), the less this modest rearrangement and amplification will be sufficient. The original themes will have to be re-expressed and new themes introduced. The new terms will, if possible, be "packaged" with more familiar and accepted ones.

Program 2 at t_2: $\underline{c}$, f, g, am, cn, go

If this does not bring the rewards attached to the leader's way of seeing the organization and its situation, new themes and new arguments are more and more likely to replace the old. And, some of these new terms are likely to be direct antitheses of the old.

Program 2 at t_3: c, m, $\underline{n}$, $\underline{o}$, p, not a, not d

Documenting such shifts in language and argument is potentially important for the broader study of organizational symbolism. My view of the documents analyzed for this paper is that they are first directly symbolic, since they were new channels of communication not previously produced in the school. More important, however, they are indirectly supportive of other symbolic action. The reassignment of office space, or new policy for allocating research funds to faculty, are examples of dramatic and memorable events in the life of a school. But such actions are given the potential for fuller significance by language, often formally expressed in documents such as those studied here. By the way they are organized, the tone they convey, and the vocabulary they provide, these documents provide organization members with important material for assigning meaning to more visible events. In the case of disagreement, the details of alternative meaning are similarly communicated by language, though often more dramatically illustrated by action.

CONCLUSION

The Dean of the School left in 1977 to accept a new position. The proposal for a new doctoral program, which used a new language to express a new strategic vision, was thus closely followed by the search for a new Dean. The candidates interviewed expressed various approaches to business education, and several people were in accord with the emphasis of the preceeding Dean. The man chosen, however, was described by the Chancellor of the University as adding an emphasis on doctoral level education to the previous emphasis on professional training. The new Dean himself indicated that

> We have a first-rate MBA program, and its going to stay that way. Our Ph.D. program is strong, but I intend to see that it gets even stronger.

The overall objective expressed by the new Dean was to make the School the number one business school in the country. His strategy emphasized the improvement of discipline-based research capabilities:

> The idea in general is to improve the academic environment, to attract the very best faculty that we can, and to make sure that we don't lose the good faculty that we do have by providing the resources for them and the kinds of activities that will make it intellectually attractive.

The choice of a new Dean thus marked a major redirection of the School; the kind of redirection that not infrequently accompanies change in organizational leadership.

The question which now bears more research is how closely the recognition, selection, and even the success of leaders who *re*formulate strategy is tied to the previous development of a language which "frames" the issues facing the organization in new ways. Language is the lens through which opportunities, including the opportunities provided by Deanship candidates, are observed. In the case presented here, I believe the language initially developed to state convincingly the needs of the doctoral program gradually extended beyond the program. This language clarified some essential weaknesses in the first Dean's vision, including the assumption that a diverse faculty could be persuaded to hold a unified view of business and education. Thus even some faculty without strong ties to doctoral education were in sympathy with the need for review and evaluation expressed more and more forcefully in the documents produced by the doctoral program.

The choice of new Dean reflected such discontent. While many other factors must be considered (including the nature of the committee making recommendations, the pool of candidates available, and campus-wide interests) in explaining the choice of new leaders, those of us interested in strategy *re*formulation might well give increasing attention to the themes articulated in organizational dialogue prior to strategic change. Such dialogue, this paper argues, serves as the "ground" which helps determine which strategic alternatives may flourish.

ACKNOWLEDGMENTS

Earlier drafts of this paper were presented at the 1979 Academy of Management meetings, Atlanta, and the 1979 AIDS meetings, New Orleans. I profited from many responses to these papers, and especially from detailed critiques made by Bob Gephart and several anonymous reviewers. A longer version of this paper is available on request.

NOTES

1. The documents are typed on standard 8 ½ by 11 paper, but the spacing between lines varies. The "line," rather than page, is therefore used as a common measure of document length. Any line with more than one word, excluding headings, is included in the length count.

2. Unless otherwise noted, words underlined for emphasis in quotations are not underlined in the original.

REFERENCES

Axelrod, Robert (Ed.). *Structure of decision.* Princeton, N.J.: Princeton University Press, 1976.

Bower, Joseph L. *Managing the resource allocation process.* Homewood, Ill.: Irwin, 1972.

Bower, Joseph, & Doz, Yves. Strategy formulation: A social and political process. In Dan E. Schendel & Charles W. Hofer (Eds.), *Strategic Management.* Boston: Little, Brown, 1979.

Churchman, C. West. *The design of inquiring systems.* New York: Basic Books, 1971.

Corbett, Edward P. J. *Rhetorical analyses of literary works.* London: Oxford University Press, 1969.

Mason, R. O. A dialectical approach to strategic planning. *Management Science,* 1969, *15,* B403–B414.

Mason, R. O., & Mitroff, I. I. Assumptions of majestic metals: Strategy through dialectics. *California Management Review,* 1979, *23*(2), 80–88.

Perelman, Ch., & Olbrechts-Tyteca, L. *The new rhetoric* (John Wilkinson & Purcell Weaver, Trans.). Notre Dame, Ind.: University of Notre Dame Press, 1969.

Smith, William R. *The rhetoric of American politics.* Westport, Conn.: Greenwood Press, 1969.

Toulmin, Stephen E. *The uses of argument.* Cambridge: Cambridge University Press, 1958.

Part V

**MAKING SENSE OF
ORGANIZATIONAL SYMBOLS**

In one sense every paper in this volume is an exercise in sense-making. Each author provides an interpretation of organizational symbolism which draws upon his or her basic assumptions about the nature of organizational life. The papers presented in Part V are concerned specifically with the question of interpretation and of how sense is made of organizational events and processes.

Richard Boland and Raymond Hoffman (*Humor in a Machine Shop: An Interpretation of Symbolic Action*) focus on the manner in which humor in the work situation provides a basis for interpreting the meaning of what takes place in that situation. They show how humor has a symbolic status, conveying significant patterns of meaning which help to frame and control difficult work situations and to re-affirm the identities of the workers. Their analysis reveals the way humor is used to counterbalance the difficulties and dangers which foundry machinists confront in the hazardous routine which constitutes their daily work lives.

The two papers which follow, by Daft, and by Frost and Morgan, should be read in tandem. Dick Daft's interpretation of the significance of organizational symbols (*Symbols in Organizations: A Dual-Content Framework of Analysis*) is derived from his notes and observations of the presentations and discussions at the Illinois Organizational Symbolism Conference. As a paper it can stand alone and its focus has much in common with the papers presented in Part III on the management of organizational symbols, in that it focusses on identifying the nature and types of symbols found in organizations, and on the general functions which they may perform. It is presented here alongside the paper by Peter Frost and Gareth Morgan (*Symbols and Sensemaking: The Real-ization of a Framework*), because the latter analyzes how Daft's scheme was used at the Illinois conference to make sense of the nature of organizational symbolism. Analyzing the transcript of Daft's presentation, Frost and Morgan trace how a problematic reality (the meaning of organizational symbolism) was made sensible for many at the conference through use of Daft's scheme. The analysis illustrates how the symbolic construction of one person can be used by others to concretize or realize a reality: a shared definition of the situation. The analysis also illustrates the interplay between dominant and counter-definitions of reality found in group situations of this kind.

In Mark Wexler's paper (*Pragmatism, Interactionism and Dramatism: Interpreting the Symbol in Organizations*) we are provided with a wide ranging discussion of the nature and foundations of the interpretive approach to symbolism. Wexler's concern is to demonstrate the relationships between pragmatism, interactionism, and dramatism, in a way that identifies potential directions for the study of organizational symbolism. He examines the nature of, and interface between public and private symbols within the context of a valuable discussion of the nature of three important schools in interpretive thought.

HUMOR IN A MACHINE SHOP:
AN INTERPRETATION OF
SYMBOLIC ACTION

Richard J. Boland and Raymond Hoffman

This paper focuses on the way humor as a form of symbolic action contributes to a process of individual and organizational control over work situations. We define symbolic action to mean communicative behavior between two or more individuals in which the intent is not merely a literal indication of specific objects or events, but a metaphorical process through which one object or event is understood in relation to another. Through symbolic action humans go beyond indicating things, and enter a different dimension of discourse in which the meaning of indicated objects or events is at issue. This distinction between literal or symbolic action should be understood as one of degree, since all human understanding is essentially symbolic (Cassirer, 1944).

The role of humor in organizations has received relatively little attention. A noticeable exception is found in the work of Roy (1960), who used an interactionist frame to show how humor marks time and makes the monotony of routine work bearable. Whereas Roy emphasizes the structure of interaction during periods of humor (e.g., over lunch), the analysis presented here emphasizes the function of humor in the construction and negotiation of a problematic work setting. The workers are involved in the ordering of their social world. Pulling and getting jokes is an interaction through which they mutually construct their social reality.

The Machine Shop

The basis for this study is a small, privately owned machine shop. Such shops are found in almost every town that has an industrial or agricultural base, but are especially prevalent in the midwest where they provide custom-tooled steel parts to nearby manufacturing firms. Typical shop size ranges from 10 to 50 machinists, working with large lathes, surface grinders, drill presses and other automatic machines to transform tubes and bars of steel into a wide variety of finished products. The shop we observed works primarily with steel tubing (from ½″ to 12″ outer diameter) producing component parts (mostly steel bushings) for agricultural and earth moving equipment manufacturers. As a job shop, almost no request is too small and their customers and order sizes range from the single individual to the largest industrial firms. This shop (M shop) has 20 machinists in 15,000 square feet of floorspace. It has concrete floors and walls, 18 to 24 foot ceilings, and overhead conduits connecting the machines. Approximately 20 percent of the shop is used for stockpiling raw steel in racks 12 feet high. Overhead cranes move the required steel stock in bundles up to 6,000 pounds to the appropriate machining areas. A given order may require a dozen or more separate machining operations.

Like most machine shops, M is characterized by noise, dirt and constant threat of injury. Machine operations and steel handling create a loud whining and clanging, and the nature of the steel and the machines gives a pervasive sense of grease, oil and dust. There is a strong element of danger in the work. Lathes rotate the steel tubing at a high speed and a stationary cutting tool is applied to the softer steel stock. The result is heat, with the machined steel turning blue hot and peeling off at the tool's edge in coiled ribbons that can cause immediate third degree burns. Other machines create equal amounts of hot steel discharge in the form of chips and shavings.

No matter how "boring" or "monotonous" a job in the shop may seem, no matter how simple and routine an operation may appear to an observer, there is an element of danger that always exists. There's an old saying that puts it well. "Take the machine for granted and it'll take your hand, pay attention and you'll be a whole man." The machines may take off an arm or hand, or severely cut an individual, while the steel itself may fall from its stacked piles and crush a foot, ankle, leg or arm. If a loose piece of clothing or long hair gets caught in a machine, the individual himself is quickly pulled in. Most injuries take place when the individual stops respecting or paying full attention to the machine. The older the machinist, the lower the accident rate. Minor accidents may be humorous to the other workers, evoking an "I told you so" look on the face. But nobody likes to get burned by blue hot steel shavings that stick to the skin. Most machinists realize that at best the machine is a double edged sword, capable of being controlled to an extent, but also capable of inflicting unexpected injury to its operator.

The steel itself is important in creating the atmosphere of the machine shop. Virtually everything the men work with is steel in one form or another. Steel tubing is the raw material. High carbon steel tools cut and shape the tubing on steel lathes and drill presses. Steel drums store the finished pieces and work in process. Steel is the scrap, and even work boots are lined with steel. Machinists live in a steel world for 8–10 hours every day. They make the steel take a certain form, and yet the steel shapes them. A machinist's hands become very strong and thick with calluses from all the cuts, slivers, and burns he receives. Nonetheless, to a machinist, his hands are a prized possession. He is proud of them, no matter what they look like to other people. The machinist is physically altered by the process of shaping the steel, and comes to respect its inert strength. It is the "immoveable object" that he struggles with.

There is also an important cognitive component to being a machinist. Steel as a raw material has a wide range of hardness, tensile strength and malleability. The machines and tools have varied rates of material feed, cutting speed and steel removal, and a specific job order may demand tolerances of plus or minus five ten-thousandths of an inch. Being a machinist includes developing the special ability to take these standard specifications plus other, more subtle aspects of a particular piece of steel, machine and tool into account in producing the desired result.

The machinists at M shop range in age from late fifties to late teens, and shop experience ranges from 35 years to no experience at all. A hierarchy exists within the shop based on experience with machines. One exception to this is the foreman, who, at 40 years of age, finds himself at the top of the formal hierarchical structure even though he has less experience than several of the machinists. The foreman does not take his position as implying that he is the most experienced, however, and often calls on the advice of older machinists in problem situations. Several other hierarchies exist in the social world of M shop, including ones based on strength and intelligence.

M shop was founded in the summer of 1972. At first, much of the work was subcontracted, but in the fall of 1973 the shop began full service operation with three machinists and one owner/manager. From that point through August of 1974 one of the authors worked in the shop as an apprentice. He continued to work as an apprentice machinist during summers and holidays for the next five years, including the most recent summer of observation. During this time, the shop had grown to 20 full time machinists and he has continued to be an accepted, though intermittent, member of the work force. The examples of humor discussed here are based on recorded observations, but they are elaborated with recollections of the five preceding years of work experience.

Machine Shop Humor

We do not pretend to have developed a taxonomy of all the instances of humor that were observed, but some natural headings would include language jokes, physical jokes and machine jokes. In this paper we will deal only with physical and machine jokes as they are the easiest to relate specifically to the work place. Language jokes, especially at lunchtime and breaks, run the full spectrum of an individual's social life, including hobbies, family, personal history, etc. Taking them into account is beyond our ability here. We would argue, however, that our narrowing to these specific behaviors is to study a particular language—a bodily and object mediated one—not to ignore language.

Purely physical jokes include one or more individuals in direct or indirect contact with another. It is significant that these physical tricks are not taken literally by the machinists. If they were, they would be seen as pranks—malicious and deserving of reprobation. Instead, they are understood as symbolic action intended to excite laughter. Each machinist has a rag tucked into his back pocket for ready use in wiping himself, the steel, or the machine. Taking his rag, without his notice, is a common and effective joke—especially when he reaches to clean a hand full of grease. Or, because lidded steel drums are put on a dolly for movement to the next machine operation, replacing a full drum with an empty one can cause the individual to fall flat on his face when he gives the heave-ho. Another frequent physical joke is the goose. A broom handle or steel tube, not so delicately placed, will bring any machinist up short. Many of the physical jokes play on the desire to keep clean in the dirty shop environment. A rag wet with machine coolant or grease set on a chair or lobbed across the shop onto a clean shirt back is one example, and dropping large pieces of steel into a vat of coolant or cleaning fluid, splashing those around it is another.

Physical humor is also evident in mimicry. While the shop is in full production with all men at their machines, an extended sequence of mimicked jokes are taking place. Imitating unique physical gestures or characteristics of those stationed at other machines or walking in the aisles is a frequent form of humor. Besides the parody of unique physical gestures or abnormalities of others, mimicry often has sexual or intellectual overtones. Other machinists are often portrayed as either sexually incompetent or as sexually perverted, using bars of steel or pieces of the machine as mock sex objects to pantomime another's missing or insatiable appetites. The pantomimes may also refer to another's mental powers as in "you are looking (acting) so stupidly".

The other major category of humor relates to the machines themselves. These are primarily jokes played on an individual through his machine. Each machinist will spend approximately 60% of his time on one particular machine. He will come to see the machine as his and will often give it a name, paint a unique decoration on it, and in general come to have an intimate understanding of its unique operating characteristics. Because of this relationship, the machine is an ideal medium for pulling jokes. It is an important element in establishing the individual's identity as a machinist, and therefore a powerful medium for pulling jokes about the definition of self. "Blueing" is a popular trick in which an indelible steel marking ink is rubbed on the handles or knobs of a machine. This is especially funny when the individual touches his face or clothes after grabbing the "blued" knob or handle. The natural blackened color of the knobs and handles makes this "blueing" difficult to detect. In a similar vein, the hose which sprays a fine stream of coolant over the raw steel as it is being machines can be adjusted to spray at high pressure directly onto the machine operator. Other machine jokes include removing fuses or gears from a machine, thus making them inoperable, or reversing the direction in which a machine rotates. Slightly more adventurous jokes include the outright removal of key operating parts from another's machine, or recalibrating the measurement instruments he uses for checking the narrow tolerances.

These machine tricks are best when pulled while a machinist is in the middle of a production run but has turned off and left his machine for a few minutes. When he returns, the trick pullers are watching for his reaction when the machine doesn't start, runs backwards, soaks him with coolant, or when he discovers he has "blueing" on his hands and has just touched his face. One joke that requires a running machine is the cannon trick. Here, the running machine becomes an amusing toy for the machinist. By plugging one end of the steel tubing with a rubber ball, the air pressure is built up until a cannon like explosion blows it out.

INTERPRETATION

In this section we will interpret these instances of body or machine mediated humor as functional in a problem solving sense. We are specifically not interested in explaining the humor to be found in the jokes themselves, or to define what they mean to the individuals involved. At this level of analysis the antics we have identified would appear childish and foolish. Our next question would have to be "how do grown men come to act in such silly ways?" But these men are not silly or childish. They are machinists, highly skilled, knowledgeable, dedicated machinists. They navigate successfully in a world of real physical danger, they handle unexpected variations in the materials, machinery and specifications within tight cost standards, and they pride themselves on the low percentage of "rejects" they produce. One major customer with especially strict quality standards is said to return upwards of 65% of the production of other shops, but less than 10% at M shop.

We will therefore keep our analysis at the level of symbolic action, and attempt to sketch the symbolic function of this humor as problem solving. If literal problem solving takes place within a frame of reference and concerns the selection of optimum or satisfactory courses of action, symbolic problem solving can be said to operate at the level of selecting frames of reference or the framing of a situation (Koestler, 1964). There are many ways in which a given situation at M shop can be framed by the participants. The individual working on a piece of steel can be seen as a skilled craftsman putting his talent on display, as an hourly worker just putting in time, as master of his machine making it perform to the limit of its possibilities, or as a mere appendage, dancing to the tune of the machine, steel stock and blueprints. Within any one of these or myriad other ways the shop situations can be framed, a literal problem solving process can be applied. Through the symbolic action of humor, the workers juxtapose two or more possible frames of reference for a given situation, and resolve them meaningfully. In this way they move across frames of reference, always entertaining several possible frames simultaneously, never reducing to just one that can be relied on for a literal analysis of the situation.

For Roy the problem in the workplace was monotony, but for us the problem is the socialization and alienation of the self. To understand the importance of self-definition to the workers in M shop we will first give a fuller description of what it is to be a machinist. A machinist is, first of all, a craftsman. His craft comes to him from a long line of journeymen who initiated apprentices to the intricacies, skills and special sensibilities that mark a machinist. Becoming a top machinist may take 15–20 years, and some men will never make it. It is not a set of procedures to be followed in robot like fashion, but a total bearing to be assumed. Walk into a machine shop and you "know" who the machinists are. Their relation to the steel, the machine, the tools, and the total work space is a way of being that can be sensed but not imitated. Attention to details, as far as command of the standard metal, tool, and blueprint specifications is just the surface of the craft. An intimate sensitivity to nuances of the materials, the machine and the tools as they interact is a slightly deeper description. But at a fundamental level the machinist is seeking a perfection in the form and texture of each machined piece. This vision of perfection calls him, and through experimentation, ingenuity and perseverance he seeks it.

We take the position that the instances of humor observed in M shop are seen as being funny by the individuals involved to the extent that each individual finds in "getting the joke", that two incongruous frames of reference for interpreting the self are meaningfully resolved. The problems of self-definition that this humor is dealing with are inferred from the frames of reference the jokes juxtapose. While this is ultimately each individual's unique experience in "getting the joke" we will summarize what appear to us to be the most conspicuous frames involved.

Each worker, over time, establishes a strong self-identity in the shop. In these self-identities, the definition of the individual as a worker is our primary concern, but this is deeply intertwined with other, more personal aspects of their life and we cannot separate them. The self-definition includes such things as his manner and type of dress, morning ritual of arrival, dressing, having coffee, checking his machine, etc. It also includes his identity as a machinist—the level of skills and capabilities he asserts. We see these self-identities as structured in sets of hierarchies. Humor plays both an initiating and reversing role in these nested sets of hierarchically structured self-definitions. It initiates structure by affirming an individual's place, and it also reverses structure when played on an individual's previously established identity. For instance, a new worker will have jokes played on him so he learns his place, but once established, the jokes are played to reverse his place. The ambiguity of self confirmed by humor allows for movement through the established hierarchies. While humor serves to celebrate an individuals existing identity it also asserts its fragility and ultimate equivocality. The machinist who prides himself on being the cleanest in M shop, with a pressed uniform and scrubbed hands, is great for a wet rag, blueing or coolant hose trick. Of course, this particular machinist defines himself by many of the structured hierarchies of the shop. He is also seen as one of the best joke pullers and one of the most difficult to pull one on. While this may or may not add to the reversal effect of a joke played on him, it does provide for multiple frames of reference that can be used as a basis for "getting the joke".

Other examples of humor used to reverse the established order are found at the lunchtable. Some men will bring exactly the same lunch everyday (salami on white bread, two carrots, two celery sticks, one packet of twinkies). They eat these items in the same order everyday, and a good joke is to divert their attention, so that they eat their food in a different order. One man went so far as to arrange with another worker's wife to pack a different lunch for her husband as part of the trick. (He refused to eat it.)

This use of jokes to deny an asserted self-identity is a major theme of the mimicry mentioned earlier. The individual's position in the hierarchies of sexual prowess, physical strength, intelligence or skilled machinist is a basis for much of the mimicry. The joker is saying "you're not so smart (strong, skilled)." The machine jokes (removing parts, changing adjustments, etc.) are also reversing the individuals position, but, like the lunch jokes, have a ritual interruption component also. That is, each machinist develops a highly rigid, sequenced set of actions for setting up his machine or for running a particular job. Any joke pulled on him while he is in the middle of this sequence will force him to go back to the beginning and start over again. This starting over again is an integral part of "getting the joke", and emphasizes the disparity of the several frames that must be involved.

There is an important sense in which the joke must "fit" the existing hierarchy. In order to pull a joke, an individual must himself be well established in the relevant hierarchy. For instance, a new apprentice cannot really pull a joke on anyone. Once he *is* seen as fit for pulling jokes, he only plays certain kinds, rag jokes or dirty and clean jokes, but not machine jokes. Only the machinists pull machine jokes. On the one hand, then, jokes are primarily directed against an individual's self-identity, but on the other, the joke is asserting or confirming the identity of the joke puller.

Thus far, the examples of humor have related primarily to the problem of socialization. For the individual this problem can be stated as "how do I maintain my independence, my unique self-identity, yet become an element in the established order?", as well as, "how am I related to the established order, where is my place in this social sphere, how is it known to me and affirmed by others, how do I move through it from one place to another?" An individual's progression through the multiple social hierarchies in the shop is paralleled by the appropriateness of different types of humor. The shared understanding of when certain types of jokes can be "made by" and "gotten by" an individual establishes and confirms his place in the shop, and the reversal of established structure through humor serves this same purpose. The role of humor in dealing with the problem of alienation has two aspects that we will now explore.

First, the same jokes we interpret as functional in socialization serve to deal with the problem of alienation in that the individual is socialized into a system which includes acceptance of some level of alienation. Once again, to the extent that the jokes we observed are allowing for multiple frames of reference to be used in defining the self-identity of the individual worker, a certain ambiguity of identity is maintained. The essence of alienation is the experience of the product of one's labor as alien from one's self. It is experienced as foreign from the self, and divorced from it. It is not an extension of one's self, but an independent object that stands against self. The product of an individual's labor, as an object alien to him, is less of a problem as the self-identity from which the product is alien is itself ambiguous. To the extent that the definition of self is equivocal, the more difficult a clear judgment of that which is alien from it becomes. Thus, the degree of ambiguity of the self constructed through humor functions to socialize the individual into accepting as nonproblematic a certain level of alienation.

Second, we can treat the problem of alienation apart from its interrelationship with that of socialization. To do this, we will refer to alienation in Marx's original sense. The product of labor stands before the worker as an alien being, and also as an independent power. The more the individual produces the more powerful the world of objects becomes, and the poorer and less significant the individual becomes (Marx, 1844).

We can see the power of the object most clearly when the completed product (a sub-assembly in a larger industrial process) is shipped to the M shop customers. When the machinist completes a product to all blueprint specifications and realizes what for him is its final form, the product is not really finished. It is merely in an intermediate stage in the total process of creating the finished product. At least one other company will use it in their own production process. These are the customers of M shop who will continue working on it until it is an acceptable subcomponent in their own product. For the product, as an object, to be acceptable to a customer, it must meet the specifications of the larger industrial process, and must "fit" with other objects from other subcontractors in forming the next level of product assembly. If, as an object, it does not fit with the larger process it is rejected and returned to M shop. The very real possibility of the rejection of his product gives it, as an object, an autonomous power over the individual—capable of denying the worker's competence as a machinist—and is the other aspect of alienation that humor deals with.

In these instances the machinists operate strictly as joke pullers. The individuals being joked with are at the customer's plant. The physical absence of the jokee, however, does not stop the machinists from anticipating his or her response and enjoying the "getting of the joke" as well. Frequently, the men who work in shipping and receiving will pack a message, in the form of a cartoon drawing, in the steel drums containing the finished pieces. The cartoons are created jointly with the machinists who worked on the pieces. Most of the time the workers at M shop have never met the receivers and inspectors who will find the messages when the drums are opened. Themes for these jokes center on questioning the competence of the inspector or the management at the customer's plant. Some examples include caricature drawings of an inspector as a blind man whose seeing eye dog is sniffing M shop parts laid on the ground, an inspector using a standard 12 inch wooden rule in checking the ten-thousandths inch tolerances, and an inspector diligently studying a set of upside down blueprints to determine the appropriate specifications.

Here we see the humor functioning to maintain as ambiguous the identity of others, outside M shop, who serve as agents in the powerful world of objects, as well as the relation of the M shop workers to them. Through humor, the intelligence, skill and judgment of these outside agents is called into question. "We at M shop know what we're doing, but our customer's workers do not." The power of their product as an alien object is made ambiguous by establishing the possibility that product rejection decisions are arbitrary and incompetently judged. Thus, humor reduces the problem of alienation by both asserting the ambiguity of the self from which the product is alien, and by declaring the power of the product in its independent existence to itself be ambiguous.

CONCLUSION

Humor is symbolic action that confirms the existence of multiple frames of reference for viewing the same social reality. "Making" and "getting" a joke is a double interact in which the meaningfulness of multiple frames is confirmed by each participant, without explicitly defining what those frames of reference are. In fact, the more possible frames that can be meaningfully juxtaposed, the more levels the joke can operate on, the funnier it is. As a result, humor is an important device for allowing participants in a social structure to reciprocally confirm the ambiguity of certain aspects of that social structure. The humor we observed at M shop is primarily aimed at the self-identity or self-definition of the workers involved, or of others in a position of power over the product of their labor.

We interpret the humor we observed as functional in solving the problems of socialization and alienation at M shop. It is a problem solving strategy that seeks an openness rather than a closure. Both of these problems are ones of accepting a structure without the surrender of self. Both are only problems in light of an asserted self-identity which they contradict. If the individual had no self-identity, no desire for self directed accomplishment or no individuality, neither would be a problem. We see humor as functional from a problem solving perspective in that it keeps these problems open by making the question of self-identity ambiguous. A good joke denies (at least on one level) the asserted self-identity that fuels the problems of socialization and alienation. The key to understanding humor as problem solving in this sense is to see it as allowing each individual to both be and not be what they assert. The multiple frames of reference resolved in getting the joke allow this ambiguity to persist. It's really not important which particular frames of reference an individual uses to get a joke. What is important is the confirmation that multiple frames of reference can be brought to bear, that multiple possibilities of interpretation do exist, and that the problems are still open problems that can be dealt with.

Without denying the usefulness of Roy's analysis, we would argue that our emphasis on humor as symbolic action can account for his observations and can also explain the "group disintegration" anomaly he reports.

Briefly, after six weeks on the job, Roy started a joke about the lead worker's relationship to a college professor. This was an important theme in the lead man's interaction with others. The joke was to see the professor as a teacher in a barber college. Afterward, the lead man became silent, and interaction among the men was limited to the formal requirements of work. As a result, all established times and themes of the group's interaction stopped. Roy interprets his action as an innovation in the use of humor that lowered the tone of the professor theme and therefore lowered the lead man's status. From our perspective, what he said about the professor was taken literally, not symbolically, by the group members, and it was the absence of a symbolic interpretation, not an innovation in the use of humor, that led to the stoppage of the normal interaction patterns.

There were no multiple possible frames of reference to support the "getting of the joke" in this situation. Because we emphasize the relationship of types of jokes one may pull and the process of socialization, we cannot expect a man six weeks on the job to be able to joke about the central aspect of the self-definition of the lead man. Roy had not worked his way up the ladder of joking relationships to be in a position to "pull" this kind of joke. This is not to say that in different circumstances, or at a different time, Roy or another worker could not have made the "professor of the barber college" into a very good joke. It does point out, however, the fine line between an action that seen literally can be cruel and almost devasting to the identity of another, but that seen symbolically, as a joke, can be wonderfully funny and saving to that same identity.

Returning to the inability to explain a joke without losing its humor, we can see a transcendental aspect to successful joking. The joke can be experienced, can be "got", but cannot be described without losing this transcendent aspect. In M shop, humor is symbolic action in which participants in the shop mutually transcend the immediate situation, however defined, for the multiple possibilities of its being experienced. The shared understanding of a multiplicity of possible frames of reference keeps the major problems of socialization and alienation open questions. It provides an ambiguity in resolving the questions of individual freedom and self-determination such that the individual both is and is not free, both is and is not self-determined, but continues to act.

REFERENCES

Cassirer, E. *An essay on man.* New Haven: Yale University Press, 1944.

Koestler, A. *The act of creation.* New York: Dell Publishing, 1964.

Marx, K. Economic and philosophic manuscripts of 1844. In R. C. Tucker (Ed.), *The Marx-Engels reader.* New York: Norton, 1972.

Roy, D. F. Banana time: Job satisfaction and informal interaction. *Human Organization,* 1960, *18*, 156–168.

SYMBOLS IN ORGANIZATIONS:

A DUAL-CONTENT FRAMEWORK FOR ANALYSIS

Richard L. Daft

Imagine going to work in an organization devoid of symbols. Only tangible, explicit, instrumental objects would exist. This organization would have no retirement dinners, no stories or anecdotes, no myths about the company's past, no annual picnic, no catchy phrases from the chief executive about the organization's mission, no differences in office size or carpet thickness, no Christmas turkeys, and no company emblem on employee ashtrays. The organization texture would be reduced to a mechanical system, nearing machine perfection, yielding goods and services with robot-like efficiency.

An organization designer's dream? More likely a nightmare. An organization without symbols would be unworkable for human beings. But an organization stripped clean of symbols would illustrate the importance of symbols for understanding the organization. Employees receive a wide range of cues from symbolic elements of organization. Symbols help employees interpret and understand the organization and their role in it by providing information about status, power, commitment, motivation, control, values and norms.

The meaning of symbolism in general, and in relation to organizations in particular, is discussed in detail in the introductory chapter to this volume. In this paper I focus attention on symbols as potentially valuable objects for organizational research, and I propose a tentative framework which organizes diverse symbols for systematic investigation. The paper should be read in conjunction with the next paper in this volume entitled "Symbols and Sensemaking." The latter describes and discusses the context of my framework presentation and audience responses to it.

Why Symbolism?

Pondy and Mitroff (1978) recently reminded us that human organizations have characteristics typical of level 7 and 8 systems on Boulding's (1956) 9-level scale of system complexity. Thus human organizations are among the most complex systems imaginable. Pondy and Mitroff also pointed out that the theoretical view dominant in organization theory tends to be about level 4 on Boulding's scale (open systems), and most empirical research sits at level 1 (simple frameworks—reflected in static, cross-sectional studies).

The disparity between organizational research and the reality of organization complexity is partly explained by organizational characteristics typically chosen for study. Static, structural properties, such as number and arrangement of organization elements, are frequent topics of analysis. A substantial amount of organization research seems devoted to mapping various aspects of organizational form and structure. These studies probably dominate because many structural variables are readily analyzed with measurement tools and statistical techniques understood by most organizational researchers. These properties of organization, however, represent low order system characteristics.

Unique qualities that distinguish human organizations from lower-order systems recognize the higher capacities of mankind. Higher order system characteristics on Boulding's scale acknowledge these higher capacities, including man's ability to use language, to attribute meaning to events and share meaning with others, to be aware of his own awareness, to make sense of things (Pondy & Mitroff, 1978). Lower order conceptions of organization structure capture countable characteristics of organizations, but often make the implicit assumption that man (system element) is mindless (Pondy & Mitroff, 1978).

The study of symbols in human organizations represents one avenue that may begin to close the gap between the complex reality of organizations and our seemingly oversimplified conception of them. Symbolism is an emergent characteristic of organized human behavior that may provide a key for unlocking new understanding of organizational activities and processes.

A Framework for Analysis of Organizational Symbols

Organizational symbolism was the topic of analysis at the conference that this volume grew out of. The conference was informal and the number of participants was small enough that everyone could sit in a large circle for presentation, although several activities also took place in smaller subgroups.

As people became immersed in the conference discussions, an implicit definition of organizational symbolism began to evolve. No one advocated a precise definition, and there certainly was no vote on the boundaries of symbolism. But many illustrations of symbols were offered that were accepted by the group as fitting the shared definition. No one had to explain why an example was symbolic; the subjective reaction was simply one of agreement.

Examples of symbols that were identified during paper presentations and discussions and accepted by group as legitimate include:

Corporate Anniversary Celebrations
Receipts (proof of expenditures)
Stories and Myths (often about organizational founder to explain start up, history
    and purpose of organization)
Organization Charts
Military Honor Guard
Metaphors (e.g., "wild duck" used by Watson of IBM to stress the type of individual
    cultivated and valued by the company)
Annual Reports
Company Logos

The striking aspect of these examples of organization symbolism is the broad range of content they represent. Conference participants seemed perfectly comfortable suggesting that a receipt for an academic conference and an honor guard at a military funeral both served symbolic functions within organizations. The scope of symbols described was perhaps greater than most participants expected. Yet, on an intuitive basis, each example fit within participants' subjective definition of organizational symbolism.

The puzzlement confronting me as a participant (and informal observer) at the conference concerned the common thread connecting such diverse symbols. What is the underlying variable that explains why each example is considered a symbol? What do a receipt and a story have in common? Some underlying phenomenon seemed just below the surface of the discussions that might organize and explain the symbolic content of these symbols.

One common thread is the notion of information. Each symbol communicates something to organizational participants. Symbols thus serve as information carrying devices. Another thread concerns the content of information transmitted. Stories and myths, for example, convey information relevant to feelings about the organization. These symbols seem to appeal to the deeper, perhaps unconscious feelings and values of participants. A receipt for expenditures, however, conveys information of a different type, which may be relevant to the intellectual, rational activities or organizations.

The wide range of symbols described at the conference provides the basis for a tentative step toward an analyzable framework. Two seemingly complementary dimensions seem to exist which reflect both a feeling and a thinking dimension of organizational symbols. These dimensions are summarized in Hypothesis 1.

> **HYPOTHESIS 1:** *Organizational symbols communicate instrumental and/or expressive information to participants.*

The relationship between the two types of symbolic content are illustrated in Figure 1. Instrumental content refers to the logical thinking aspect of the organization, and this content helps the organization do its work. The function of an instrumental symbol is to serve a rational purpose, to convey information or meaning that will achieve some rational need for the organization. Expressive content, on the other hand, pertains to underlying feelings and emotional needs of individuals. Expressive symbols are hypothesized to appeal to the deeper needs of organization participants, perhaps by removing uncertainty or providing an object for the individual to identify with.

The key notion in this framework is that symbols may differ substantially in the purpose they serve within organizations, and some symbols may serve both an instrumental and an emotional function. Symbols on the right hand side of Figure 1 perform primarily an instrumental function for the organization. Receipts or other tangible objects convey information to meet rules and requirements within the organization. These symbols help the organization accomplish immediate, legitimate work activities. At the other extreme (left hand side of Figure 1), the symbol doesn't seem connected to immediate work activities. Stories and myths may appeal to an individual's need to associate with something meaningful. These symbols also provide generalized information on scope, purpose and history of the organization and may provide a sense of tradition and organizational culture for organization members.

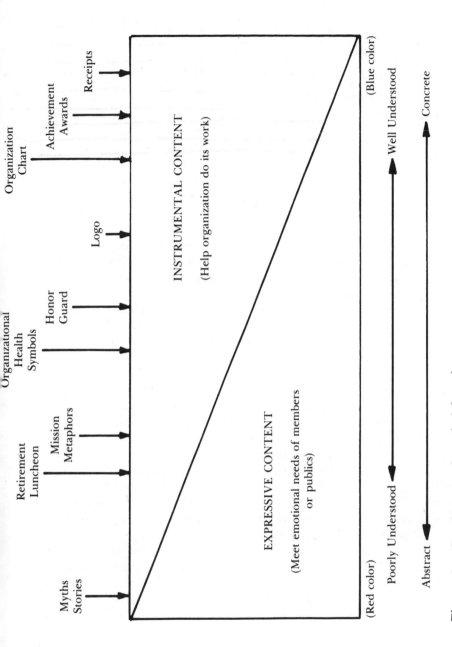

Figure 1. Continuum of symbol functions.

Discussion

Toward the middle of Figure 1, symbols may serve dual purposes. Organizational health symbols (annual reports, public relations statements) often are widely circulated to reassure various publics about the organization and to help people understand the status and well-being of the organization. These reports also convey instrumental information because facts and figures are necessary for government regulations or customer expectations. Honor guards provide ritual and meaning to a soldier's death, but they also provide a mechanism to achieve the soldier's burial in a way that is acceptable to families, perhaps removing resentment from the loss of a loved one, and reducing inhibitions among others about joining the military. Toward the instrumental end (right side) of the continuum in Figure 1, organization charts are an example of a symbol that serves the instrumental purpose of organizing work by letting people know their role and place within the organization system, but may also communicate expressive information about status, prestige and power. Toward the expressive end (left side), a retirement luncheon serves primarily the feelings of participants, but also may influence rational behavior by rewarding long service.

The novelty of Figure 1 compared to other work on symbolism is the integration of expressive and instrumental functions. Most frameworks stress the emotional, expressive role of symbols (Dandridge, Mitroff & Joyce, 1980). But based on the array of symbols described by conference participants, a dual role seems plausible. Symbols may be more widespread within organizations than we realize, carrying a variety of meanings and information, helping the organization do its day-to-day work. From this perspective the role of symbols in organization becomes magnified. Symbols may help accomplish tangible day-to-day activities, not just serve the softer, qualitiative needs of organization members. Perhaps symbols are so everpresent that we have taken them for granted, like the air we breathe or the language we speak, and hence have not noticed them as objects for systematic inquiry. The dual-content framework illustrates that symbols may truly represent an important source of new knowledge about organizations.

Two additional variables also may be related to the continuum in Figure 1. These variables, the degree of understanding and concreteness of the symbolic phenomena, represent two characteristics of symbols that are hypothesized to vary along with expressive and instrumental content. These variables and the relationships are hypothesized as follows.

HYPOTHESIS 2: *Instrumental symbols pertain to well understood organizational phenomena and expressive symbols pertain to poorly understood phenomena.*

HYPOTHESIS 3: *Instrumental symbols describe concrete organizational phenomena and expressive symbols describe abstract organizational phenomena.*

Hypothesis 2 relates symbolic function to the notion of "understanding" in organization theory. Degree of understanding was described by Thompson (1967) as knowledge of cause-effect relationships. Perrow (1967) described a similar notion in terms of problem analyzability. Generally, when a task or problem is well understood, an objective, computational procedure can be used. When problems on activities are poorly understood, however, solutions may require intuition, experience, and trial and error, and participants may experience uncertainty about how to reach desired outcomes. Hypothesis 2 suggests that expressive symbols tend to relate to and communicate about poorly understood aspects of organizations. These symbols may be ambiguous to some extent and can be interpreted to meet individual needs of participants. Instrumental symbols, on the other hand, are expected to describe and communicate about well understood phenomena, and provide cues that are relatively clear cut and unambiguous in interpretation.

Hypothesis 3 proposes that symbols may vary in degree of abstraction of concepts being communicated. This is similar to Hypothesis 2 because degree of understanding may be related to abstraction. Expressive symbols may tend to operate at a high level of abstraction, while instrumental symbols are more concrete and closer to the phenomena communicated about. Stories are abstract, but organization charts are tangible and concrete. In some cases, a tangible object may be a symbol for expressive needs (the cross as a symbol of christianity), but the phenomenon represented still may tend to be abstract and intangible.

CONCLUSION

The ideas represented in Figure 1 are extremely tentative, but the notion that organization symbols serve both emotional and instrumental functions seems to provide a logical explanation for the diverse symbols that were described at the symbolism conference. Emotional and rational dimensions of organizational life have also been discovered and described in other research (Mitroff & Kilmann, 1975; Mintzberg, 1976). Rationality and emotionality may represent core dimensions of human groups, although the rational, easily definable dimensions are most frequently studied in organization theory. Perhaps many observable outcroppings of organizations, such as organization charts or policy manuals, represent more than their face value implies. These items may also signal other images and meanings to organizational participants.

Viewed in this way, seemingly mundane symbols may represent a rich source of new knowledge about higher level properties of organizations (Pondy & Mitroff, 1978).

REFERENCES

Boulding, K. E. General systems theory: The skeleton of a science. *Management Science*, 1956, *2*, 197–207.

Dandridge, T. C., Mitroff, I. I., & Joyce, W. F. Organizational symbolism: A neglected topic on organizational analysis. *Academy of Management Review*, 1980, *5*, 77–82.

Mintzberg, H. Planning on the left side and managing on the right. *Harvard Business Review*, 1976 (July–August), 49–58.

Mitroff, I. I., & Kilmann, R. H. Stories managers tell: A new tool for organizational problem solving. *Management Review*, 1975, 18–29.

Ott, R., *Are wild ducks really wild: Symbolism and behavior in the corporate environment.* Unpublished manuscript, Suffolk Community College, 1978.

Perrow, C. A framework for the comparative analysis of organizations. *American Sociological Review*, 1967, *32*, 194–208.

Pondy, L. R., & Mitroff, I. I. Beyond open system models of organization. In Barry M. Staw (Ed.), *Research in organizational behavior* (Vol. 1). Greenwich, Conn.: JAI Press, 1978.

Thompson, J. D. *Organizations in action.* New York: McGraw-Hill, 1967.

SYMBOLS AND SENSEMAKING:

THE REAL-IZATION OF A FRAMEWORK

Peter J. Frost and Gareth Morgan

Weick has argued that "believing is seeing", that people make sense of things by seeing a world upon which they have already imposed what they believe (Weick, 1979, p. 135). People, in effect, read into things the meanings they wish to see; they vest objects, utterances, actions and so forth with subjective meaning which helps make their world intelligible to themselves. One important aspect of symbolism in organizations is the way people use symbols to make sense of situations which are problematic, ambiguous or unsettling. Such sensemaking may take place alone or in group situations such as in formal or informal meetings.

The purpose of this paper is to trace the way the sensemaking process in a group situation may occur, by focussing upon the emergence of a symbolic construct which was created at the conference on Organizational Symbolism. The construct commanded considerable attention and provided grounds for establishing consensus among some members of the group to which it was presented. The construct introduced was a conceptual framework for analyzing symbolic forms. It was presented orally by Richard Daft and has subsequently been described formally in the paper which precedes this one in this volume.

In providing an analysis of the process whereby this construct was presented and evaluated in the group session, our intention is not to evaluate its substantive significance or its contribution to knowledge. Our purpose, rather, is to attempt to reveal the symbolic and socially constructed significance of the process which produces such frameworks or schemes in a group setting. To accomplish this aim, we have drawn upon the transcript of the Conference Session at which the scheme was presented and developed.

Our analysis itself stands as a form of sensemaking, an "after the event" reconstruction. The study was not planned in advance. The idea to which it gives form emerged during the process of the session, when the authors independently realized they were witnessing the emergence of a symbolic form through which many of those present were attempting to concretize and to give significant form and meaning to their experience and understanding of the conference proceedings up to the time at which it was introduced.

Our plan in presenting our interpretation of this process is:

- to provide some background on the nature of the Conference and of the context in which the session analyzed was placed;
- to provide an analysis drawing on transcript data, of the way the symbolic construct emerged, and was concretized;
- to identify significant themes which arose from the presentation and sensemaking process;
- to draw some tentative conclusions regarding the role which symbols may play in the sensemaking process in group settings.

THE CONTEXT—BACKGROUND TO THE CONFERENCE

The Conference was informal and brought together approximately 24 people from a number of academic institutions in North America who in one way or another had heard about the event and were sufficiently interested in the topic to attend. Disciplines represented at the Conference included Accounting, Anthropology, History, Organizational Behavior, Psychology and Sociology.

The keynote of the Conference was informality, symbolized by the fact that it was held at Lou Pondy's home rather than at a formal institution and by the fact that discussion about organizational symbolism was to evolve rather than follow any predetermined structure. A conference plan and timetable had been prepared, with groups of speakers listed for different sessions to symbolize that the meeting was a Conference, to satisfy bureaucratic requirements of sponsoring organizations. However, it was made clear from the beginning that the printed program would not be followed in anything other than a general sense.

Members of the Conference were welcomed by their host at the first session on Friday evening, May 4, 1979. The session was opened immediately to anyone who wished to offer their views as to why they were there and what they hoped would happen. The meeting was characterized by a sensitivity to the need for an open exchange of views rather than a focus on specific detail and content on one or a limited number of perspectives on organizational symbolism. Three people offered to initiate discussion on organizational symbolism at the first session the following morning.

At the morning session, a number of divergent points of view were expressed as to the nature of symbolism and a coffee break was taken at a point when most present confessed that they were fairly confused and perhaps somewhat frustrated about what organizational symbolism comprised. The next session was led by a historian who focussed on the theme "Symbols of Rationality" and generated a wide-ranging discussion of the way in which organizations manipulated symbols of rationality.

The two afternoon sessions which followed lunch were based on small group discussions, each led by someone who had not made a formal contribution in earlier sessions. People wandered from group to group "shopping" for ideas and dialogue according to their interests. These discussions were followed by the final "wrap-up" session of the day which is the session on which our detailed analysis will focus.

THE TRANSCRIPT[1]

The session which lasted approximately 40 minutes began with some 15 people present. The group as a whole was in high spirits, exchanging a great deal of cross talk and laughter. Earlier in the day, Lou Pondy had invited Dick Daft to lead this session. This invitation was made known to the group when the person opening the session introduced Dick Daft to them.[2]

The introductory remarks and Daft's presentation began as follows (lines 1–63).

A: 1   Someone in the group has listened to every single word spoken at the Conference so far, and has understood all of it, and has been able to place it in just a marvellous perspective, and his name is Dick Daft, and he is going to tell us what he's heard and so on, about things—labelled a summary.

aft: I'm afraid you are going to be disappointed (banter, laughter) you'd better have another drink (laughter). Well, I heard a lot of deep and profound

and interesting things today, and I confess that at this point, I've forgotten
half of them (laughter), and I'd say I didn't understand the other half (laughter).
BB: Make up a story (laughter).
Daft: 10   So I'll talk about some of the things I have had on my mind for some time.
I've been wanting an audience. I guess I was looking for common threads today
and I found two. I'll just offer them. I'm sure you have more ideas than I
do to build onto them.

Daft: This morning, we talked about this notion of symbols. We talked about the
Star of David as a symbol in the same breath with a receipt for this
conference and it was difficult for me. (Laughter). Maybe you didn't have
that kind of problem. Symbolism for me didn't incorporate all those things
(laughter), so I tried to take the various uses of the symbol. . . .

CC: It is the deep structure! (Laughter).

Daft: 20   . . . and I tried to organize the various best examples of symbols that came
out this morning into a simple little continuum which I have here for your
benefit (See Figure 1). What I tried to do . . . the organization which popped into
mind was a notion of what we might call expressive content of the symbol as
opposed to an instrumental content. And so this end tries to capture the
notion of instrumental content or what can help the organization do its
work. It might be a symbol that is used in that way, as opposed to a deeper
underlying emotional content for individuals, which is over here and which
might meet the emotional needs of the public. So on this end is expressive,
on this end is instrumental or rational. You notice the colors in that—

30   that's an underlying symbol. This is the cool, rationality here (blue) and
this is the hot emotion (red)—the red and the blue—colors are supposed
to have meaning. (laughter) Two examples then, the dental receipt, you
remember the tooth as opposed to the receipt that the IRS wanted, and the
receipt for the Conference? That kind of symbol has a very rational purpose.
It conveys information, meaning about an event that can be used to help
the organization do its work. Off on the other end, stories and myths may have
some sort of deeper content that appears deep to the individual; not to the
intellect or to the rational, or to the organizational but to some underlying purpose

Then I tried to take some of the other examples which might contain both
40   and array them along this continuum. Organizational health symbols that
come up—you know, the annual reports, the organizational structure, as they
are advertised to the outside world perhaps, are mostly expressive in nature.
They help reassure, they help people understand the purpose of the
organization, although, there may be some small amount of instrumental content
there in terms of the organization doing its work. By the way, this is all very
tentative. If you disagree and I take . . . you are certainly welcome to the
ideas. Along the middle here, I put the example of the honor guard
and closed casket—I saw both kinds of symbolism loaded on that. There
is the work of the military, the instrumental value of it—to get the work
50   done, to get the body in the ground and so on. And yet there is the sort of,
the deeper meaning, the serving the country, the loss of a loved one.
It has both, I thought that might have both. Then I added one in here that is
mostly instrumental which I called the internal financial statements, the
kind of internal workings of the organization, which help the organization
do its work—the organization chart as it is used internally, not for
external reassurances and so on. The symbol that helps people to know where

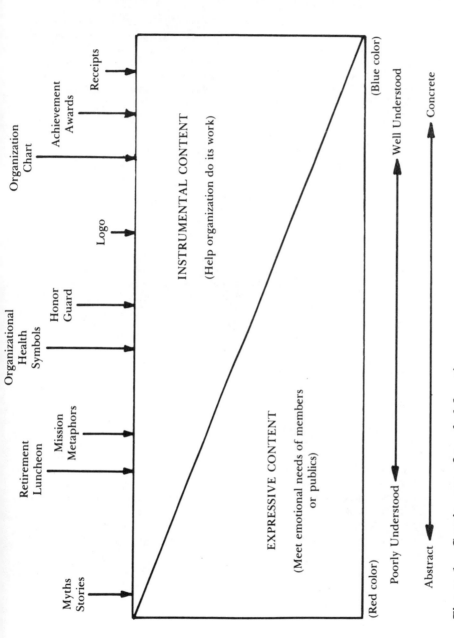

Figure 1. Continuum of symbol functions.

211

they are, what they do, their role in the organization for effective performance
. . . and it might have a small load here of expressive content. And, a couple
of ideas that came out just in brainstorming a bit this morning, is that this
60   relates more to people perhaps (pointing to expressive end of continuum), more
to the human dimension of organizations and perhaps this relates more to things
(pointing to the instrumental end) or the concrete tangible ideas. That's
63   what I got from this morning.

At this time, a member of the group (BB) intervened and made a comment which questioned the basis of the scheme which Daft had presented (Lines 64–85). The point raised was that symbols are constituted differently by different people rather than having a single or universal meaning.

BB: 64   Just a comment. You know we talked about different levels within the organization,
and _____'s comment about looking at the worker versus the manager in the
organization. (And) In some respects you could flip various of those symbols
into expressive versus instrumental depending on whom you look at. For example,
you asked me for an example when we talked about it this morning and I thought
about it. Suppose you took that receipt (for the conference), which I take back
70   and (which) for the organization is largely instrumental and supposedly not
very emotional, expressive. But suppose that that receipt had a lot of
symbolic meaning, of a great conference, of friends. . . .
AA: A ha!
BB: and so on. I could turn it around . . .
AA: It becomes then very evocative.
BB: That's right, and so depending where you are in the organization, the
organization chart—which is functional and instrumental for the organization,
to me, again looking at it, I might say well, "Here I am in this chart,
why am I not there?" or, "I'm up here" and so I think again . . .
Daft: 80 You might take it home and put it on the wall to show people the organization?
BB: It would have a different meaning. So, I think the scheme, the way that
runs, and the amount of expressive versus instrumental would change with the
different levels in the organization.
Daft: So this is . . . What would this (model) be biased toward? I guess the top
85   view, perhaps of the organization? From the top down perhaps?

The discussion continued with Daft explaining how the scheme had aided him, and its relevance as a framework was reinforced by interjections and examples provided by other conference members (lines 86–108).

Daft: 86 Anyway, to me it helped organize the wide variety that I heard, and the kinds
of symbols that were (unintelligible) and I had always thought, I came here, thinking

that symbols were here (pointing to the expressive end of Figure 1)—were
these deeper, expressive symbols of things that we identify with. And a lot of
examples were not here, they were more concrete, more instrumental
and more communication devices.

A: Concrete things serving other purposes.

Daft: Yes, instrumental kinds of purposes.

D: Seems like a prime example of that is the dollar bill.
You go into a lot of small stores and somebody
has taken their first dollar bill and pinned
it up on the wall. Basically, its purely instrumental,
except for that one purpose when a person
takes their first dollar bill and pins it on the wall
—which has nothing to do with its amount of value.

A: I would say that that's expressive.

D: Ok, in that form.

(General scramble of voices—high intensity and enthusiasm. Considerable response)

D: It has nothing to do with the present value of that dollar.

Daft: So this is a very fuzzy kind of thing, I guess, individual symbols can vary
widely in terms of where they can be placed or the purposes for which they might . . .

?): Another person in fact, might ask why, what's the decoration on something
that's supposedly purely a functional instrument?

At this time, another member (EE) intervened with an interjection which
links back to the earlier conversation relating to the subjective construction of symbolic forms (lines 65–87). EE suggested that symbols have no
meaning on their own account, but derive meaning from the interpretation which people make of what they see (lines 109–112).

EE: 109 What we are saying also is that they don't have any meaning or meaning on their own
account. Like, a symbol doesn't have meaning in itself.

AA: It's not inherently a symbol.

EE: 112 No, it's only the way it's interpreted. It becomes symbolic.

Thereafter the discussion switched immediately back to a discussion of
the symbol scheme which had been presented (see lines 113–119 in
Appendix 1). The switch was away from an examination of the problematic nature of symbols (and hence of classificatory frameworks of
symbols) to further discussion of the framework itself as a source of
explanations of organizational phenomena.

The conversation then proceeded (24 lines) as an exchange between
the informal chairman of the meeting (AA) (13 lines) and Daft (11 lines)
exploring the meaning Daft intended in some aspects of his scheme

(lines 120–143; reproduced in Appendix 1). The conversation, thereafter moved to a discussion of the way in which journal articles must be dressed up with an acceptable mode of symbolic expression to fit the journal style for the article to be deemed suitable for publication. This issue was debated with regard to whether it is possible for organization theorists to adopt the methods of anthropology and still get their work published. Discussion of these points occupied 76 lines of transcript and ends in laughter. (Lines 144–220 reproduced in Appendix 1).[4]

At this point AA offers the following comments (lines 221–242) on the symbol framework presented by Daft ending with a statement that it's a hell of a good starting point (from which to study organizational symbolism):

```
AA:      221  I want to . . . I'd like to say a couple of . . . First of all, I find
              this scheme very appealing. I'd like to try to make it explicit
              why I find it appealing. One is that it doesn't try to resolve
              the issue of what really is a symbol and admits the notion that
              there are a whole variety of things that can serve as symbolic
              functions, and provides a kind of organized, systematic scale
              for arranging symbols, from some kind
              of concrete to . . . uh . . . I've forgotten what you call that other—
              you don't have a word on the other end—ephemeral. ? . .
Daft:    230  Yes.
AA:           . . . end of the scale. And I think that is extremely helpful. The
              other thing that's helpful is the implicit functional analysis.
              That in fact there is a kind of instrumental versus expressive
              function in the symbols - ? symbols can be both. And in fact that
              there is a correlation. That the concrete symbols tend to serve
              the more expressive functions. So there is a hell of a lot
              of content and substance in that, and even if I at some point disagree
              with it and modify it, it itself is a very concrete symbol with
              which I can work and begin operating and changing. It is a hell
              of a good starting point.
```

From this point onwards in the session (lines 243–522, Appendix 1) conversation focuses in large measure on ways people try to make sense of the framework presented.

DISCUSSION

Making Sense of a Framework

The process through which Daft's scheme for understanding symbols has emerged can be understood as a process of sense-making, through which many of those present at the "wrap-up" session were attempting to clarify their understanding of the Conference, and to achieve some form of structure which could serve as a point of departure for their future work. The scheme, which initially is presented as a very tentative one, is increasingly concretized and endorsed by members contributing to discussion, even though some questions are raised which challenge the underlying premise that symbols can be classified in this way. These points are clearly illustrated in the elements of the transcript presented above.

The scheme is introduced by the person opening the session (AA) as a form of sense-making scheme, as evidenced by the statement that it places the conference proceedings in "just a marvellous perspective", (lines 1–3) and that it is a "summary" (line 4). These sense-making aspects are reinforced by the presenter, in saying "I guess I was looking for common threads today and I found two. I'll just offer them. I'm sure you have more ideas than I do to build onto them" (lines 11–13) . . . "Maybe you didn't have that kind of problem (i.e., of making sense of different definitions of symbols). Symbolism for me didn't incorporate all those things. . ." (lines 16–17) . . . "I tried to organize the various best examples of symbols that came out this morning into a simple little continuum . . . (lines 20–21) . . . "That's what I got from this morning" (lines 62–63), and elsewhere, (e.g., lines 86–91, 147).

The presenter also continually emphasizes in the early part of the discussion that the ideas are very tentative, and provide his own personal view of the situation (e.g., lines, 10–13, 45–47, 63, 86). However, as the ideas are reinforced by others, they are increasingly concretized, a point clearly illustrated in the comments of AA in a summarizing statement that the scheme is "very appealing", (line 222), "helpful" (line 231) and "itself is a very concrete symbol with which I can work and begin operating and changing. It is a hell of a good starting point" (lines 240–241). Endorsement and concretization of the scheme did much to refocus attention upon the scheme, which had been diverted to other issues (lines 144–220).

In the presentation and development of the scheme up to that point, eight different interpretations of what the scheme stood for were presented in discussion. The scheme is presented as one for distinguishing between (1) the "expressive content of the symbol as opposed to an instrumental content" (lines 23–24); (2) hot "emotion" versus cool "rationality"—symbolized in the red and blue colors in which the scheme was drawn (lines 30–31); (3) to "people and the human dimension of organizations" as opposed to "things" (lines 61–62); (4) "breadth or size of the audience" i.e., small for expressive, high for instrumental (lines 120–129); (5) the idea that the scheme may be of use for dealing with symbols in an organization which has "multiple publics" (lines 138–143); (6) that the scheme provides a "systematic scale for arranging symbols" (line 227); (7) that the dimensions are "ephemeral versus concrete" (line 228–229), and that it has (8) an "implicit functional analysis" (line 232).

In the remainder of the discussion which followed AA's summarizing statement, no less than 23 other interpretations of the scheme were made by members of the Conference. These were (9) "substitute" consensual for "ephemeral" (line 243); (10) substitute "abstract" for ephemeral (line 252); (11) the dimension is about the "non-physical" representation of things. They are "linguistic. . ." (lines 254–256); (12) some symbols are "representative" (lines 258–259); (13) the dimensions reflect the "degree of understanding" of the symbol—whether the reality is "poorly understood" or "well understood" (lines 263–274); (14) the dimension reflects "high variety" and "low variety" (lines 279–280); (15) the term high variety carries "a lot of meaning, a lot of punch . . . a lot of richness" (line 291); (16) "there is a component of cause-effect, analyzable-unanalyzable" (lines 296–297); (17) the distinction in the framework reflects the idea of "bimodal consciousness" . . . between the "instrumental left brain and the expressive right brain" . . . and "the possibility that there are multilevel languages. That our rational, descriptive sort of language, isn't the same as our symbolic language. One is a right brain language the other is a left brain language. And maybe there is a continuum between these two" . . . (lines 317–329); (18) the right brain relates to an "affective" dimension (lines 329–331); (19) the dimension may distinguish between the symbolism found in different "types of organizations" (lines 333–336); (20) the dimension may reflect "information processing (at different levels) in the hierarchy" (lines 336–341); (21) the scheme is "a bit of sense-making" (line 346); (22) the dimension parallels the "formal versus the informal organization" (lines 349–353); (23) the scheme links to discussions of symbolism in anthropology, which focus upon symbols towards the (expressive) end of the continuum, devaluing the instrumental (lines 370–372); (24) the scheme helps to "chunkify (store information) about a whole bunch of the meeting" (lines 379–380); (25) A point could be made regarding the possibility of researching the way in which "expressive (symbols) are used instrumentally" (lines 404–405); (26) the scheme may distinguish between "business organizations . . . rational/instrumental, and . . . other types of organizations—families, religious organizations, and others in the culture (where) you'll find a larger and larger reliance upon expressive dimensions for what goes on" (lines 438–443); (27) the different kinds of symbolism may reflect the newness or degree of stability of an organization, or crisis, versus non-crisis—there being more expressive symbolism in new, unstable crisis-oriented organizations (lines 450–456); (28) the types of symbolism may reflect openness to the environment (line 457); (29) it may reflect the ambiguity of technology (line 473); (30) the dimension may reflect the symbolism found in different kinds of college, e.g., the "liberal arts college and the conservative arts college" (lines 481–485); (31) images such as those produced by photography can be a concrete artifact and at the same time have "enormous expressive content" (lines 512–519).

Analysis of the pattern of the presentation and discussion is instructive. In the initial stages the presenter and AA (who while not explicitly designating himself as the group leader or as chairperson of the session, was an informal chairperson) play dominant roles, contributing 17 or the first 20 sensemaking ideas. Most of the sensemaking ideas contributed by other conference members were put forward once the scheme had already been discussed extensively. This point is illustrated in Table 1. Most of the contributions from conference members other than the presenter and the informal chairperson came in the latter part of the session. The presenter (10) and the informal chairperson (8) contributed 18 of the 31 sensemaking ideas articulated. One other member contributed four ideas and another 9 members each contributed one idea.

The sensemaking process which unfolded in this session, illustrates the way in which a dominant reality (that is, that this scheme provided an effective summary of the ideas presented at the Conference) may emerge and be sustained. The framework is presented tentatively, but strong support for it, initially by the informal chairperson and subsequently through the enthusiastic efforts of other members to interpret the framework and in effect "try it on for size," helped to sweep away the early tentativeness and to concretize the framework. Of the 15 people present at the session, 12 made a contribution, the relative length of each person's contribution being indicated in the final column of Table 1.

Interventions: Supporting Alternative Views of Reality

This analysis of activity at the meeting suggests that "a reality" is defined by those members taking a lead in the discussion, and is then endorsed in varying degrees by others present. The extent to which non-contributing members at the session actively agreed or disagreed with what was being put forward because they favored other ways of making sense of the Conference cannot be determined accurately from the materials available. However, there is some evidence in the transcript to suggest that "alternative realities" may have been favored by certain conference members. This can be more clearly illustrated diagramatically in Table 2 which seeks to reconstruct the pattern of interac-

Table 1
Matrix of Sense-Making Points[1]

	Sense-Making Points	Total Contribution to Meeting / % of Contribution Lines[2]
AA	1 2 3 4 5 6 7 8 10 11 14 18 19 20 31	17.8
Daft	9 13 15 24 26	37.3
GG	28 30	6.8
Unidentified Contribution[3]	12	3.3
DD	17	3.9
EE	21	1.2
FF	22	4.9
HH	23	0.6
JJ	25	8.2
BB	27	5.5
II	29	2.3
CC	16	8.4

Notes:

[1] Numbers refer to sensemaking *points* identified in the text—in order of presentation.

[2] Percentages are estimated values, given missing tape segment. GG's contribution is most significantly under-represented since GG's comments alone were on the missing segment.

[3] Contribution to meeting of unidentified participants was 3.3.

Table 2

Principal Patterns of Interaction

CONTRIBUTOR
(CODED)

AA
DAFT
BB
CC
DD
EE
FF
GG
HH
II
JJ

● Interactions on the *primary* sensemaking theme of the session.
◇☆ *Diversionary* sensemaking themes grouped in terms of commonality.
▼ Sensemaking *interventions* (discussed in text)
1,2,3, . . . ,11: attempts to show patterns of interaction in a very general way.

Note—this table only attempts to show patterns of interaction in a very general way.

219

tion reflected in the transcript in terms of the concerns and issues to which the speakers were attempting to give form. As can be seen from the Table, 11 potentially diversionary issues were introduced during discussion, but each is fairly quickly subordinated to the main process of making sense of conference proceedings in terms of the scheme being presented. It is worth discussing the nature and significance of the eleven interventions.

Interventions 1, 2 and 8

Intervention 1 (lines 64–85 of the transcript) points to the fact that the classification of the symbols presented in the scheme, may have *different* meaning for different people in the organization, i.e., be symbolic in different ways. This intervention thus contains within it the idea that it is not possible to classify symbols in any objectively meaningful way, because symbols are subjectively constructed. It thus challenges the very foundations of the type of understanding of symbols which the scheme is trying to provide.

The problem here is recognized by the presenter and leads him to assert the tentativeness of the scheme (lines 86–91). Discussion is then refocussed upon the usefulness of the scheme by the informal chairperson, and a conference member who provides an example of how the scheme may work.

Intervention 2 (line 109–112) quickly returns to the latent issue raised by the first intervention. EE states that (the discussion implies) symbols have no meaning on their own account. The meaning of this point is restated by AA, the informal chairperson (line 111)—"it's not inherently a symbol", but the discussion stops here, since another member (FF) interjects and refocusses the discussion upon the diagram. The issue remains dead until member EE raises it again in intervention 8 by suggesting that the framework and discussion is all a "bit of sense-making, isn't it?" (line 346). Here again this line of questioning is halted by an interjection from the conference member (FF) who intervened earlier. FF produces an example which again focusses attention upon the use of the framework.

In these exchanges we find different perspectives being brought to the study of symbolism, and a classic illustration of people *talking past one another*. Interventions 2 and 8 in effect continue the argument that symbols have no objectifiable status, that they are social constructions, and that the scheme being put forward and supporting discussion is itself to be seen as a sense-making process.

The ideas underlying interventions 2 and 8 occur largely without impact on the group. They express an *interpretive* perspective on the meaning of symbolism (that is, they treat symbols as problematic, and are concerned with the meaning of symbols given the premise that different people constitute reality differently) embedded in a context of meaning in which symbols are being discussed from a *functionalist* perspective, that is, symbols as concrete artifacts rendering themselves open to some form of objective classification. Because of this context, in which one perspective has emerged as a dominant reality in the group, the underlying substantive content of the intervention is not developed. Individuals operating from the two different perspectives in effect "talk past" each other. This talking past is rooted in the different sets of paradigmatic assumptions (interpretive vs. functionalist) upon which participants in the group seem to be operating.

Interventions 3, 4, 5, 6, and 7

These interventions introduce another theme which is explored for a while and then abandoned. This time the focus of interest is upon the way in which academic journals may be seen as requiring certain symbolic signs of acceptability in the articles which they publish. The discussion begins with intervention 3 (lines 144–167), formulated by the presenter in response to a sense-making idea by AA, that organizations may have multiple publics. The presenter links the idea that different publics may respond to different symbols to a discussion earlier in the day as to whether organization theory could draw upon the methods of anthropology as a means of investigating symbolism. He points to the fact that these methods may not be regarded as legitimate by the organization journals, which tend to favor quantitative, comparative studies, regression analyses, etc. as a basis for judging what is acceptable research. He also points out that the legitimacy of such quantitative methodology is an aspect of the mythology to which these journals subscribe. The point here is taken up by another member in Intervention 4 (lines 172–186), who emphasizes that the journals reflect competing rhetorics, and that it is valid to borrow from other disciplines. The presenter, in Intervention 5, responds (lines 192–212) by suggesting that there is still a problem in getting work on symbolism published until the new methods required for such research have become acceptable. He re-emphasizes the idea that organizational symbolism cannot "steal wholesale" from anthropology until these methods have acquired symbolic respectability in the eyes of journal referees and readers.[4] This prompts Intervention 6 from yet another member HH who suggests that "anthropology has it's own issues and battles going on within the discipline" (lines 213–214). The discussion then fades out, and the informal chairperson returns attention to the scheme with a strong endorsement of it (lines

221–242). The issues involved in Interventions 3–6 are now put completely aside, until Intervention 7 (lines 296–312) raised by CC, the same person who made Intervention 4. CC returns discussion towards the idea that the acceptable ideas in organization theory, about cause-effect, analyzable-unanalyzable, etc., are all a kind of myth based upon a particular kind of subjective belief. Attention to this theme is again diverted by another member (DD) introducing another sensemaking idea in relation to the scheme—that it reflects the idea of bimodal consciousness (lines 317–319).

Interventions 9 and 10

Intervention 9 was made by the informal chairperson when he suggested that the meeting should listen to the views of someone (JJ) who had not said much at the general gathering, but who had come to the Conference "with a very specific agenda in terms of looking to the Conference as a means of helping her to tie together her thesis" (lines 382–386). JJ was asked "How much sense-making has this done for you, in terms of pulling together the experience?" (lines 386–387). Taking up the question JJ starts by saying, "It's done some sense-making and some problem-causing" (line 388) and proceeds to discuss the problems, and then uses the scheme to make sense of her work by explaining that she is interested in studying how "expressive stories are used instrumentally" (line 405). In developing her ideas, she then proceeds to focus attention upon the details of her research (Intervention 10, lines 415–422) which orients discussion towards a discussion of different types of educational organizations, and provides the basis for sense-making ideas 26, 27, 28, 29 and 30. The effect of Interventions 9 and 10 served to change the focus of discussion, in that it involved a new person and a new set of issues, but the dominant sense-making theme of the whole meeting provides the structure within which it is set.

Intervention 11

The final intervention occurred near the end of the session (lines 491–500). One individual, GG observed that in all the enthusiasm for the symbol scheme presented he felt that the group had *created a construct* which had now developed a life of its own. It had been reified. GG had touched on one very important issue raised in this paper, that symbols and ideas may have tentative beginnings but that with articulation and encouraging responses from people, particularly in terms of "usefulness" to them for answering questions, solving problems, revealing meaning and so forth, these same symbols and ideas become concretized and treated as *real.*

The intervention by GG is supported by EE who was associated in earlier interventions which argued for an appreciation of the subjective nature of symbols (Intervention 1, 2 and 8). His comment was "Perhaps now we can attack it!" (line 506). There was general laughter at this point when people appeared to realize how concrete the construct had become. The suggestion that it now be attacked was offered in this spirit of amused awareness. The issue once again faded as attention was drawn to the main framework by AA with a discussion of photographs which capture symbols on paper, these symbols being "in one sense concrete" (line 516), in another sense expressive, they "tell a story" (line 519).

One final intervention occurred—the session was adjourned when Dick Daft suggested amidst laughter and agreement that the group adjourn for a drink before proceeding to dinner.

General Issues Raised by This Analysis

The purpose of the foregoing analysis is to provide a fairly elementary illustration of the way in which a focus upon the sense-making process in interactive situations provides a means of analyzing the way in which situations may become structured and given meaningful form. In essense, the Conference upon which we have focused can be seen as an emergent organization, with the members present searching for some meaningful definition of what organizational symbolism stood for, and what concrete possibilities it offered. The opening session discussion revealed that people were attending the Conference for a variety of reasons. While a few were there out of curiosity to find out what organizational symbolism stood for, others were there to find confirmation and support for what they were doing, to exchange ideas, to build up contacts with those interested, to discuss problems relating to the legitimacy of their research, and so on.

An important uniting theme which ran throughout most discussion was an acute awareness that the problems and methods of studying symbolism run counter to what was likely to be endorsed by the orthodoxy within organization studies. From the first evening's discussion it became clear that those present were very much aware that in focussing attention upon the field of symbolism, they were running the danger of stepping outside and placing themselves against the positivist orthodoxy. It was also recognized that it would be a mistake to simply focus upon criticism of the positivist camp, and at the very first meeting it was resolved that discussion should seek to avoid this. As such, attention was devoted to a discussion of organizational symbolism and its possibilities.

As will become clear from a reading of the other papers in this volume, symbolism can be approached in many different ways according to the underlying paradigm or reality assumptions to which the researcher subscribes. Discussion at the Conference brought out this range of divergent possibilities in a very piecemeal and informal way, contributing by the time of the session analyzed above to a degree of confusion. This, no doubt, was a powerful influence shaping the discussion which we have analyzed. It is perhaps reasonable to assume that many of those present did not want the Conference to close without at least some clarity about the nature of organizational symbolism, and that given the expressed need by many at the Conference to pursue the study of organizational symbolism, people would want to find some form of direction so that they would have some clear point of reference in conducting their future work.

Our analysis of the Conference session provides a great deal of impressionistic evidence as to the way in which this desire for some sort of structure was found. We find important roles being played by the presenter and the informal chairperson in structuring the form and content of discussion. They articulated ideas about a structure of organizational symbolism which had meaning for them. Once these ideas had been made explicit, many other people in the session then re-constituted the structure to shape understanding of their own concerns.

The transcript also reveals that others present may not have shared the same perspective on the scheme as a uniting theme. Interventions 1, 2, 8 and 11 for example, raised substantive issues which if followed to a conclusion, would have questioned whether it is possible to classify symbols in terms of the scheme presented—for they imply that the symbolic significance of a phenomenon rests not in its intrinsic content, but in the pattern of meaning attributed to it; that symbols are not inherently symbols lending themselves to objectified forms of classification.

The substantive content and implications of the various interventions were not taken up in any significant way, the discussion being returned in each case to the principal sense-making theme. The transcript thus reveals a number of parallel processes of sense-making based upon different kinds of underlying assumptions with regard to the nature of symbolism. While those engaged in the dominant sense-making process can be seen as subscribing to a fairly compatible view of what symbolism stood for, we may speculate that others who remained silent throughout the discussion, or intervened along contrary lines, were more skeptical and perhaps subscribed to other views. By examining the way in which sense-making processes unfold, it is possible to identify some of the different kinds of reality assumptions which underwrite different perspectives represented at the meeting.

The focus on sense-making themes also reveals the way in which patterns of argument follow non-linear and sometimes random and illogical paths. As illustrated in Table 2 and in the analysis of interventions provided earlier, the path of discussion is often broken by interventions which lead in a new direction, and which are never resolved, the discussion being switched back by one or other contributors to the primary theme. Discussion also often follows false trails. A good example of this is found in sense-making idea number 7 which introduced the word "ephemeral" to describe the "expressive" end of the continuum. This was the first time ephemeral had been introduced into the discussion although the person who introduced it clearly thought it had been introduced earlier. ". . . I've forgotten what you call that other . . . you don't have a word on the other end . . . ephemeral?" (lines 228–229). Debate about this word then led to debate about terms which led to sense-making ideas 10, 11, and 12. These ideas thus emanated from a confusion about what had already been said. This is not atypical of what happens in meetings, particularly those involving complex and ambiguous concepts and information.

CONCLUSION

The focus upon sensemaking leads to a search for the key themes which structure a situation, and the symbols which are created and used towards this end. The scheme which was used to structure the conference session analyzed here, can be seen as a symbolic form which evolved as those present vested it with various patterns of meaning as a means of making sense of a problematic situation. The process involved here may well be typical of other situations in which people are brought together with a view to arriving at some form of consensus or shared frame of reference. People going off at tangents to a main theme being developed, or entering discussion at apparently random or irregular times may be signalling in the issues they raise, the language and gestures they use, and the ideas they express, realities which are different from those of others and the dominant reality constructed or maintained in the group. Attempts by leaders to establish a consensus in such cases may ignore the fact that organization members with different world views are asking and attempting to answer fundamentally different questions from one another. The drive for consensus may prevent important elements of discovery for members of such groups. An awareness and analysis of the symbolic sense-making nature of group discourse may improve our insights into its process. Various kinds of meetings, decision-making systems, organizational change and development programs, etc., could be studied in these terms.

A focus on sense-making processes will do much to reveal the nature of the reality assumptions which underlie discourse, and the way in which the use of symbolic forms plays an important part in achieving consensus and agreement, which in large measure rests upon a process of creating acceptable patterns of symbolic meaning. Even the briefest knowledge of meetings and decision-making systems reveals the importance of symbolic action in these spheres. In many regards those who are concerned with managing meetings and decisions are in essence concerned with managing the symbolic consequences of their actions.

The methods used in the present analysis of sense-making processes are somewhat crude and ad hoc, intended to provide an *illustration* of what may be possible, rather than a code of practice which gives a model point of departure. Research experience in other fields of inquiry will undoubtedly prove of much value here. In particular, a great deal can be learned from experience gained in the fields of hermeneutics and literary criticism, where the analysis of argument and discourse has a long and distinguished history. The works of Burke (1966), Gusfield (1976), Huff (pp. 167–183, in this volume), and Toulmin (1958) illustrate a variety of approaches and methods which may well provide those interested with further ideas for developing the analysis of sense-making processes, in clear and rigorous terms.

NOTES

1. The session produced 522 lines of transcript. Due to an oversight, approximately 5 minutes of recording was lost. Side one of the tape had ended and this was not realized immediately. Side two of the tape was used for recording once the error was recognized.

2. Letter codes identify the different contributors to the group discussion to preserve anonymity. Dick Daft's contribution remains public. His paper on the symbol framework is published in this volume. We are grateful to Dick Daft for his permission to use his name in the analysis.

3. The material discussed here has been reconstructed from notes and from our conversations with the person who originally uttered the missing words.

4. Lines 196–204 have been omitted. They involve a comment which is of an "off the record" personal nature, shared with the group by the person speaking. The person wishes it to be treated as confidential.

REFERENCES

Burke, K. *Language as symbolic action*. Berkeley: University of California Press, 1966.

Gusfield, J. R. Literary rhetoric of science: Comedy and pathos in drinking driver research. *American Sociological Review*, 1976, *41*, 16–34.

Toulmin, S. E. *The uses of argument*. Cambridge: Cambridge University Press, 1958.

Weick, K. E. *The social psychology of organizations* (2nd ed.). Reading, Mass.: Addison Wesley, 1979.

Appendix 1

Segments of the transcript not reproduced in the text are reproduced here. The segments are as follows:

Lines 113–490; Reconstructed portion of the transcript representing a gap between lines 490–491; 491–522.

Lines 113–221:

F	113	There's also an ambiguity. It's like . . . People . . .
	114	I think what you are saying—that, that diagram could be flipped
	115	around—sort of spun on a central axis. But I think there is also
	116	an ambiguity as to whether it's in the center or on the ends. So—
	117	unintelligible . . . there's the training into the rules, the procedures
	118	for manipulating this machine. And on the other hand there's the
	119	story? the relationship (unintelligible).
AA	120	Dick, what do the two poles say—breadth of what? Is it breadth
	121	of audience?
DAFT	122	Oh, ah, that's . . . I was thinking. I was trying from the thing
	123	I couldn't work out in my own mind that this morning . . .
	124	whether other variables that might be here were the breadth or the
	125	size of the audience.
AA	126	Uh huh!
DAFT	127	I often think that this might have wide, be widespread if you like
	128	within the organization or outside, whereas this over here might
	129	have more limited, immediate . . .
AA	130	Yeah!
DAFT	131	Small number . . .
AA	132	Aah! Like you were carrying the tooth . . .
DAFT	133	Yes
AA	134	to a single person, whereas, stories and myths in some senses . . .
DAFT	135	Yes have widespread . . .
AA	136	were, were broadly available.
DAFT	137	Yeah!
AA	138	Someone, maybe it was _____ again in his paper was talking about
	139	the difficulty of an organization dealing with multiple publics and
	140	the fact that you may . . . (pause) it was _____, that there are problems
	141	with the fact that you can create a set of symbols for one public
	142	and not be able to segment it in a sense, and it would mean a
	143	different thing to another public.
DAFT	144	Yeah, and you might need a different set of symbols for each public.
	145	O.K. Well then in terms of this afternoon, the symbol thing for
	146	various publics, I have one thread this afternoon that I would like to
	147	. . . this explains a couple of things that I heard this afternoon. One
	148	was _____'s idea from anthropology and why not just
	149	borrow, or steal the methods from anthropology? Why agonise? Why
	150	go through all this within ourselves? And then, I began to realize
	151	that the methodologies that are popular and are hot and are widely
	152	used in organizations I guess, and I talked about this a bit
	153	last night, are myths and stories of a sort. In other words,
	154	the, let's say that the number of quantitative, comparative studies,
	155	longitudinal, regression analyses, is widely accepted and very

156 legitimate, as an acceptable means of researching in organization
157 theory. And I think that's a widespread kind of a myth. And if
158 you are going to publish a paper in many of the journals, you have to
159 add in enough of this to give it the gloss or the look of a legitimate
160 piece of work. You have to add the symbolism in of a rigorous,
161 thoughtful, quantitative research, systematic examination of the
162 issues, in order to make it stick. And I think the reason we can't
163 borrow is because if we take these—we can't take these, I don't
164 know what they are called, ethno . . . methodological . . . Is that
165 one of the words? or
166 (Some comments from some group members, inaudible . . .)
167 Includes

CC   168 That's not what anthropologists would call it.
Some else: 169 Symbolic analysis . . .
DAFT   170 Well, these, er . . . (other voices dominate)
??   171 Symbolic analysis
CC   172 If you write in a sufficiently obscure fashion (someone laughs) that
173 it's just a matter of competing rhetorics, and . . . (laughter).
174 There is this marvellous article in the American Sociological Review
175 by Joseph Gusfield. It was a couple of summers ago where he did
176 a rhetorical analysis of a typical technical report. And they
177 published it—sort of with great protest, in which he looked at a
178 report which talked about alcoholism and he talked about the way the
179 problem was framed. It was inherently biased toward making it a
180 problem. And he looked at the way the issue, the study was designed
181 which was to maximize finding if it was there. And he just went . . .
182 I think it's the sort of thing this group could find useful. Because
183 he takes Burke—and he sort of says how would Burke look at the
184 rhetoric of something like this, sort of like . . . ? does. And the
185 style that, the regression will be involved with is just a result of
186 having stolen from the biologists.

DAFT   187 But it's in . . .
CC   188 So I think it is perfectly reasonable to go steal stuff from other people.
DAFT   190 No, but it . . .
CC   191 If you make it obscure enough, people will think you know something.
DAFT   192 O.K., that's very likely. But obviously, we have to work through our
193 own in order to make these new methodologies legitimate. For the
194 symbols, the stories, the methodologies and so on to be, that are
195 now in vogue and are now acceptable, to be replaced.
196)
197)
198) Lines omitted as confidential—see note 4.
199)
200)
201)
202)
203)
204)

CC   205 I agree with you. I certainly think. . . (unintelligible) . . .
206 Anthropology is becoming fashionable.

DAFT	207	O.K. as soon as it's. . . .
CC	208	It's the same thing!
DAFT	209	But my proposal was, right, that we can't steal wholesale, because
	210	we have to work through and develop our own legitimate . . . it has
	211	to develop a legitimacy, a symbolic content within our field
	212	before it is acceptable to journal referees and to readers.
HH	213	Another thing, anthropology has it's own issues and battles going
	214	on within the discipline.
CC	215	That's their problem!
HH	216	Yes, but if we're borrowing you know like we could get . . .
CC	217	A used car.

(Audience reacts: Laughter)

II	218	Well, at least you ought to know that you are driving a used car.
	219	(General audience noise, laughter—In the background
		next voice emerges. Initially crowd
	220	noise predominates.)
AA	221	I want to . . . I'd like to say a couple of . . . First of all, I find
	222	this scheme very appealing. I'd like to make it explicit
	223	why I find it appealing. One is that it doesn't try to resolve
	224	the issue of what really is a symbol and admits the notion that
	225	there are a whole variety of things that can serve as symbolic
	226	functions, and provides a kind of organized, systematic scale for
	227	arranging symbols, from some kind
	228	of concrete to . . . uh . . . I've forgotten what you call that other—
	229	you don't have a word on the other end—ephemeral. ? . .
DAFT	230	Yes
AA	231	. . . end of scale. And I think that is extremely helpful. The
	232	other thing that's helpful is the implicit functional analysis.
	233	That in fact there is a kind of instrumental versus expressive
	234	function in the symbols—symbols can be both. And in fact that
	235	there is a correlation. That the concrete symbols tend to serve
	236	more instrumental functions and the ephemeral symbols tend to serve
AA	237	the more expressive functions. So there is a hell of a lot
	238	of content and substance in that, and even if I at some point disagree
	239	with it and modify it,
	240	it itself is a very concrete symbol with
	241	which I can work and begin operating and changing. It is a hell
	242	of a good starting point.
GG	243	Rather than ephemeral, how about putting consensual at the other
	244	end?
AA	245	Consensual?
Pause		
DAFT	246	That gives it a different image, where concrete captures
	247	the nature of the image. (Some audience comment going on at same time
	248	—unintelligible)
AA	249	Ah!
DAFT	250	No, consensual doesn't do that, that captures more of a process rather
	251	than a . . . .

(Audience participation—indistinct)

AA	252	How about abstract?
DAFT	253	Okay.

(Pause)

AA	254	I mean, you know sort of what characterizes stories and myths is,
	255	in fact, they are non-physical representations of things. They are linguistic . . .
DAFT	256	The one . . .
AA	257	Whatever.
??	258	Perhaps representative
Several Voices	259	Representative
DAFT	260	Actually, I'd like to close on that note, But I will add one more
	261	notion that I heard this afternoon and that seemed to be the image . . .
	262	I've been doing some work recently on Perrow's idea of technology and
	263	I thought I heard this notion of the degree of understanding coming
	264	up in different terms. In other words, one of Perrow's dimensions
	265	you recall is the search dimension? There's the analyzable search
	266	versus the unanalyzable search, which relates to how well understood
	267	the technology is. And if its well understood you can do the
	268	analyzable research, and use computational procedures, and if it's
	269	not well understood you use wits and gut reactions and so on. It's
	270	similar to Thompson's notions of cause-effect and means-end. Sometimes,
	271	they are clear and other times they are vague, fuzzy. And
	272	somehow a lot of the ideas coming through today, I thought captured
	273	that kind of underlying reality. If the reality itself is well
	274	understood, or crystallized, as opposed to vague and poorly understood
	275	. . . I would just add that on here. Perhaps this end (pointing to left hand side of Figure 1) tends to work best where things are vague and ambiguous and this end, (pointing to right hand side of Figure 1), this
	276	crystalized (next word unintelligible) where things are measurable,
DAFT	277	understandable, tangible and you can then use more concrete symbols
	278	to express (unintelligible final words(s) in sentence).
AA	279	Another dimension that characterizes that is high variety and low
	280	variety. Where the variety is not necessarily ambiguous, you don't
	281	know . . . It's not a case that you don't know what's there.
DAFT	282	I tried to work that out . . . I just couldn't! It keeps going
	283	on the same . . .
AA	284	I think so . . .
DAFT	285	High variety here, low variety there! (Pointing to left side and then right hand side of Fig. 1).
AA	286	Yeah! that a tooth doesn't capture much variety.
DAFT	287	Oh yeah! In that, this is high variety at the
	288	end. The high variety
	289	content . . .
AA	290	Yes.
DAFT	291	It carries a lot of meaning, a lot of punch . . .
AA	292	Yeah!

DAFT	293	A lot of richness.
AA	294	Yeah! It's thick
DAFT	295	Yeah thick!
CC	296	There's a component, there is a component to the comparison of
	297	cause-effect, analyzable—unanalyzable that Thompson stuck in that
	298	is useful. He had, in trying to pull together some of your
	299	earlier discussion, he had what he called beliefs about cause
	300	effect relations.
DAFT	301	Actually Perrow did too when you think about it. He talked about
	302	perceptions of technology.
CC	303	O.K., but all of that can be mythical . . . I think that's the point
	304	about getting together. That, if that was really crystallized. If
	305	it really made sense, then most of that entire . . . would drop out.
	306	The stories and myths are the only part that don't have an instru-
	307	mental component. And so its really a debate between believing
	308	that the thing makes sense and those who would argue that it clearly
	309	does, because they take these parameters as fixed, because they
	310	(unintelligible). But I think it brings it back to symbolism.
	311	If we actually think about whether we believe it, not we, but
	312	whether the system will believe.
AA	313	That's useful. . . .
CC	314	Rather than believed?
	315	Well, I don't know about useful, but I know about beliefs. Because
	316	the jargon in the field is framed in terms of beliefs about (things?).
DD	317	Another difference that I have heard a couple of times during the
	318	last day and a half and that's the idea of bimodal consciousness.
	319	Left and right brain that you could almost represent.
DAFT	320	I'll buy that! Yes.

Some positive audience response.

DD	321	The instrumental left brain, and the expressive right brain
	322	tie that in with the possibility that there are multi-level languages.
	323	That our rational, descriptive sort of language isn't the same
	324	language as our symbolic language. One is a right brain language,
	325	the other is a left brain language. And maybe there is a continuum
	326	between those two. Two different kinds of languages which we
	327	are representative of, taking a cross-section of the two different sides
	328	of the head, or (remainder of sentence is unintelligible).
DAFT	329	You are catching the right brain on this side? (Pointing to left
		hand side of Figure 1).
DD	330	Yes.
DAFT	331	The affective.
DD	332	unintelligible.
DAFT	333	Also just some of the other things that came up to me . . . that this
	334	is type Z, you might find more of this in a type Z organization,
	335	and more of that in a type A . . . Would that be correct or am I going
	336	off at . . . the deep end? One of the ideas in the information pro-
	337	cessing . . . yeah! in the hierarchy. This would be stressed at the
	338	top of the hierarchy, this more at the bottom or in the middle of the

	339	hierarchy. This er . . . well various ideas that came out today. I
	340	guess I can't put everything on, that I . . . saw. That's my
	341	summary.
AA	342	That's terrific! One of the really neat ideas which came out in
	343	_____'s session was the whole notion of the storyteller and the
	344	story producer and so forth. You sound like a story producer. The
	345	story.
EE	346	Also, it's a bit of sense making isn't it?
AA	347	Yeah!
EE	348	Trying to make a sort of ah . . . unintelligible . . .
FF	349	Isn't there something like formal versus the informal . . .
AA	350	Yeah! Oh good!
FF	351	organization. And somehow, the informal is over on that left hand
	352	side. It's something that once you've reached that middle, it's
	353	like the end of the earth on the left. You know there's this big
	354	waterfall—you just sort of drop off. And my question is. Why
	355	is all the emphasis on the right-hand side of your diagram?
DAFT	356	Your diagram. I don't think it is.
AA	357	What do you mean the emphasis being on the righthand side?
DAFT	358	That's right. It's supposed to be a continuum.
FF	359	I'm talking about the way people . . .
AA	360	Not why is *our* emphasis,
	361	but why is the *field's* emphasis?
FF	362	It seems to me that everybody . . . if we have made the distinction
	363	between formal and informal, it's O.K. to talk about the formal,
	364	from the center of that diagram over to the right. But talking
	365	about the informal is something you just don't do and you know and
	366	you . . .
BB	367	(unintelligible)
FF	368	know you mention but you don't develop it, you don't give it
	369	really any legitimacy.
HH	370	The interesting thing is that you see much emphasis on the right.
	371	Which is, in anthropology . . . everyone talks about the right hand
	372	as the valued hand the left hand is disvalued.
FF	373	Right.
HH	374	And what's on the top is superior and what's on the bottom is
	375	inferior—which (determines?) positional meanings and symbols.
FF	376	(talking simultaneously with HH.) and the way you constructed
	377	the diagram, to put that on the right as opposed to the left.
	377	Pause.
GG	379	This has also helped to "chunkify" a whole bunch of the meeting.
DAFT	380	Yes. This is one chunk for me from today's activities.
	381	(some laughter).
AA	382	I'm going to propose a different kind of intervention. JJ
	383	hasn't said much at our general gathering. And I know she
	384	came with a very specific agenda in terms of helping her to tie
	385	together her thesis. If it wouldn't (unintelligible) I would ask
	386	her. "How much sensemaking has this done for you, in terms of
	387	pulling together the experience?"
JJ	388	It's done some sense-making and some problem causing. First of

	389	all, a lot of the talk here has been more philosophical than I
	390	had been in my own thinking about stories and myths. Having read
	391	mostly Burton Clark and having been influenced by FF
	392	because of hearing about his research while it was going
	393	on. You know, I had a more kind of episodic thing in mind. And,
	394	thinking through some of the philosophical implications that people
	395	have been arguing here, I'm not sure I want to deal with all of that.
AA	396	That's the problematic side.
JJ	397	Yeah! If I get into that, it may be another year before I'm ready
	398	to write a proposal I can show to anybody because it's going to
	399	have to be cleared up in my head and it's not. On the other hand,
	400	I'm down at the expressive end with what I'm thinking about. There
	401	have been a lot of conversations that have talked about these kinds
	402	of things. But, what I am interested in looking at. I'm interested
	403	in looking at liberal arts colleges and their myths and
	404	stories. Part of what I'm interested in looking at is how those
	405	expressive stories are used instrumentally. I expect that they
	406	are used in recruiting. I expect they are used in
	407	fund raising. I expect that they may be used in faculty socialization. And . . .
	408	So part of what I'm interested in, is dealing with, is pulling
	409	some of the things from each of those two ends together. And I
	410	guess I hadn't gotten . . . This thing really helps, because I
	411	hadn't gotten all those differences in my head.
AA	412	Yeah! There is a kind of content-function difference.
JJ	413	Umm Humm! and I hadn't differentiated that very well for myself.
AA	414	Yeah!
JJ	415	And so I now have a little more to go on there. Now, the next
	416	thing I have to decide is . . . given that . . . I have to pick some
	417	Places to look at. And . . . . got to pick his by using another
	418	dimension to decide two extreme points to look at. He had the
	419	control dimension, the A & Z thing. I don't have that kind of
	420	dimension. Yet, I would like to look at some extreme cases so I
	421	could get some . . . The problem with Clark is that all his schools
	422	were very similar. You know, secular . . .
AA	423	Small elite . . .
JJ	424	Small elite.
AA	425	Liberal arts.
JJ	426	A lot of those things. And I think I've got to restrict it somedays,
	427	or I'll . . . or people will say: "She's measuring size, she's measuring
	428	selectivity. So I've got to group in someways, but I'd like to have
	429	some differences within a fairly select group and that's where I'm
	430	falling apart, I don't know what that might be. And, if anybody's
	431	got any ideas.
DAFT	432	Do you have to limit yourself to business-type organizations?
JJ	433	No . . . Universities is what I'm looking at. Liberal arts colleges,
	434	actually.
DAFT	435	I was thinking Clark's studies might have caught a unique kind of
	436	organization that had a larger share of the stories and myths than
	437	many other organizations.
	438	Business organizations in my mind, are rational, instrumental. And I

	439	may be on this half. (Pointing to right hand side of diagram). And as you
	441	get onto other types of organizations, families, religious organizations,
	442	and others in the culture, you'll find a larger and
	443	larger reliance upon expressive dimensions for what goes on. If you
	444	take a cut across, even you know, formal organizations.
JJ	445	Sure
DAFT	446	Business organizations and other types of human communities might
	447	give you a richer variety in terms of the kinds of symbols that
	448	dominate in the system.
	449	(Some audience indications of agreement.)
BB	450	What about those that are starting up or have come off a more recent
	451	change versus those that have stabilized? Because it seems to me,
	452	that the stability function may provide you with more and more of the
	453	instrumental.
AA	454	Machine like.
BB	455	That's right. Whereas those starting out, there has got to be a good
	456	deal of the kind of expressive aspects. Or in crisis versus non-crisis.
GG	457	Another dimension may be openness to the environment. And it seems
	458	to me that in terms of picking a dimension, you don't just want to
	459	pick a dimension which would give you convenient samples, sample units.
	460	But it should be tied to a theory of differences in symbols either
	461	in terms of content or function in some particular way. If you think
	462	of the environmental openness as the independent variable of your units
	463	of analysis, then, the differences of symbolic forms of management, of
	464	symbolism, could be argued on the basis of some ecological adaptation to
	465	the environment. That is, the more closed the college is to the
	466	environment, the less need there is to be instrumental and the more
	467	the expressive content will be used. Or maybe the expressive content
	468	will be used to maintain, to solidify the boundaries between the college
	469	and the environment.
II	470	Or it could be the opposite hypothesis that I would think would be
	471	confirmed. That the more closed the organization is, the more likely
	472	you could maintain a very instrumental orientation. I would suggest
	473	that the more ambiguous the technology of a liberal arts college is . . .
	474	If you could find an experimental type of liberal arts college where
	475	they are providing a programme which is experimental, using a rather
	476	less known classroom technology, and contrast that with one that is
	477	more closed in that they already know the technology, they have an
	478	autocratic type of system, closely regulated in terms of the requirements
	479	on (unintelligible) you'll probably find a suitable
	480	difference.
GG	481	Another dimension which, since we are throwing around ideas of looking
	482	at the expressive functions of symbols in two different kinds
	483	of colleges . . . The liberal arts
	484	college and the conservative arts
GG	485	college. (Laughter)
GG	486	I understand that X left a job from a conservative arts college
	487	where his account is that there is a lot of expressive symbolism in
	488	there. There are some reactionaries there. To take an example:

489   He got into big trouble when he gave a take home exam because it
490   violated their norms about academic control.

END Side 1.

Some discussion missed. Tape was not turned over immediately. Estimate: 5 minutes.

The material written as a bridge between lines 490–491 follows:

RECONSTRUCTED SEGMENT

The material entered here is a reconstruction of conversation missing on the tape. GG, who spoke during this taped period, recalls saying that X (see lines 485–489) was criticized for not conforming to the college's academic norms. GG pointed out that this particular college had been criticized by the Federal Government for not providing information pertaining to hiring and treatment of minority groups and was told to comply or risk loss of federal funding. The college refused to comply and sealed itself off from criticism by giving up these funds. GG suggested that when organizations become insulated from environmental influences they can maintain a stronger symbol system. GG suggested also that organizations wishing to insulate themselves from the environment can use symbols and symbol systems to create and maintain barriers against intrusion and investigation.

GG then moved to the more general observation that the presentation of the symbol scheme had created a great deal of enthusiasm and excitement in the group. GG suggested that the group had set up a straw man and wondered at what point such a straw man, the symbol scheme, comes to life. GG felt that by talking about and working with a symbol there is a time at which we reify the symbol—it becomes real—we talk about it as if it were true. GG then went on to suggest that it might be time to tear down the straw man.

The transcript continues . . .

TAPE SIDE 2

GG   491   . . . Tear down the straw man. It's interesting how the straw man has
         492   become a symbol. But, before I had said that symbols may interpret
         493   and sometimes define reality. But in the process of the last 15 minutes
         494   I think, it also constructs reality (unintelligible) Because
         495   what we . . . some of the straw men that we have in terms of conventional
         496   science is that we've set that up and that's a symbol and thereby

	497	setting up the symbol, we attack the hell out of it (laughter)
	498	and we attack that symbol so that no longer is it the preferred, the
	499	conventional wisdom. It's the old, traditional, fuddyduddy wisdom,
	500	(laughter) And now we've constructed a new symbol.
??	501	After barely thirty minutes (much laughter).
GG	502	And so that we have now another brighter . . .
BB	503	And we've worked the hell out of this one and attacked the hell out
	504	of the first one and we've worked the hell out of this one.
	505	Not necessarily unproductively but er
	506	(Some audience comments of agreement)
EE	507	Perhaps now we can attack it!
		(General laughter)
AA	508	The other interesting thing is that maybe more contribution is taking
	509	place on the left (hand side of Figure 1) than we either realize or are
	510	willing to acknowledge. _____'s recent research has been much on the left
	511	in terms of. . . . at the far end. I was thinking more of the work on the _____
	512	Institute. Photography is an interesting case because in one sense it
	513	produces a concrete artifact. A piece of paper with a captured symbol.
	514	On the other hand, it can have the enormous expressive content. I mean,
	515	the pictures I was taking today (couple of words which follow
	516	are unintelligible) in one sense are concrete, but in another sense, for
	517	the people here when I produce a selection of shots and send them
	518	around to people, will have this evocative . . . They are very
	519	selective, they will tell a story.
DAFT	520	Yeah, well we are supposed to . . . aren't we going to meet at the
	521	. . . Restaurant in about an hour? I think we ought to break and have
	522	another drink.

PRAGMATISM, INTERACTIONISM AND DRAMATISM:
INTERPRETING THE SYMBOL IN ORGANIZATIONS

Mark N. Wexler

> Man cannot escape from his own achievement. He cannot but adapt to the conditions of his own life. No longer in a merely physical universe, man lives in a symbolic universe. Language, myth, art, and religion are parts of this universe. They are the varied threads which weave the symbolic net, the tangled web of human experience. All human progress in thought and experience refines upon and strengthens this net. No longer can man confront reality immediately; he cannot see it, as it were, face to face. Physical reality seems to recede in proportion as man's symbolic acitivity advances. Ernst Cassirer (1944, p. 25)

In line with Cassirer's statement there is a growing agreement among social scientists that the organizational society (Presthus, 1978) is one increasingly understandable through a comprehension of man's symbol making activities (Boorstin, 1975; Duncan, 1962; 1968; Seidenberg, 1950). Within this perspective the organizational society, like the organization itself, is conceived of as a uniquely fabricated or man-made environment. Being man made it is encrusted with and developed as an extension of man's meaning systems. It is, as such, an abstract society (Zijderveld, 1970). To penetrate it, within the context of social scientific scholarship, one must grapple with the centrality of the symbol. It is in this spirit of investigation that Boulding has (1956) argued for a new science of the symbol, and Langer (1963) and Ogden and Richards (1945) for the inclusion of symbolism as a central construct in theories of human behavior.

However, as this volume makes apparent, symbolism remains a lacuna in the growing and amoebic like contours of organizational theory and research. In this paper I intend to address this neglect. To accomplish this goal I have set myself the task of investigating the conceptual roots of the social scientific treatment of symbolism.

THE LOGICS OF DISCOVERY

The logic of discovery underlying and leading to the study of symbols has one basic theoretical root, and three important research orientations. The root of symbolism is grounded in the principle of extension (Frye & Levi, 1941; Rapoport, 1955; Sapir, 1934; Werkmeister, 1940); the research orientations can be located in the distinction and combination of methodologies required to gain an understanding of the private and public nature (Bok, 1978; O'Neill, 1972, pp. 3–37; Sennett, 1977) of another's symbolic expression (see Figure 1).

The principle of extension is the belief that unites all analyst's interested in pursuing the study of symbolism. It is a belief that when person(s) create either things or ideas about things or indeed ideas about ideas, an investigation of these human creations will reveal information about the creator(s) of that product. The analytic emphasis is upon interpretation. While the type of interpretation varies, the principle of extension and concomitantly the reliance upon symbolism remains. Thus in Freud's hands the products of interpretation are dreams, verbal slips and jokes (Freud, 1953), in Durkheim's (1951) they are the French government and Church's data on the frequency of suicide, while in Malinowski's (1929) they are the gift giving practices and daily activities of the Trobriand Islanders.

From the principle of extension the analysis of symbolism can be pursued in three very distinct manners depending on the purpose and temperament of the analyst. They are:

1. the analysis of public symbols;
2. the analysis of private symbols;
3. the analysis of the interaction of public and private symbols.

This dichotomy of public and private concretizes the abstract nature of the principle of extension by compelling the analyst to adopt distinct research assumptions. Recent research documents the pervasiveness of the public/private distinction in the historical development of western culture, yet its very "taken for granted" nature masks important research assumptions (Schwartz, 1968; Zerubavel, 1976, 1979a, 1979b).

Research into the public symbol, as will be exemplified by an examination of the logic of discovery in the pragmatists' treatment of symbolism (Dewey, 1929, 1934, 1946; James, 1907; Peirce, 1966), focuses upon the manner in which shared meanings lodged in commonly shared symbols move persons to act in a relatively predictable and orderly manner. The image best used to exemplify research on the publicly held and shared symbol is the cohesive culture. Here meaning is not problematic; the consensus upon action is.

To exemplify the logic of discovery of the private symbol one can look to the working assumptions of the dramatists (Burke, 1963, 1968, 1972, 1975; Duncan, 1962; Goffman, 1963, 1971). Research into the private, but conscious symbol, focuses on the way meaning is selectively conveyed

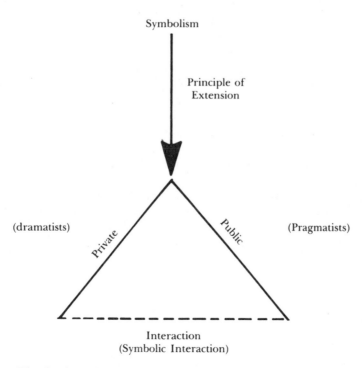

Figure 1. The logics of discovery.

and interpreted. To study the private symbol, the researcher must employ other symbols. Private symbols exclude, and carry with them a key to the distribution of meaning and the politics of membership.

Research into the interaction of publicly shared and privately held symbols, as will be exemplifed in the discussion of interactionists (Blumer, 1954, 1969; Mead, 1934), focuses on the interface between the personally held meanings resonating in the concept of the "self" and the publicly shared symbol system of the collective. Interactionists express a developmental and dialectical analysis of the symbol. The two processes occur simultaneously and in this joint process the idiosyncracies of the self are made reasonable to the shared meaning system of the collective and vice versa.

Pragmatism

Understood technically and not in its frequently perjorative common usage, pragmatism is an orientation to meaning, action, and evaluation which treats the public or commonly shared symbol as a central analytic construct (Morris, 1970; Thayer, 1968). The pragmatists' (Dewey, 1929, 1934, 1946; James, 1970; Peirce, 1966) effort to conceptualize the action potential of the public symbol reveals that these theorists were struggling with the issues of their time. Briefly, pragmatism bears the clear marks of the cultural and intellectual forces at play in America in the last quarter of the nineteenth century (Ayer, 1968; Bruce, 1970; Kennedy, 1950). In this sense, pragmatism can be viewed as part of a general revolt against the intellectual and somewhat fastidious closed system of idealism in 19th century thinking. Idealism had totally extended man's subjective experience of mind until it became a metaphysical principle of cosmic proportions. The pragmatists balked at this image. They felt that the theory of evolution, then new, with its emphasis upon change, called for a new interpretation of nature, life and reason—one that emphasized how life adapted to the environment (Wiener, 1949). This new interest and fascination with the ubiquity of change and the necessity of adaptation led the pragmatists to two large concerns. First, a concern to understand how humans mediate between action and meaning, and secondly, how the ensuing integration of meaning (mind) and action (body) is instrumental in developing techniques for instituting change favorable and "useful" to human existence.

In general there are two types of thought on the mind-body question, excluding the mediating viewpoint adopted by the pragmatists. The first, as in the aforementioned idealists, consider mind and the mental process of humans as paramount. The second, as in the philosophical materialists or scientific empiricists, consider the body and the observable, hence measureable processes of humans at the forefront. William James (1907) in his seminal work entitled *Pragmatism,* draws out the distinction and with Peirce and Dewey attempts to mediate the polarities. James depicts the differences as:

MIND	BODY
the tender minded	tough minded
rationalistic (following principles)	empiricist (following facts)
intellectualistic	sensationalistic
idealistic	materialistic
religious	irreligious
free willist	fatalistic
monistic	pluralistic
dogmatical	skeptical

The pragmatists' mediation of this schism is unique. Fundamentally the pragmatists develop a theory of meaning wherein humans use of publicly shared symbols mediate between the mind-body separation. Symbols, within the pragmatic tradition, represent intended meanings (mind) and are important because they orientate action (body). The argument, simply put, is that individual lines of meaning are worked out among persons as they develop symbols to communicate their desires and intentions. The study of shared symbols reveals the thinking of those sharing the symbols. Persons and collectivities act on the basis of these abstractly communicated aspects of social life. Central to this lively position is not that people react to the acts of others but that they act on the basis of communicated intentions or symbols of others.

The mediation is complete. Symbols assist persons to define their situations and rest assured that others, due to the public nature of symbols, share it. Of course any actual situation has a specific existential reality—that is, it exists apart from what anyone knows or does not know about it. But within the pragmatic mediation, things unknown, unconsciously held or forgotten by participants are not part of their definition. Thus the salient features of situations are those seized upon by the person(s) involved in giving that situation meaning (symbols). It is this symbolically defined situation, as distinct from the existential (the two may or may not be similar), that is the operative factor in how persons and groups construct their actual behavior. Thus a situation, as it comes to be defined among group members, surrounds each member with a meaningful context of action. The pragmatic mediation of the classic mind-body problem is achieved; meanings, understood through the study of publicly held symbols are derived from action and action is in turn invested with meaning.

Interactionism

The interactionists, particularly George Herbert Mead (1934), and his followers (Blumer, 1954, 1969; Hewitt, 1976; Kuhn, 1964; Shibutani, 1955), further the pragmatists' mediation of the traditional dualisms stemming from the mind (meaning) and body (action) dichotomy. The interactionists integration is primarily social psychological, unlike the pragmatists they proceed by establishing a dialectical conception between the self (private symbol) and the collective (public symbol). In this conception human beings are neither creatures of impulse nor simple victims of external stimulation; they are active organisms who guide and construct their line of action while continually coming to terms with the demands of an ever-changing world as they interpret it.

Both pragmatism and interactionism are efforts to reformulate the conception of the human sciences in terms of the revolutionary implications of evolutionary theory. However, unlike the pragmatists' reaction to the mentalism of German Idealism, the interactionists seek to modify the strict psychological behaviorism (body) of Watson (1924, 1930), and in a more contemporary fashion, of Skinner (1953, 1974).

Mead's thinking upon this subject is clear. Evolution is the ongoing process wherein humans both individually and collectively meet and either solve or fail to solve problems. In "Homo sapiens" adaptation occurs due to such clearly mental (minded) powers as thinking in abstractions, self consciousness, purposive and moral conduct. A science of human life which proceeds by studying merely overt behavior, such as that forwarded by Watson, misses the central aspect of human life. "Watson", says Mead;

> insists that objectively observable behavior completely and exclusively constitutes the field of scientific psychology, individual and social. He pushes aside as erroneous the idea of 'mind' or 'consciousness' and attempts to reduce all 'mental' phenomena to conditional reflexes and similar physiological mechanisms—in short, to purely behavioristic terms. The attempt of course, is misguided and unsuccessful. . . (1934, p. 10).

To rectify this misguided emphasis, Mead suggests that by focusing upon the conscious symbol, one can achieve an exacting empirical investigation of both overt and covert human behavior.

Thus interactionism is a kind of correlational enterprise. It seeks to show the correlations between the conscious experience of individuals and indeed of collectivities and the conditions under which these arise. Following William James, Mead argues that consciousness must be understood as a thought-stream in the ongoing relationship (interactions) between people and their environment. Experience in this thought-stream is not first individual and private, then social and public. Rather the two, as studied through consciously held symbols, occur simultaneously. In this perspective, each individual is continuously involved in a succession of joint enterprises with others. The "jointness" of enterprise, whether it be a simple dyadic interaction or a multiple interaction sequence in a complex organization, is dependent upon shared meanings achieved through commonly held symbols. These enterprises and one's membership in them alter the individual, his experience and the environment in which he acts and from which he derives meaning. While this occurs, the individual helps reformulate the enterprise. This dialectic of the individual with his private world and the collective with its public realm is the clearest sense in which the interactionists further the work of the pragmatists.

To place the interactionists within an understandable perspective it is vital to differentiate between symbolic and non-symbolic interaction. The distinction is vital as the former necessitates the inclusion of mind (and as we shall see, self and society) whereas the latter can be treated simply and effectively within the stimulus response model posited by the behaviorists. Briefly, non-symbolic interaction takes place when one responds directly to the action of another without actually interpreting the action, whereas symbolic interaction involves the interpretation of action. As a practical and easily visualized instance, suppose we have two boxers in a bout. One begins to move his arm in the initial phase of a body blow: the other responds automatically with a defensive reaction. This "conversation of gestures," as Mead (1934, p. 61) terms it, is non-symbolic. However if the boxer were to identify the forthcoming blow from his opponent as a feint intended to trap him, he would be engaging in symbolic interaction. In this instance of symbolic action, the boxer adapting to the feint is capable of taking the role of the other. He attempts to ascertain the intended meaning of the blow, that is, what the blow signifies to this opponent's plans and then act in accordance with his perception of his opponent's intended line of action.

It is through symbolic action that humans create meaning and formulate their lines of action, trying all the while to take into account the intended lines of action of others. The symbolic interactionists emphasize aspects of personal and collective development by focusing attention on action and the ongoing interpretation of differently shared symbols. They refuse to view the process of socialization as some monolithic pouring of societal and cultural values into apparently empty human vessels. Indeed the interactionists balk at efforts to study humans as an amalgam of attitudes and values. They prefer to highlight how, in the process of minded (symbolic) action, we create a collectivity which aligns ongoing action, permitting individual differences (private symbol) to exist within the orderliness of the shared public realm.

The interactionists believe tht we come to understand and further develop ourselves and the society we live in through the "minded" aspects of interaction. If in *Mind, Self and Society* Mead (1934), and subsequent interactionists (Blumer, 1954, 1969; Kuhn, 1964; Lauer & Handel, 1977; Quarantelli & Cooper, 1966) had stopped at the analysis of mind, we would be left with a solid criticism of psychological behaviorism; however, Mead and his adherents pressed on, attempting to indicate how symbolic interaction is instrumental in the development of both "self" and "society".

At the micro-analytic level, one investigated empirically, the interactionists focus upon the development of the "self" (Ames, 1974; Hewit, 1979; Kinch, 1963; Kuhn & McParland, 1954; Miyamoto & Dornbusch, 1956). Nothing esoteric is intended by the term. It merely denotes the "process" whereby persons learn to look at and act towards themselves as social objects. My ability to sit here at my desk and think about myself as a professor working on a paper on a bright sunny Sunday, a young man in need of a haircut and a negligent son who has once again forgotten to make his biweekly phone call to his parents, are facets of my "mind" existing through the development of my "self". It is vital in this context to emphasize that the possession of a self is not only the capacity to observe oneself but moreover to respond to one's observations and direct one's own behaviour. This self observation and self direction is tempered by the exigencies of adapting to the courses of action we believe others about us are adopting.

The interactionists' image of the person is complex. The "self" reflects the dialectical treatment of the public and private character of the symbol in that it is a process composed of the "I" and the "me". The "I" is the unpredictable, the novel and the quixotic aspect of the self while the "me" is the organized community as reflected in one's ability to hold and interpret symbols. The self is a dialectical process with the "I" calling out the "me" and then responding to it. The dialectics of the self do not originate at birth but emerge during childhood (Mead, 1934; Denzin, 1972; Charon, 1979) in three stages—preparatory, play and game. The interactionists resemble Piaget (1932, 1951) in emphasizing the stages of becoming uniquely social through shared meanings and symbols. However, unlike Piaget, in the interactionist perspective, to come to experience one's self as an object, one is required to take the viewpoint of another toward the self. This process, that of role playing, is how we learn to both quell the disquieting imbalances between the "I" and "me" and how to create lines of intended action acceptable to the collective. Indeed it is from the imagining standpoint acquired during role playing that one learns to view the self as it is and becomes aware of reality as it appears to generalized others (Mead, 1934; Strauss, 1959).

At the macro-analytic level, the interactionists address the nature of societies or the large collectivities and groups in which individuals act (Blumer, 1954; Mead, 1934; Shibutani, 1961; Warriner, 1970). This larger entity is composed of "minded selves" acting with both public and private symbols to construct meaning and orient to lines of action in the pursuit of both individual and collective goals. What is important in the macro-analytic emphasis of the interactionist is the emphasis on society as an ongoing and altering system of human action. Structure is clearly of limited importance. Structure achieves status as a topic in that it symbolizes the intended meanings the collective adheres to. These collective intended meanings are however, tentative. Human action, as is clear in Gouldner's (1954) study of the gypsum plant, often circumvents structure and rules.

In the interactionist perspective, "role playing" and its active cousin "role taking" and concomitantly the "generalized other" and its extension the "reference group" are central in comprehending the movement from micro to macro theory. Role playing, as we have suggested, is the ability to become aware of the self and its reality as it appears to others. To the symbolic interactionists, role playing is an incomplete or perhaps superficial play of one's self in the role of another. The idea of "playing" a role suggests that the role is truly not "me". Although "I" adopt the public symbols, meanings, and lines of action inherent in my interpretation of the role, "I" doubt whether they are truly "me". In "role taking" this battle of authenticity is resolved. The more profoundly one accepts the definitions of self derived from the viewpoint of others, the more the role is taken as one's own—not just played.

It is important in this brief discussion of the interactionists' perception of society to note that the self is not passive and receptive. It simply is not a matter of accepting other's definition of one's self that determines that one have "that" self. Rather, Mead calls for the "realization of the self in action" (1934, p. 200). Taking the role as opposed to only playing it, means doing it with conviction. This "self realization" in activity, is of course a common thread that the interactionists share with their pragmatic predecessors, and one that calls into play the crucial manner in which individuals ("minded selves") in collectivities (societies) test the reality of both their environment and their perception of their place in it.

Both "role playing" and "role taking" relate in Mead's scheme with the concept of the "generalized other" (1934, p. 160) and his adherants extension of it to the "reference other" and "reference group" (Shibutani, 1955). As in the micro-analytic discussion of socialization, at the macro-analytic level the collectivity is not simply one of homogeneity achieved by shared symbols. Rather there are two ongoing and co-existent levels of analysis. Each collectivity (organization, society) has at some level a relatively coherent set of shared symbols that permit those within to develop lines of action consistent with both their self-images and desired outcomes. This public realm of shared meanings among relatively anonymous others stems from the Meadian concept of the "generalized other". Briefly, in role playing we learn to abstract and generalize the symbols and meanings of others not only to "significant others"— those who we know and who are key in the development of our self—but also an abstracted general other. Thus as "minded selves" we enter a situation, define it from our perspective and appreciate how others, even those we have not yet met, might define it. We act in line with the meanings we attribute to our own definition of the situation, taking into account that of the generalized other. It is through the "generalized other" that the interactionists embrace the cohesiveness of the collective. It is also a means of refining and discussing the "they" or "establishment" as it reveals itself in daily discourse.

The abstract other, in keeping with the interactionists' roots in pragmatism, is tempered by the reality testing of "role taking" and the ensuing reference group or sub-cultural perspectives that stem from it (Kuhn, 1964; Shibutani, 1955; Wallace, 1966). This perspective rounds out and places another level of mediation between the public and privately held symbolism in interactionism. As in the "I" and "me" the private and public levels of meaning co-exist, so to in the "generalized other" and "reference other". Briefly, in the reference others we act in a specific context and hence relate to specific, often chosen, others. In the ongoing interaction with specific others, particularly given increasing frequency and intimacy we share specific nuances of meaning, learn shorthand methods and at times idiosyncratic methods of aligning our action with specific others. Thus while the collective and society is united by symbols mediated through the internalized "generalized other", it is differentiated in the private symbols of ongoing action between members of specific reference groups.

Dramatism

Kenneth Burke's system of inquiry (1962, 1968, 1972, 1975), called dramatism, is distinguished from Mead's and the interactionists' in that it seeks to account for symbols symbolically. While the interactionists functionally sandwich symbols between the private aspects of self and the public realm of the collectivity, the dramatists use the metaphors of art and especially of theater to capture the "how" of symbolizing (Brisset & Edgely, 1975; Gordon, 1969; Messinger, et al., 1962; Rueckert, 1963). The logical position inherent in the diversity of styles adopted by the dramatists has been encapsulated by Shakespeare's perception that "all the world's a stage." The dramatists concur. Their agreement is based upon the belief that the dramatic stage is virtually unique as one of the areas of life where the task of sustaining a reality is a conscious concern.

The dramatist notion of science is artful: it sensitizes rather than sharply delineates. In Burke and his social scientific adherents like Goffman (1959, 1961, 1963) and Duncan (1962, 1968) the theatre provides an interpretive background wherein actors, acting singly or jointly, scripted or improvising, construct and sustain reality. It is important to realize in this context that like the phenomenologists or the ethnomethodologists, the dramatists view human reality as symbolically negotiated and not as a given and set order (Berger & Luckmann, 1966; Farberman & Goode, 1973). Actors consciously sustain meanings through their actions and in so doing provide clues to both other actors and the audience as to the nature of the reality being negotiated.

Mainstream behavioral analysis has not been adverse to including "role" in the conceptualization of the relationship between the individual and his or her position. The dramatist begins with the concept of "role" and seeks to discover how reality is meaningfully constructed through the ongoing analysis of "symbols in use". This apparent extension of the theatrical metaphor has been applied to settings as diverse as the American Temperance Movement (Gusfield, 1963), the insane asylum (Goffman, 1961) the political party (Edelman, 1967) and the modern corporation (Thompson, 1963). What these authors, working in different "theaters" have in common is a reliance, albeit a loose and roughly hewn one, upon the works of the father of dramatism—Kenneth Burke.

Burke is a literary critic and unlike either the pragmatists or interactionists, his is an approach to the artfulness of the conscious but closely held symbol. Burke's prose exemplify his method; associative rather than linear reasoning is used to depict dramatism. Briefly, Burke makes a key distinction between action and motion. Whereas Mead begins with the "mindedness" of symbolic interaction in distinction to the "mindless-ness" of imitation, Burke begins by relating "action" to conscious humans and "motion" to things and lower animals. Things move, humans act. The logic is persuasive. In Burkean terminology, we must develop "terministic screens" (paradigms) to uncover the human as actor. To forfeit this opportunity and turn to physicalistic metaphors (models) is to abandon the essential definitional criterion of humans.

To Burke and his adherents the implications of these ideas extended by illustrations from literature, history and art lead to the dramatists' perspective (Rueckert, 1963). This perspective is founded upon the belief that humans build symbolic structure on nature, adding art to life. Language and symbol manipulation give our species a "moral sense". Burke argues that homo sapiens (man and wise) is the only animal able to conceive of and act upon "negatives" and in so doing can control and structure "actions" upon the basis of symbolic meanings not reducible to "natural" motives. Humans do not simply have sex, they create love; they do not simply kill for food, but also for deities and homeland; the physical body is not only protected, it is adorned. Humans then separate themselves from their natural condition and in so doing a symbolic world, capturable in dramatic metaphor, overlaps the natural one.

For the dramatist the inference is clear; life is drama. Society is a drama in which actions, in terms of symbols are the crucial events. The difference between "staged" drama and the drama of every day life is seen as the difference between human conflicts and their resolution imagined by an artist (playwright) and those actually experienced. In the dramatist perspective, the two are homologous: life and art both deal with the fundamental problems of human existence. Therefore inquiry into human life, framed dramatistically, reflects or sensitizes one to distinctively human problems in a humanly constructed setting. The dramatists do not denigrate physicalistic metaphors (system, equilibrium, boundary-spanning, encoding, decoding, field, forces, etc.) but view them as meaningful when limited to inquiries into nature, not human nature.

The dramatistic frame is more than merely a caution against inappropriate metaphors. There is a method to this artfully extended theatrical metaphor. The dramatists (Duncan, 1962; Foote, 1957; Lyman & Scott, 1970; Klapp, 1968; Rueckert, 1963), taking their lead from Burke, "fill out" the dimensions or "moments" of action in a formal sense: Scene, Act, Agent, Agency and Purpose.

These dimensions are what the dramatist as inquirer needs to focus upon to "understand" action, whether it be in the context of staged or real life drama. Briefly, actions occur within the framework of a social scene or setting; the action is conducted by an agent with a conception about what is appropriate to the scene; the actor uses the means at his disposal to accomplish the action; and action is done for some purpose.

In this deliberately Aristotelian paradigm, the dramatists, like good contemporary mystery writers, coordinate the classical questions: "where" and "when" was something done, "what" was done, "who" did it, "how" was it done, and "why" was it done. To get to these on-going problem frames Burke and adherents focus upon the world of human motives. Burke views motives not as biological, psychological or social forces but rather as the basic forms of personal thought by which human beings experience their world. To arrive at a program for the study of "motives", Burke places the questions into three broad categories: the "grammar of motives", has to do with the forms of inquiry which seeks to comprehend the types and forms of motives in themselves; the "symbolic of motives" is that form of inquiry which concerns itself with the expression of motive through symbols; and the "rhetoric of motives" seeks to comprehend the basic strategies that individual and collectivities employ in their attempt to manipulate one another.

CONCLUSION

We, in organizational research, must be cautious of "neophilia" or the love of novelty. Ours is a field constantly pressed by the practical demands and exigencies of corporate and organizational clients. This demand, when pressed often and in the intellectual market place, produces a tendency to generate new ideas for the sake of marketing the novel. This must be resisted. However in resisting "neophilia" we must remain open to intellectual innovation.

Symbolism, particularly the emphasis on conscious symbolism in organizational research is, in my opinion, just such an intellectual innovation. Symbolism is no panacea. It is an orientation to formal organizations that will produce no instant miracle firm nor increase productivity and reduce absenteeism. Symbolism is an intellectual approach to comprehending, describing and delineating the nature of action and interpretation in man-made or fabricated environments. It deals with the complexities of organizational life without assuming that humans are simple stimulus—response mechanisms. It broadens both theory and methods, mellowing out the highly "perscriptive" nature of organizational research; tempering this with a practical but descriptive emphasis.

Intellectual innovations unlike products of "neophilia" exist in the process of being constructed. We in this volume are "struggling to articulate" a perspective which can reflect the richness of organization and the life within them. The symbol is the key. Through it we can comprehend how organizations struggle to achieve order, how goals and our understanding of them alter. Indeed, rather than assuming that organizations are purposefully coordinated systems of two or more people, we can with organizational symbolism, begin to probe the manner in which orderliness, and at times the loss of it, is rendered meaningful in organizations.

REFERENCES

Ames, V. M. No separate self. In Walter Cortz (Ed.), *The philosophy of George Herbert Mead.* Switzerland: Amriswiller Buschse, 1973.

Ayer, A. J. *The origins of pragmatism.* San Francisco: Freeman Cooper, 1968.

Berger, P. L., Luckmann, T. *The social construction of reality.* New York: Doubleday, 1966.

Blumer, H. Society as symbolic interaction. In Arnold Rose (Ed.), *Human behavior and social processes.* Boston: Houghton Mifflin, 1954.

Blumer, H. *Symbolic interactionism: Perspective and method.* Englewood Cliffs, N.J.: Prentice-Hall, 1969.

Bok, S. *Lying: Moral choice in public and private life.* New York: Pantheon, 1978.

Boorstin, D. *The image: A guide to pseudo-events in America.* New York: Atheneum, 1975.

Boulding, K. *The image: Knowledge in life and society.* Ann Arbor: University of Michigan Press, 1956.

Brisset, D., & Edgley, C. *Life as theater: A dramaturgical sourcebook.* Chicago: Aldine, 1975.

Bruce, A. *Rationalism, empiricism and pragmatism.* New York: Random House, 1970.

Burke, K. *A grammar of motives and a rhetoric of motives.* Cleveland: World Publishing, 1962.

Burke, K. Dramatism. In D. L. Sills (Ed.), *The international encyclopedia of the soical sciences* (Vol. 9). New York: Macmillan, 1968.

Burke, K. *Dramatism and development.* Barre, Mass.: Clark University Press, 1972.

Burke, K. *The philosophy of literary form: Studies in symbolic action* (3rd ed.). Berkeley: University of California Press, 1975.

Burns, E. *Theatricality.* New York: Harper and Row, 1972.

Cassirer, E. *An essay on man.* New Haven: Yale University Press, 1944.

Cassirer, E. *Language and myth* (1st ed.). (S. K. Langer, trans.) New York: Dover Publications, 1946.

Charon, J. M. *Symbolic interactionism: An introduction on interpretation, and integration.* Englewood Cliffs, N.J.: Prentice-Hall, 1979.

De Grazia, S. *Of time, work and leisure.* New York: Pincher Books, 1964.

Denzin, N. L. The genesis of self in early childhood. *Sociological Quarterly,* 1972, *13,* 291–314.

Dewey, J. *The quest for certainty: A study of the relation of knowledge and action.* New York: Minton Balch, 1929.

Dewey, J. *Art as experience.* New York: Minton Balch, 1934.

Dewey, J. *Problems of man.* New York: Philosophical Library, 1946.

Duncan, H. D. *Communication and social order.* New York: Bedminister Press, 1962.

Duncan, H. D. *Symbols in society.* New York: Oxford University Press, 1968.

Durkheim, E. *Suicide.* (J. Spaulding & G. Simpson, trans.) Glencoe, Ill.: Free Press, 1951.

Edelman, M. *The symbolic uses of politics.* Urbana: University of Illinois Press, 1967.

Farberman, H. A., & Coode, W. *Social reality.* Englewood Cliffs, N.J.: Prentice-Hall, 1973.

Foote, N. N. Concept and method in the study of human development. In M. Sherif and M. C. Wilson (Eds.), *Emerging problems in social psychology.* Norman: University of Oklahoma Press, 1957.

Freud, S. *The standard edition of the complete psychological works of Sigmund Freud* (James Strachey, trans.). London: Hogarth Press, 1953.

Frye, A. M., & Levi, A. *Rational belief: An introduction to logic.* New York: Horcourt, Brace and Javonovich, 1941.

Goffman, E. On cooling the mark out. *Psychiatry,* 1952, *15,* 451–463.

Goffman, E. *The presentation of self in everyday life.* Garden City, N.Y.: Anchor Books, 1959.

Goffman, E. *Asylums.* Garden City, N.Y.: Anchor Books, 1961.

Goffman, E. *Behavior in public places.* New York: Free Press, 1963.

Gordon, G. N. *Languages of communication.* New York: Hastings House, 1969.

Gouldner, A. *Patterns of industrial bureaucracy.* New York: Free Press, 1954.

Gusfield, J. R. *Symbolic crusade.* Chicago: University of Illinois Press, 1963.

Hall, E. T. *The hidden dimension.* New York: Anchor Books, 1966.

Hewitt, J. P. *Self and society: A symbolic interactionist social psychology.* Boston: Allyn Bacon, 1976.

Hook, S. *Pragmatism and the tragic sense of life.* New York: Basic Books, 1974.

Ichheiser, G. *Appearances and realities.* San Francisco: Josey-Bass, 1970.

James. W. *Pragmatism.* New York: Longman Green, 1907.

Kennedy, G. *Pragmatism and American culture.* Boston: D.C. Heath, 1950.

Kinch, J. W. A formalized theory of the self concept. *American Journal of Sociology,* 1963, *68,* 481–486.

Klapp, O. *Symbolic leaders: Public dramas and public man.* Chicago: Aldine Publishing, 1968.

Kuhn, M. Major trends in symbolic interaction theory in the past twenty-five years. *The Sociological Quarterly,* 1964, *5,* 61–84.

Kuhn, M. H., & McPartland, T. An empirical investigation of self attitudes. *American Sociological Review,* 1954, *19,* 68–76.

Kuhn, T. S. *The structure of scientific revolutions* (2nd Ed.). Chicago: University of Chicago Press, 1970.

Lauer, R. H., & Handel, W. H. *Social Psychology: The theory and application of symbolic interactionism.* Boston: Houghton Mifflin, 1977.

Langer, S. *Philosophy in a new key: A study in the symbolism of reason, rite and art.* Cambridge, Mass.: Harvard University Press, 1963.

Lindesmith, A. R., & Strauss, A. L. *Social psychology* (3rd ed.). New York: Holt, Rinehart & Winston, 1968.

Lyman, S., & Scott, M. *A sociology of the absurd.* New York: Appleton-Century-Crofts, 1970.

Malinowski, B. *The sexual life of savages in northwestern Melanasia: An ethnographic account of courtship, marriage and family life among the natives of the Trobriand Islands and British Guinea.* New York: Liveright Publishing Corp., 1929.

Manis, J., & Meltzer, B. (Eds.). *Symbolic interaction: A reader in social psychology* (2nd ed.). Boston. Houghton Mifflin, 1972.

McHugh, P. *Defining the situation: The organization of meaning in social interaction.* Indianapolis: Bobbs-Merrill, 1968.

Mead, G. H. *Mind, self and society: From the standpoint of a social behaviorialist* (edited with an introduction, by Charles W. Morris). Chicago: University of Chicago Press, 1934.

Meltzer, B. *The social psychology of George Herbert Mead.* Kalamazoo: Western Michigan University, 1972.

Merton, R. K. *Sociological ambivalences*. New York: Free Press, 1976.

Messinger, S., Sampson, H., & Towne, R. Life as theater: Some notes on the dramaturgic approach to social reality. *Sociometry*, 1962, *25*, 98–110.

Miller, D. *George Herbert Mead: Self, language and the world*. Austin: University of Texas Press, 1973.

Mills, W. C. *Sociology and pragmatism*. New York: Paine Whitman, 1964.

Miyamoto, F. S., & Dornbusch, S. M. A test of interactionist hypothesis of self-conception. *American Journal of Sociology*, 1956, *61*, 399–403.

Moore, E. C. *American pragmatism*. New York: Columbia University Press, 1961.

Moore, W. E. *Man time and society:* New York: John Wiley, 1963.

Morris, C. W. *The pragmatic movement in American philosophy*. New York: Braziller, 1970.

Ogden, C. K., & Richards, T. A. *The meaning of meaning: A study of the influence of language upon thought and the science of symbolism*. New York: Harcourt, Brace and Company, 1945.

O'Neill, J. On private troubles and public issues. In J. O'Neill (Ed.), *Sociology of a skin trade*. London: Heinemann, 1972.

Park, R. E. The concept of social distance. *Journal of Applied Sociology*, 1924, *8*, 339–344.

Piaget, J. *The moral judgment of the child* (M. Gabaiv, trans.). New York: Harcourt, Brace, 1932.

Piaget, J. *Play dreams and imitation in childhood* (C. Galtegno & F. M. Hodgsen, trans.). New York: W. W. North, 1951.

Pierce, C. S. *C. S. Peirce: Selected writings* (Phillip P. Wiener, Ed.). New York: Dover, 1966.

Presthus, R. *The organizational society* (rev. ed.). New York: St. Martin's Press, 1978.

Quarantelli, E. L., & Cooper, J. Self-conceptions and others: A further test of Mead's hypothesis. *Sociological Quarterly*, 1966, *7*, 281–297.

Rapoport, A. The role of symbols in human behavior. *ETC: A Review of General Semantics*, 1955, *12*, 180–188.

Rescher, N. *Methodological pragmatism*. Oxford: Basil Blackwell, 1977.

Rock, P. *The making of symbolic interactionism*. London: MacMillan, 1979.

Ross, R. *Symbols and civilization*. New York: Harcourt, Brace and World, 1962.

Rueckert, W. H. *Kenneth Burke and the drama of human relations*. Minneapolis: University of Minnesota Press, 1963.

Rueckert, W. H. *Critical responses to Kenneth Burke: 1924–1966*. Minneapolis: University of Minnesota Press, 1969.

Sapir, E. Symbolism. *Encyclopedia of the social sciences* (Vol. 14). New York: Macmillan, 1934, pp. 492–495.

Scheffler, I. *Four pragmatists*. New York: Humanities Press, 1974.

Schellenberg, J. A. *Masters of social psychology: Freud, Mead, Lewin, and Skinner*. New York: Oxford University Press, 1978.

Schwartz, B. The social psychology of privacy. *American Journal of Sociology*, 1968, *73*, 741–752.

Scott, M., & Lyman, S. Accounts. *American Sociological Review*, 1968, *33*, 46–62.

Scott, M., & Lyman, S. *The sociology of the absurd*. Los Angeles: Goodyear Publishing, 1970.

Seidenberg, R. *Posthistoric man: An inquiry*. Chapel Hill: The University of North Carolina Press, 1950.

Sennett, R. *The fall of public man*. New York: Alfred A. Knopf, 1977.

Shibutani, T. Reference groups as persepctives. *American Journal of Sociology*, 1955, *60*, 562–569.

Shibutani, T. *Society and personality: An interactionist approach to social psychology*. Englewood Cliffs, N.J.: Prentice-Hall, 1961.

Shibutani, T. *Human nature collective behavior: Papers in honor of Herbert Blumer.* Englewood Cliffs, N.J.: Prentice-Hall, 1970.

Skinner, B. F. *Science and human behavior.* New York: Macmillan, 1953.

Skinner, B. F. *About behaviorism.* New York: A. Knopf, 1974.

Skinner, B. F. The steep and thorny way to a science of behavior. *American Psychologist,* 1975, *30,* 42–49.

Stone, G., & Faberman, H. *Social psychology through symbolic interaction.* Lexington, Mass.: Xerox College Publishing, 1970.

Strauss, A. (Ed.), *The social psychology of George Herbert Mead.* Chicago: University of Chicago Press, 1956.

Strauss, A. *Mirrors and masks.* New York: Free Press, 1959.

Swanson, G. Toward corporate action: A reconstruction of elementary collective processes. In Tomatsu Shibutani (Ed.), *Human nature and collective behavior.* Englewood Cliffs, N.J.: Prentice-Hall, 1970.

Thayer, H. S. *Meaning and action: A critical history of pragmatism.* Indianapolis: Bobbs-Merrill, 1968.

Thompson, V. *Modern organizations.* New York: Alfred Knopf.

Turner, R. The self-conception in social interaction. In C. Gordon & K. J. Gergen (Eds.), *The self in social interaction.* New York: Wiley, 1968.

Van Gunstern, H. Public and private. *Social Research,* 1979, *46,* 255–271.

Wallace, S. E. Reference group behavior in occupational role specifications. *Sociological Quarterly,* 1966, *7,* 366–372.

Warner, L. W. *The living and the dead: A study of the symbolic life of Americans.* New Haven: Yale University Press, 1959.

Warriner, C. K. *The emergence of society.* Homewood, Ill.: Dorsey Press, 1970.

Watson, J. B. *Psychology from the standpoint of the behaviorist* (2nd ed.). Philadelphia: J. B. Lippincourt, 1924.

Watson, J. B. *Behaviorism.* Chicago: University of Chicago Press, 1930.

Werkmeister, W. H. *A philosophy of science.* New York: Harper and Brothers, 1940.

Whitehead, A. N. *Symbolism.* New York: Macmillan, 1958.

Wiener, P. *Evolution and the founders of pragmatism.* Cambridge, Mass.: Harvard University Press, 1949.

Zerubavel, E. Timetables and scheduling: On the social organization of time. *Sociological Inquiry,* 1976, *46,* 87–94.

Zerubavel, E. *Pattern of time in hospital life.* Chicago: University of Chicago Press, 1979. (a)

Zerubavel, E. Private time and public time: The temporal structure of social accesibility and professional commitments. *Social Forces,* 1979, *50,* 38–51. (b)

Zijderveld, A. C. *The abstract society.* Garden City, N.Y.: Doubleday, 1970.

Part VI

SYMBOLS AS SOURCES OF
DOMINATION IN ORGANIZATIONS

In Part I of this volume we discussed two paradigms for studying organizational symbolism—the radical humanist and radical structuralist, both of which are concerned with analyzing the role of symbols as sources of domination and constraint on individual and organized action. The radical humanist perspective focusses on how people may create and sustain symbols which, whatever their original intent, eventually serve to control and alienate their creators. The radical structuralist perspective focusses on the way symbols may be systematically manipulated and controlled by those in power in organized settings, to create cohesive ideologies that control those subject to such power.

In Gordon Walter's paper (*Psyche and Symbol*) we are presented with an illustration of the radical humanist perspective. Drawing upon the work of Christopher Lasch (*The Culture of Narcissism*) and other psychoanalysts, Walter argues that many characteristics of behavior in modern organizations symbolize a neurotic organizational personality. He discusses the symbolic manifestations of narcissism in organizations, and the need for researchers to trace the unconscious roots which "trap" behavior in unresolved processes of the psyche.

The paper by Abravanel (*Mediatory Myths in the Service of Organizational Ideology*) provides us with a view of symbolism consistent with the radical structuralist perspective. He focuses on ideology as an organizational resource which may be used and manipulated for various organizational purposes. He discusses the role of myths in resolving organizational contradictions, in particular, between what an ideology prescribes and what organizational members must do to accomplish organizational tasks.

PSYCHE AND SYMBOL

Gordon A. Walter

Humanists take the nature of man as the cornerstone of organizing and assert that the best organization is that which allows the most for the individual. When explaining his accomplishments, Albert Einstein asserted another humanistic notion, "For the most part, I did what my inner nature demanded of me." His statement puts in perspective the fact that organizational factors such as "motivation" cannot create greatness. Psychoanalytic theory offers one perspective within the humanistic paradigm and one from which a startling view of modern organizations and the individuals who populate them is beginning to be articulated. Increasingly the psychoanalytic critique emphasizes the high propensity of modern organization inhabitants to suffer from a particular type of fixation or arrested development. They term this character problem "secondary narcissism" and this paper considers narcissism in relation to symbolism in organizations.

The humanist critique of modern society and organizations, emphasizes the inherent limits of the attainment of full personhood. Symbols play a major role in this influence process. Consider, for example, the history of structures which raise the eye toward the sky. Early were Mesopotamian temples with ziggurates of ascending stairs, symbolizing the wisdom of the priests who governed. Egyptian pyramids symbolized permanence and the nobility of upward striving on a barren desert landscape. Obelisks of pronouncements and principles, pillars in temples built on hilltops (e.g., the Parthenon) are other ancient examples. More recently Gothic Cathedrals whose interiors and exteriors communicate the grandure of God's kingdom are surrounded by spires which point upward to even greater and more incomprehensible grandure. The symbolic meaning in such structures has changed, but the profundity of their skyward pointing character remains. Today's equivalent is the "city scape", with its sky-scraper business towers, but a different message is carried with these signs. These communicate the smoothness and elegance of SUCCESS through their gleaming metal and glass exteriors. Even more immediately, these buildings communicate the viability of basking in the temporal glory of being *looked at;* being seen, being visible, being *somebody*. This is the symbolism of narcissism (Lasch, 1978), and psychoanalysts note that not only were the 70's the "me decade" but we are living in a virtual Age of Narcissism. Our organizations are both the producers and the product of this era.

Modern materialistic organizations and society eschew the "naive" idealism of the past. Paradoxically while their claim is of pragmatism and realism the symbolism of those very organizations is of a scale which dwarfs the individual. By contrast in, say, Greek mythology symbolism is of explicit human scale (Graves, 1960; Campbell, 1972, 1976a,b,c). According to psychoanalytic thought, the symbolism of success provides a critical link between modern materialistic organization and the narcissism of this era.

THE SYMBOLISM OF SUCCESS

As noted in the first chapter of this volume, a symbol is the combination of a sign with the meaning that is attached to the sign. Modern bureaucracies are pervasively peppered with symbols which hook into deep places of the psyche and thereby evoke, guide, and channel both the action of the psyche and its final nature. Three categories of signs from the world of work provide a point of departure. These are the exteriors of offices, the interior of offices, and the presentation of self within offices.

Modern office buildings now dominate most urban centers. Their volume, scale and height tend to define the skyline. They dwarf Gothic Cathedrals whose spires and gargoyles shrink into insignificance by comparison. They combine the solidity of Romanesque churches with the spiritual lightness of the Gothic in a new way. According to Barthes (1972), the smoothness and shinyness of flush-mounted glass and anodized metal exteriors, communicate an ethereal and eternal quality (e.g., Bauhaus School of Design). That such structures are also assertive and thus phallic in character is perhaps so obvious as to not require elaboration.

Interiors are more varied and complex. Entries are often grand, open and reminiscent of Greek temples whose columns were arranged to allow the gods to blow in and out unseen and unhampered. The eternal again is implied as is a high assessment of one's importance. The express elevators to the "higher" floors provide a "rush", as one observes the 'X' on the floor marker indicating that 2,000 or more souls are being left below during the momentary ascent. A graciously and perhaps even sumptuously decorated office reception of a company communicates oppulance and self-assurance. This is especially convenient for lawyers, financial consultants, and corporate headquarters officials who must deal with a vareity of others. It is assertive and emphasizes the natural advantages of home turf. So too does the presence of a comely lady receptionist. These individuals are clearly not of goddess stature but are reminiscent of the nymphs who served as handmaidens to mythological gods in a variety of ways. They also often provided aid and comfort to the troubled (e.g., the Sea Nymph who saved Odysseus from Neptune, and the daughters of the Evening Star who gave essential aid to Perseus in his efforts to decapitate the Medusa [Campbell 1972, 1976a,b]. Fine furniture plus tasteful and obviously expensive art add to the "perfection and completeness of the domain." Fourteen foot high ceilings, floor to ceiling doors and windows, plus marble walls add to the success/ competence motife. Looking out over the mass of the city from this aerie emphasizes not only superiority, assertion and dominance over those beneath, but also encourages a rich awareness that "all those people down there" can also gaze up and see *you!* Visibility equals assertion and thus relates closely to the issue of narcissism. Finally, it is obvious that size of office, quality of furnishings, number of windows, quality of view and a corner location also communicate relative status. The important point, however, is that not only is status communicated via these signs but so to are ideals.

The presentation of self has fascinated social scientists and hucksters for decades (e.g., Goffman, 1959; Malloy & Humber, 1975). The exclusivity of one's "private" secretary, the brought coffee, the perfectly washed and pressed "fresh" shirt, the elegantly tailored suit (also perfectly pressed), and the highly impractical thin-soled shoes all say something. For example, an expensive and "tasteful" suit is quietly assertive and also communicates modesty while demonstrating self-restraint and a commitment to the status quo. By contrast a sport coat of bright colors or a loud pattern can symbolize unbridaled self-assertion, a willingness to engage another at a moment's notice, or a capacity for outright aggression and rebellion. The message? The first says, "We don't make mistakes." The second says, "You had better not."

Different subcultures have different templates for symbol building and interpretation. Thus for the loud sports coat, some might call the individual adolescent, while others might use adjectives like honest, brave, and open. Academic institutions, with their anti-materialistic myth, use dress as well. The shabby tweed jacket and baggy trouser syndrome in England, for example, has generated a strategy of dress captured by the following tongue-in-cheek advice to assistant professors. "Go out to the Salvation Army or Goodwill and buy the oldest tweed jacket you can find, preferably a few sizes too small. Then take 10 kilograms of stones and place them in the pockets. Then, hang the jacket out in the rain for one week." Lack of concern for dress signals a different symbol system but it is interesting to contemplate how much effort might go into appearing to invest no effort into one's outward appearance.

IMPLICATIONS FOR HUMAN BEHAVIOR

Success has been important in all eras, yet the symbolism of success is particularly pervasive today and the definition of the ultimate form of that success is, generally, more materialistic than ever before. People are bombarded by highly tangible (materialistic) signs, symbolizing the proper direction for life. According to humanists, success has shifted from an inward to an outward experience and, in fact, from existence to spectacle.

Spectacle, according to the modern existentialist Roland Barthes, (1972) involves overt signs which capture and communicate archtypical arrangements and thus constitute living symbolism. For wrestling, the public "abandons itself to the primary virtue of spectacle; which is to abolish all motives and all consequences: what matters is *not* what it *thinks but* what it *sees*." (Emphasis added, Barthes, 1972, p. 15). The spectacle of wrestling illustrates how pure gesture can capture the universal human experiences of, in this case, suffering, defeat and the hunger for justice. Brilliant lighting, without shadow, creates emotion without reserve and the observer gets the pure image of passion rather than passion itself. Wrestling is not a sport but a source of emotion. Thus when a wrestler is down he is exaggeratedly down "so that he completely fills the eyes of the spectators with the intolerable spectacle of his powerlessness" (Barthes, 1972, p. 17). Grandeloquence of gesture in wrestling, as with primitive masks in ancient theater, provides signs of absolute clarity and thus allows broad emotional resonance.

Similarly, in the world of business organizations, numerous unambiguous signs symbolize the gratifications of success such as the temporal gratifications of power, assertion, and pleasure. They also include the more ephemeral, eternal, and spiritual gratifications of a higher, more significant, more meaningful and lasting existence. In short, modern bureaucratic success-symbol systems communicate a rich and pervasive modern mythology of materialism. Those who most fully accept this new mythology tend to describe themselves as "realists" and "economic pragmatists", but they are far less self-defining than they think. They are the product of an effective influence system which is implicit in our advanced, post-industrial, affluent society. Further, in addition to influencing values, the symbolism of success also plays a fundamental role in character formation.

One perspective on character formation comes from psychotherapists who tend to be humanistic because of self selection and the values of the profession. Their symbolism is a living one, since daily they see enormous evidence that the gratifications promised by the Materialistic Myth seldom yield the state of happiness and peace-of-mind implied or assumed. In today's upper classes, pleasure is high, self-importance is high, and possession of the trappings of success is high, yet personal problems abound. Bob Slocum of Joseph Heller's *Something Happened* is illustrative of the consequences of the total "buy in" to the myth of materialism. Bob is a successful insurance executive with a Connecticut suburban estate and, paradoxically, a near *panic* level of continuous *depression*. The "something that happened" over the period of his professional life was the suffocation the inner self or to be more psychoanalytically precise, of *the self*.

The symbolism of success does not cause the problems of today's Bob Slocum's and his many corporate brethren but, according to psychoanalytic theory and practice, this symbolism influences the maintenance of these disorders and their associated misery. Lasch (1978) explains the phenomenon in his book *The Culture of Narcissism* as one in which individuals, fixated by early separation trauma, (a) are driven by unrealistic images of perfection (archaic superego) and (b) adopt grandiose patterns of behavior to impress and manipulate others. In Freud's time the chief pathologies were hysteria and obsessional neurosis but in our time it is the "borderline" personality and these pathologies express, in exaggerated form, the underlying character structure of the era (Lasch, 1978, p. 87). Since World War II the trend in psychopathology has been toward narcissism, in which infantile impulses are characterized by stimulation and perversion rather than the suppression of Freud's era.

. . . These patients suffer from pervasive feelings of emptiness and a deep disturbance of self-esteem. For all his inner suffering, the narcissist has many traits that

make for success in bureaucratic institutions, which put a premium on the manipulation of interpersonal relations, discourage the formation of deep personal at-
tachments, and at the same time provide the narcissist with the approval he needs in
order to validate his self-esteem (Lasch, 1978, p. 91).

Thus, the symbolism of modern organizations appears to contribute
to the culture of narcissim by rewarding and even requiring narcissistic
behavior. It thereby limits the development of many individuals and
reduces the chances of attaining an integrated and balanced self. According to the thinking of humanists, life or reality should challenge
individuals to overcome fragmented and fixated portions of the personality. But in this era no such healthy discipline is exacted. With all the
complaining about shortages and inflation, it may be that the central
problem for individuals is actually affluence and the related absence of
real fundamental challenge. To see the manner in which symbolism
affects the individual, a deeper treatment of narcissism is now needed.

NARCISSISM

Narcissism is a clinical term which implies more than self-absorption and
less than self-love, in contrast to its colloquial usage. The leading psychoanalytic theorist, Heinze Kohut (1971, pp. 26–27) discusses the concept
in its modern significance as follows:

> The equilibrium of primary narcissism is disturbed by the unavoidable shortcom-
> ings of maternal care, but the child replaces the previous perfection (a) by establish-
> ing a grandiose and exhibitionistic image of the self: *the Grandiose self;* and (b) by
> giving over the previous perfection to an admired, omnipotent (transitional) self-
> object: *the idealized parent imago* (p. 26–27).

This is a highly technical statement which may at first seem to obscure
our consideration of symbolism but remember that symbolism is heavily
defined in the depths of the observer. All children experience primary
narcissism or as one humourist metaphorically put it, "Every puppy
thinks it's the center of the universe." Rage is experienced at the breaking of the omnipotent illusion of the mothers' relation to the child and
the disappointment can drive efforts to re-create the wished for love
experience. Secondary narcissism, then, is the result of attempting to
reverse the disappointment and frustration of separation and involves
either creating a tyranical idealized self-image or the incorporation of
tyranical idealized parent image for the self. Further "Love rejected
turns back to the self as hatred" (Lasch, 1978, p. 78).

Thus the narcissism treated here is a response constellation that serves as a defense against aggressive impulses rather than self-love, even though the issue is closely related to the original self-love from which the title derives. The defence can either be experienced as savage self-criticism or as grandiose striving. The profound significance of this phenomenon for this paper and its relevance to the study of organization is that success symbolism *buttresses* the demanding superego, *stimulates* grandiose strivings, and *legitimates* the underlying fixation. The issue of grandiosity is key here because grandiosity involves fantasies of wealth, beauty and omnipotence which displace underlying aggresive feelings of rage or envy owing to separation from the mother. Thus the grandiose images of a modern city center can find profoundly deep resonances with narcissistic aspects of the individual.

Affluence, hyperstimulation and narcissism in one's parents create conditions sponsoring greater narcissism in subsequent generations. The absence of the father in serving as an ego ideal or an indulgent, shallow or unpredictable mother can contribute to narcissism. It is self evident that consuming professions or careers reduce the availability of fathers. In such families the mother must compensate for the desertion, and the child becomes even more dependent on the mother. In these it is less likely that the superego will develop and merge properly with the ego. The result is an "archaic" and unrestrained ego, and hence savage self-criticism. The resulting alliance between the superego and the id (Thanatos) creates what Freud envisioned as a "pure culture of the death instinct" because the rage which is repressed by the ego is ultimately inculcated in the superego.

Divorce and unstable marriages exacerbate all these dynamics and the trend over the last 100 years has been of increased atomization of the family. Thus narcissism is on the rise. Sport and entertainment have alligned themselves to the realities of a narcissistic age and have concomitantly contributed to its development. Sport has become a spectacle and is manipulated and loaded with added meanings such as national honor and million dollar bonus babys. The result, according to Lasch, is to remove the freedom element from sports. In this way, the "self-imposed challenge" aspect is lost, and thus, so too is escape or simple fun. It is the uselessness of a game that makes it game, but the trend is toward spectacle rather than involvement.

Simultaneously, entertainment is increasingly directed at titilating (activating) instincts rather than satisfying them. The result is a populace with desire but without the habit of acting on that desire. Wishers rather than takers. Saul Bellow's hero in *Henderson the Rain King* wanders the world, detached, primarily aware only of an inner craving voice gasping,

"I want, I want, I want". And here again is a recognizable quality of the modern narcissist.

The cumulative effect of such formative forces is a personality in which superego-ego-id conflicts are escalated and in which inner peace is unlikely. Simultaneously, because of the primitiveness of these aspects of the self (their uncivilized, unintegrated, or undeveloped quality) mere "self awareness" based self-help is unlikely to be effective because the conflicts tend to be repressed and thus out of consciousness. The consequence is a hyperactive flight from the deep to the superficial. Typical here is fascination with entertainment "personalities". Celebrity banalities become newsworthy only because of the source. Thus life is experienced as spectacle and in this way symbolism further dominates life. Individuals become increasingly responsive to external symbols rather than internal signals and images because the former are clear, unconflicted and sometimes hold a promise of fullment of inner cravings. Spectacle, however, creates distance or alienation between subject and object and thus removes the truly human element. Its appeal is the evoked intense response that allows action without responsibility. Spectacle fills the void in the shell of narcissism. For, in fact, the narcissistic personality is so focused on manipulating others and satisfying personal cravings for stimulation that interpersonal relations are devalued or, one might even say, impoverished.

THE TROUBLE WITH NARCISSISM

Contrary to the Greek myth of Narcissus and the colloquial stereotype of the narcissist, the fundamental problems of narcissism are not smugness and self-adulation to the exclusion of activities or other people which do not "mirror" the subject's beauties. Organization-related factors include misuse of power, depletion of work satisfaction, waste, and alienation. Strictly personal factors include a chronic unsuccessful search for happiness, inner-directed hostility and boredom. These issues are elaborated below.

Organizational Factors

The character of work and one's relation to it has changed dramatically in the last 100 years. With the rise of bureaucratic complexity and with increasingly ambiguous (not necessarily narrow) jobs there has been a loss of the tactile, palpable quality in work. One view emphasizes that people are less likely to transform matter into useful results as a result of effort and ingenuity (Lasch, 1978). The result is an abstract, subjective, and ultimately impersonal experience at work that leads to self protection, a fixation on comparisons with others, and on "winning" over others as the only practical yardstick for self-evaluation. This too is a subjective matter and thus symbolism enters as a powerful force in defining reality. Materialistic "symbolism of success" is particularly powerful in evoking the grandiosity of the narcissist and in giving form to the primitive and tyranical superego. Self protection can become obsessive and is pursued by withholding devotion to task accomplishment. In general, concentration of effort shifts from "task orientation and task mastery to control over other players' moves" (Szasz, 1961, p. 275).

Closely allied to this and sponsored by the simultaneously changing culture is a rising sense that *having* "it" is more important than *doing* "it". Being a somebody requires that success be ratified by publicity so that celebrity status can be attained. For this the surface dominates over the substance and image manipulation absorbs the energy of the ambitious narcissist. Of one famous narcissist its has been said that although he had a very interesting surface "he was surface clear through". Perversely, since image is transitory, fragile and ultimately seen to be hollow, the narcissist experiences high anxiety. The prototype of this genre is the Hollywood "personality" about which has been said that if one scratches the artificial tinsel on the outside one will find genuine tinsel on the inside. Perhaps more to the point, one finds a child on the inside who is unable to commit to others. As with Hollywood, the style consciousness, youth emphasis, and image orientation of today's "pop" culture yields unstable arrangements and fleeting satisfactions.

The exercise of power can now be related to these observations and some of the outcomes are surprising. McClelland (1978), discusses four types of individual power, each typified by an action modality, associated feelings, sources and objects of power and other critical descriptive terms. These are here labeled types 1 to 4 for simplicity. Type 1 power (support) is experienced as coming from outside one's self and correlates to Freudian oral fixations. Eat and drink are activities that *feel* powerful and the individual may think "It gives me power". The alcoholic or the tranquilizer addict, and the hysteric represent pathological manifestations here. Type 2 power (autonomy) relates to the Freudian anal period of development and in this mode the individual may say, "I make myself powerful". Simple healthy examples of this factor would be jogging and getting an education. At a pathological level, obsessive-compulsive neurosis is the observable consequence of fixation. Type 3 (assertion) corresponds to the Freudian phallic stage and the descriptive power experience here is, "I have impact on others". Physical and mental competition is the mode of experiencing this power. At a pathological level, criminal behavior results, and it is relevant that this phenomenon too is also on the rise in the age of narcissism. The Type 4 (togetherness, moralized action) relates to transcending fixations at earlier phases of the Freudian developmental hierarchy. Here power is experienced as, "It moves me to do my duty". Even, here, however, the action can be taken to pathological extremes such as when an individual believes he is, say, a new messiah. Level 4 power involves a rather self-detached experience since others are both the source and the object of power.

The narcissist, as the reader may have imputed, has not reached level 4. Level 3 power is dominant for the narcissist as is the concentration of cathexis in the genitals. The individual attempts a variety of maneuvers to have impact on others; from the "commercialized friendship" of Dale Carnegie, to "winning through intimidation". Assertiveness training or therapy tends to be directed at people who have not yet learned how to cope in the narcissistic culture and aspire to transcend their passivity, self-limitations, and isolation (level 1 and level 2 respectively) and thereby to enter the game. Lasch argues a profound point here. It is that such "personal development" experiences exploit the individual's anxiety and advance the belief that success depends on psychological manipulation and exploitation rather than, say, task accomplishment. In modern organizations where complexity and ambiguity make evaluation of task accomplishment particularly difficult to measure, the emphasis turns to intensified, yet sophisticated identifying and cultivating of mentors, protegies, coalition partners, and capacities to cultivate more (see, for example, Pfeffer, 1981).

> In earlier times, the self-made man took pride in his judgment of character and probity; today he anxiously scans the faces of his fellows not so as to evaluate their credit but in order to guage their susceptibility to his own blandishments. He practices the classic arts of seduction and with the same indifference to moral niceties, hoping to win your heart while picking your pocket. The *happy hooker* stands in place of *Horatio Alger* as the prototype of personal success (emphasis added, Lasch, 1978, p. 107).

Organizational participants get trapped in a narcissistic power dynamic that is protected by the myth of the role of competition in the enterprise and in capitalism, and are thus driven by the symbolism of success.

> In Joseph Heller's novel *Something Happened,* the protagonist's boss makes it clear that he wants from his subordinates not 'good work' but 'spastic colitis and nervous exhaustion.' 'God dammit, I want the people working for me to be worse off than I am, not better. That's the reason I pay you so well. I want to see you right on the verge. I want it right out in the open. I want to be able to hear it in a stuttering,

flustered, tongue-tied voice. . . Don't trust me. I don't trust flattery, loyalty, and
sociability. I don't trust deference, respect, and cooperation. I trust fear (Lasch,
1978, p. 121).

The "loyalty ethic" has declined in American business because (among
other reasons) loyalty can be too easily simulated or feigned by those
most desirous of winning.

The image presented by modern novelists, playrights, and other critics in this age is that less and less is accomplished with more and more
effort. Effort is wastefully directed at the maintenance of hierarchical
relations and the only constant consequence for most participants in
organizations is anxiety. Sadly, this anxiety precipitates further "secondary narcissism" episodes in the individual and a self-perpetuating cycle is
created.

This entire process is sponsored and maintained by narcissistic illusion
(embers of grandiosity kept glowing by the winds of success symbolism)
and it is at this nexus that the various streams of thought in this paper
converge. Many individuals today accept and believe the manufactured
fantasies of total gratification. Even *Business Week* contributes to the success spectacle, as on its pages steely-eyed executives sit confidently behind enormous desks and stare aggressively yet contentedly at the reader. To summarize, anxiety leads to regression and regression leads to
grandiose hunger for a glorious illusion. The symbols of success fill the
need for illusion and exploit the susceptibility. A subsequent dependen-
cy relationship in the organization is created which in one way or another maintains and perpetuates the cycle.

Personal Factors

The narcissist not only tends to strive grandiosely, but also creates and
perpetuates (enacts) a world in which the anxiety which fuels the strivings, ties him or her to his or her own slavish goals. The only obvious
escape is into romantic illusions, but these compound the problem and
the

disparity between romance and reality, the world of the beautiful people and the
workaday world, gives rise to an ironic detachment that dulls pain but also cripples
the will to change social conditions, to make even modest improvements in work and
play and to restore meaning and dignity to everyday life (Lasch, 1978, p. 174).

The whimsical yet nihilistic humor of Woody Allen as he laughs at
Woody Allen exemplifies this ironic self detachment. He ridicules his

own imagining that he can be a Bogart or other romantic figure. Such detachment differs greatly from the "passionate detachment" to which George Santyana referred as a goal for self-management. In passionate detachment there is no element of self-directed sadism. Passionate detachment implies high awareness of desires and values (or, more deeply, id and superego) and an intense commitment to these things. It also requires high ego strength. The latter allows creative and constructive integration and elaboration of the self without inward directed hostility. Whether or not such hostility is perceived to be humorous is extraneous, as even Allen might admit if his most recent movies are an indication.

When not consumed in fantasy, auto-eroticism, or anxiety; the narcissist faces the ultimate psychological cost, boredom. The lack of meaning in work, the lack of commitment to principles and people leave everything other than "the game" blank and unstimulating. Bob Slocum in *Something Happened* is sufficiently successful that he can delegate the routine and trivial and keep the creative portions of the work for himself. Even with these advantages and many opportunities for escaping, boredom still stalks him. Kierkegaard (1922) captures the "bleakscape" thusly,

> The gods were bored, and so they created man. Adam was bored because he was alone, and so Eve was created. Thus boredom entered the world, and increased in proportion to the increase in population. Adam was bored alone; then Adam and Eve were bored together; then Adam and Eve and Cain and Abel were bored *en famille;* then the population of the world increased, and the peoples were bored *en masse.* To divert themselves they conceived the idea of constructing a tower high enough to reach the heavens. This idea is itself as boring as the tower was high, and constitutes a terrible proof of how boredom gained upper hand. . . (Kierkegaard, 1946, pp. 22–23).

A fundamental problem, then, is the emptiness of experience in the absence of commitment to purpose and meaning, that is to the pivotal imagery of the superego. (Recall the watchwords of Type 4 power, "It moves me to do my duty.") This emptiness and the vague dissatisfaction noted earlier are hallmarks of the modern condition and plays such as *Waiting for Godot* disturbingly show the impact on the individual. In that treatment, Beckett's two characters endlessly consider doing something "real" but, dependently, wait to be told what that real thing might be. In the vacuum they casually consider hanging themselves because it might cause an erection. Not a pretty picture of narcissism but not as unrealistic as it first appears. In the absence of hyperactivity, boredom and emptiness confront the hungry grandiose self.

THE ALTERNATIVE

Mental health is relatively simple to articulate. Of pivotal significance is the adoption or development of a sense of meaning in life which is congruent with primitive superego imagery and with the requirements of reality. Also important is the integration, through the ego, of id or libido with the rest of the personality so that the individuals' desires and impulses are not out of control and do not generate cycles of punishment, guilt, or shame. The ego is governed by the reality principle—that acts have consequences. In Eric Fromm's (1947, 1955) view, this state is attained when one turns away from one's animal nature and asserts one's human nature. Here one seeks relatedness to others, transcendence of dependencies, a clear identity, and a frame of reference by which to exist with the self and deal with the world. The "Receptive" orientation of the passive oral person is discarded. The "Hoarding" of the anal person is left behind. The "Exploitation" (aggression) and "Marketing" (seduction) orientation of the narcissist is transcended and a "Productive" approach to one's self and others is cultivated. Here modesty, adaptability, trust, activeness, pride (not glory), confidence, practicality, patience, loyalty, flexibility, and open mindedness are emphasized.

What is needed is letting go of phallic fantasies and embracing some meaningful goal. Perversly, the costs of narcissism—vague dissatisfaction, free floating anxiety, boredom, depression—actually discourage this. To allow change the narcissist needs experiences which are optimally disillusioning, but it is just here that modern corporate paternalism, societal affluence, and the welfare state insulate the individual. The individual may fear punishment from the restrained hierarchy but this confirms rather than disconfirms a fixation on "looking out for #1." When the bad news (reality) is finally delivered, half of the individual's career may have past and it may seem too late to adjust constructively. Bitterness, withdrawal, resignation, and regression may result, rather than progress to the next "higher" level. Hence one sees fixation or self protection rather than task accomplishment.

The individual's higher level of functioning would be one in which the individual makes decisions in life which contribute to developing and maintaining an integrated personality (e.g., Binswanger, 1963). In this state, according to existential psychologists, the individual is continuously in touch with being in the world (biological experience or *Umwelt*), being with others (social experience or *Mitwelt*), and being one's self (personal experience or *Eigenwelt*). Clearly this is not a state attained by the narcissist, for whom reality beyond the self and its incessant hungers appears insignificant. Others are important in the narcissist's struggles for self-definition and self-validation but intimacy is foreign and tends to be avoided. Paradoxically, in the inner reaches of the narcissist exists the overarching storm of "self-against-self".

As a step toward concluding this paper, consider the role of the grand "symbolism of success" in this society, the city scape. Impervious and unalterable by a single individual, the superego symbolism of modern society is uncompromising. The standards so massive that few can possibly actually win and thus most must lose. Having lost, they have no one to blame but themselves. Success options look solid and substantial but subsequent narcissistic striving is existentially tantamount to "walking up the down escalator." The narcissist never really gets anywhere. A New Yorker cartoon shows two executives in first class air travel looking out and down. One says to the other "you know, when you stop to think about it, we only own a small percentage of it."

A comparison with the Greeks is worthwhile as this paper closes. For the Greeks the ideal city had a population of 5,000 to 6,000. Games were a center of community activity and were engaged in (*sans* clothing) for exercise, simple fun, and the development of a "properly" proportioned body. They were humanists, at least with regard to fellow citizens in a given city. Their heroes and their myths had a human scale in contrast to the scale of modern materialistic symbolism as discussed above. Even the great hero Odysseus was humanly embraceable. In this myth, Odysseus and his men wander at the hand of fate for 20 years following the Trojan wars and only Odysseus survives and makes his way home. In disguise, he participates in a contest among a score of unwelcome wooers for the right to marry his wife, Penelope. For years the wooers have abused his son, squandered his estate, and violated his wife. She had attempted to avoid their overtures by weaving a funeral shawl for her father-in-law all day and unravelling it during the night. Only Odysseus passes the test of marriage by stringing his prodigeous bow and shooting an arrow through the holes in twelve axe handles. Then, with the aid of his son and the only two remaining loyal servants from his household, he fights the suitors to the death. He survives and triumphs and consequently regains his home and the respect of his fellow citizens of Ithaca. Of utmost importance, however, is that the hero's reward is "a loyal son and a constant wife."

How different, indeed, from today's enormous cities with mass society, mass media, mass transit, mass production, mass education, and so forth. The human scale is hardly noticeable in urban centers where enormous office towers congregate. Odysseus is merely quaint in contrast to today's corporate world 'hero' who has a 900 square foot, 57th floor, corner office. Appointments include floor to ceiling glass, 14 foot high doors, marble walls, original designer furniture and original art. Too good for Odysseus, but perhaps, just right for you and me?

REFERENCES

Barthes, R. *Mythologies*. New York: Hill & Wang, 1972.

Beckett, S. *Waiting for Godot*. New York: Grove, 1954.

Beldoch, M. The therapist as narcissist. *Sal Magundi*, 1972, *20*, 136–138.

Bellow, S. *Henderson the rain king*. New York: Penguin, 1976.

Binswanger, L. *Being-in-the-world: Selected papers of Ludwig Binswanger*. New York: Basic Books, 1963.

Campbell, J. *Myths to live by*. New York: Bantam, 1972.

Campbell, J. *The masks of God: Oriental mythology*. New York: Penguin, 1976. (a)

Campbell, J. *The masks of God: Occidental mythology*. New York: Penguin, 1976. (b)

Campbell, J. *The masks of God: Creative mythology*. New York: Penguin, 1976. (c)

Fromm, E. *Man for himself*. New York: Holt Rinehart & Winston, 1947.

Fromm, E. *The sane society*. New York: Rinehard, 1955.

Goffman, E. *The presentation of self in everyday life*. New York: Doubleday, 1959.

Graves, R. *The Greek myths* (Vol. 1). Middlesex: Penguin Books, 1960.

Graves, R. *The Greek myths* (Vol. 2). Middlesex: Penguin Books, 1960.

Heller, J. *Something happened*. New York: Knopf, 1974.

Jennings, E. *Race for the executive suite*. New York: McGraw-Hill, 1971.

Kierkegaard, S. *Fear and trembling and the sickness unto death*. (W. Lavie, Trans.) Princeton: Princeton University Press, 1968.

Kohut, H. *The analysis of the self*. New York: International Universities Press, 1971.

Kovel, S. *A complete guide to therapy*. New York: Pantheon, 1976.

Lasch, C. *The culture of narcissism*. New York: Warner, 1979.

Lowenfield, A., & Lowenfield, Y. Our permissive society and the superego. *Psychoanalytic Quarterly*, 1970, *39*, 590–607.

Maccoby, M. *The gamesman: The new corporate leaders*. New York: Simon & Schuster, 1976.

Malloy, J. T., & Humber, T. *Dress for success*. New York: Peter H. Wyder Pub., 1975.

McClelland, D. *Power: The inner experience*. New York: Wiley/Halsted Press, 1975.

Moore, E. Toward a clarification of the concept of narcissism. *Psychoanalytic Study of the Child*, 1975, *30*.

Pfeffer, J. *Power in organizations*. Marshfield, Mass.: Pitman, 1981.

Szasz, S. *The myth of mental illness*. New York: Harper Row, 1961.

MEDIATORY MYTHS IN THE SERVICE OF ORGANIZATIONAL IDEOLOGY

Harry Abravanel

This paper examines the work of myth in the mediation of contradictions between components of organizational ideology. Two central ideas are developed. First, that contradictions are inherent in the nature of ideological belief systems. Second, that the only effective mechanism that can bridge such contradictions is *faith* in a suitable organizational myth. Organizational processes are observed and 'interpreted' within a framework that incorporates the ideological and mythical beliefs of dominant interests, that is, a control perspective.

The inclusion of ideological and mythical beliefs in any theory of organizations is essential. Ideology develops as an important organizational resource, and is used, manipulated, exalted and undermined for numerous purposes. Ideological considerations are part of management practices and, more generally, organizational methods. Patterns, decisions and actions cannot be reduced simply to technical arguments about priorities, for the latter embody values, that is, they are ideologically determined.

This paper addresses the above issues in three stages. In the first part of the paper ideology is defined in terms of its components and their interrelationships. Next, the work of myth in the mediation of contradictions is described. Finally, the concepts developed are exemplified in several cases.

THE ORGANIZATION OF IDEOLOGY

Definition of Organizational Ideology

Although discourse on ideology has a long history, discourse on organizational ideology does not. Common to discourse on both ideology and organizational ideology is agreement on, first, a system of interconnected beliefs and second, a set of action implications or consequences.

Berger and Luckmann describe ideology as 'a particular definition of reality that comes to be attached to an organization or group' (1966, p. 123), not to an individual, who exhibits ideology only in common with others in an organization or group. Following Wilson we can adopt the following broad definition of ideology:

> a set of beliefs about the social world and how it operates, containing statements about the rightness of certain social arrangements and what actions would be undertaken in the light of those statements. An ideology is both a cognitive map of sets of expectations and a scale of values in which standards and imperatives are proclaimed. Ideology thus serves both as a clue to understanding and as a guide to action, developing in the mind of its adherents an image of the process by which desired changes can best be achieved (Wilson, 1973, pp. 91–92).

Schurmann (1968) points out that most organizations cannot rely on an ambiguous underlying belief system because they must make directives and take purposive action. He adds that organizational ideology is the particular way of thinking characteristic of an organization, which serves the interests of those who are influential within the organization.

For our purposes, then, *Organizational ideology* can be defined as a set of fundamental ideas and operative consequences linked together into a dominant belief system often producing contradictions but serving to define and maintain the organization. The development of this definition, related concepts and their application is our prime concern, but before proceeding, four considerations need to be clarified: (1) domination and control, (2) what ideology is not, (3) the relationship between individual and organizational ideology, and (4) the source of ideological validity.

1. Domination and control. When we speak of domination, we ask whose purposes or interests are being served, who defines the organization. Collectivities articulate values, purposes and interests in an ideology and through action. Inevitably, if a collectivity is to survive it must adopt an organizational form. For instance, a secret society must have at least some rudimentary organizational characteristics. Even an anarchist collectivity must evolve temporary divisions of labour, and temporary roles, rules and relations to be managed. Such organizational actions not only have an affect on the internal distribution of influence but also have a bearing on organizational ideology.

In organizations distinct constituencies make competing claims. For example, management may articulate purposes and objectives relating to profit and market share, while labour unions may articulate competing interests in terms of the quality of working life. The recognition of legitimate constituencies and their interdependence often results in official rhetoric that includes the interests of all significant partners, but not always, since the relative influence of various constituencies may shift. That is, organizational ideology tacitly refers to the dominant group or groups, those interests that are in control. Any investigation of organizational ideology must recognize the likely coexistence of different internal constituencies whose definitions of reality can change significantly due to internal shifts in the balance of power or discontinuities.

2.   *What ideology is not.*   How do we distinguish ideological belief systems from other kinds of belief systems? First, action that is completely without any pattern is *non-ideological*. Next, it is possible (and common) for individuals and groups of individuals to engage in social action that is patterned or rule-guided without being ideological. They are merely practiced beliefs that are not self-consciously rationalized, although they can form a role or set of roles contributing significantly to social cohesion. Without self-conscious rational argument, practiced beliefs are merely *pre-ideological* belief systems that can sometimes be transformed into the 'ideological' (Seliger, 1976, p. 97).

Meta-ideologies, including abstract social and analytical philosophic belief systems, do not usually serve action purposes directly and hence are also outside our purview. These include 'ultimate considerations' and abstract notions like the greater good associated with justice, freedom, and progress, common to most ideologies. Rather, these notions are generally part of the larger culture. Their significance is problematic to specific situations (Seliger, 1976, p. 112).

Ideology is the intermediary required to apply or enact universally valid ideals at specific times and places. Ideology often finds justification in the *meta-ideological*. The history of nations and organizations is replete with examples of ideologies co-opting philosophies that can serve the action purposes at hand. For example, the revolutionary Marx was in-

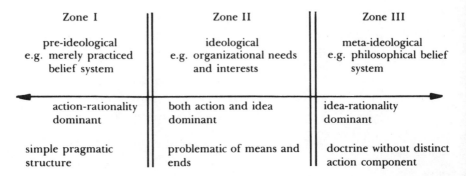

Figure 1.   Distinction between the ideological *vs* the non-ideological.

terested in the action import of Hegel's Phenomenology while Hitler and the Nazi Movement invoked Nietzche in their cause.

The final belief system that should be distinguished is the *quasi-ideological*. It involves the production of responsible ideology, for example, the application of the scientific method. Procedure within a quasi-ideological system such as the scientific method requires that tested, testable and untestable empirical claims be objectively distinguished, that the role of any value judgments be identified, and that there exist some external standards of methodological rigour.

Figure 1 may be helpful in distinguishing the purely ideological from other belief systems. The three zones are distinguished from one another by the action-idea continuum. Each zone is separated by a double line which delineates an area that defines an important job for ideological leadership. The purely ideological (Zone II) seeks legitimation by co-opting the pre-ideological (Zone I) and/or the meta-ideological (Zone III). Successful leadership uses co-optation to increase legitimation for purposes of increasing membership, commitment or confidence in the dominant ideology.

3. *Individual and organizational ideology.*   What is the relationship between individual beliefs and ideology? Ideology is a response to the need to take justifiable, legitimate action. It is a consequence of dialectical tension between what is desired and what is available, and a response to individual and collective needs for meaning, congruency, truth, security and order. It helps make sense of reality for the individual. For example 'both the struggling small businessman rehearsing his boundless confidence in the inevitable justness of the American system and the neglected artist attributing his failure to his maintenance of decent standards in a Philistine world are able, by such means, to get on with their work' (Geertz, 1964, p. 55). Ideology, in this case, bridges the gap between the ideal and the real. From this perspective ideology serves and preserves individual role performance.

The beliefs of an individual and the beliefs of the group or organization are different. The latter beliefs are displayed only intermittently, that is, only when individuals adopt certain attitudes and engage in certain actions as members of a group or organization. Nonetheless, individual beliefs may be related to and affected by group beliefs. A leader or leadership cadre may claim individuals as belonging to a constituency though they may have widely varying beliefs. Union leaders, management executives, and tribal leaders, for example, can be spokesmen for an ideology which makes specific claims, but it cannot be assumed that all individual members of their constituency share the same ideology. The extent of similarity or difference depends on diverse factors occuring over time and according to location.

Support for any existing organization can take widely varied forms over time. Leadership must legitimate either the status quo ideology, or change, when it is required. However, any re-interpretation of the past must normally support actual outcomes as part of the acceptable definition of reality. Ideology translates official organizational priorities into the sensible, appropriate, and necessary. In short, the argument is that if one sells the ideology, "proper" commitment will follow. There can be no effective organization without justification and legitimation of ideology, nor the possibility of "belonging" to the internal organizational culture. Active membership and effective participation in modern organizations require a "putting-on" or "wearing" of the accepted ideology (or a competing ideology where one coexists). In an important sense, "membership" requires that participants allow a given ideology to dominate their definition of reality in their official roles, and if they are ambitious, in their unofficial roles as well. In order to be upwardly career mobile, it is helpful to become a purveyor of the dominant ideology and to accept one's incumbent obligations.

4. Ideological validation. Ideology, though not directly observable, is a construct that requires empirical validation of it is to be taken seriously. The meanings given by actors to their world, the content and significance of what is known, and the character of the actor's way of reasoning are influenced by the actors' ideological affiliations. All ideological systems posit and assume values and commitments. As Max Weber suggested, action cannot be understood as simply an adjustment to external influences. Rather, action is motivated by values (Kalberg, 1980, p. 1170).

Validation of actions for the actor can only be maintained by his determination to act according to ideological commitments. The validity of an ideology is reinforced by the perceived internal consistency between its components and by the extent of the individual's motivation or need to be faithful to the tenets of the ideology. Similarly, organizations reinforce the validity of their actions by affirming enduring values and preferences, orchestrated within a coherent ideological belief system. Coherence is a quality that describes the fit between components of ideological systems. The components of ideology may now be identified.

Components of Ideology

Ideologies can be seen as having two components: structural components common to *all* ideologies, and legitimating components that vary according to need in different circumstances. Figure 2 depicts these universal-structural and contextual-legitmating components of ideological belief systems. The structural components define the situation and produce modes of action requiring legitimation via appeals to "logic", "emotion", or "myth" (the legitimating components).

All ideologies are composed of partisan statements which fall into one of the following structural components: Description, analysis, moral prescriptions, technical prescriptions, implements and rejections (Seliger, 1976, p. 102). Description of phenomena or "what one notices" is determined by direct and practical experience within a given social context. Analysis involves a diagnostic process that identifies what is wrong, inadequate or demanding, in a particular context. Moral prescriptions or "what should be done" present a value or moral judgment on the de-

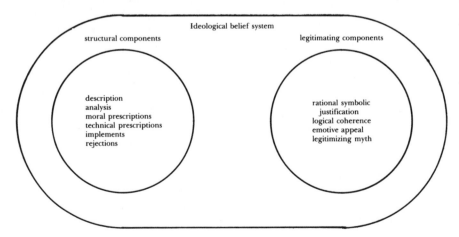

Figure 2.   Structural and legitimating components of ideological belief systems.

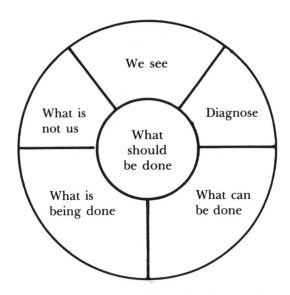

Figure 3.   The centrality of moral prescriptions.

scription and analysis which may run counter to and prevail over technical prescriptions. Technical prescriptions or "what can be done" are
more or less directly derived from the immediate perception of actual
possibilities. Organizations and their methods are implements or means
to accomplish "what is to be done". Finally, rejections or "what is not us"
include what is negated or opposed *vis-à-vis* divergent or counter
ideologies.

Briefly, the structural components on the left can be translated to read
as a story on the right side from top to bottom as follows:

description	"we see"
analysis	"diagnose"
moral prescription	"what should be done"
technical prescription	"what can be done"
implements	"what is being done"
rejections	"what is *not* us"

Obviously in real life these components are interdependent and too
complex to be formally determined. According to Seliger, and in agreement with the centrality of ethical values in Weber's sociology, moral
commitment must be accorded centrality. To illustrate this centrality,
and to affirm interdependence between components, we may arrange
the components in a circle around the element of moral prescription (see
figure 3).

CONTRADICTIONS BETWEEN FUNDAMENTAL AND OPERATIVE DIMENSIONS

When ideology is made to fulfill its functions, to guide concerted action and everyday decisions, it loses its moral purity in deference to practical considerations (such as expediency and compromise). No political party has ever been able to avoid committing itself to some lines of action which are at odds with the basic principles and goals of its ideology.

A conflict emerges not only between ideology and action but within the structure of ideology itself. Seliger has summarized this notion as follows: "Out of the interdependence of thought and action, action-oriented thought arises; and out of the permanence of the interaction, a tension evolves within action-oriented thought itself" (Seliger, 1976, p. 108). It may become impossible to invoke the logic of central moral principles in the official version of the ideology to account for the logic of actual policies that are carried out or proposed.

Thus ideology operates in two dimensions; it maintains allegiance to a purity of moral principles (the fundamental) and to practical and immediate considerations (the operative). Like the Church, ideology must be faithful both to its central beliefs and to its immediate concerns about survival. Ideology applied in action inevitably bifurcates into fundamental and operative concerns. The fundamental dimension includes princi-

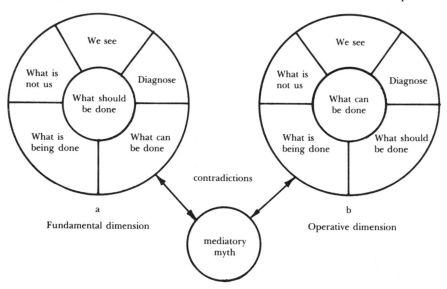

Figure 4. Bifurcation of ideology into the fundamental and operative dimensions.

ples that determine the final goals, the ends towards which the organization is working, the vision of what should be done. The operative dimension includes principles that underlie actual policies and support the means used to pursue immediate ends.

Fundamental and operative dimensions are based on somewhat different lines of ethical action. Fidelity to different concerns requires a shift in the relationship between structural components. In the operative dimension, norms of efficiency or expediency give technical prescriptions priority over moral prescriptions. What *can* be done is juxtaposed with what *should* be done.

Figure 4 indicates that, while the components of a and b are identical, a shift in the relationship between components has occurred.

Ideology is often treated as a unit whereas it is in fact a system whose components are asymmetrical and fluctuating. Principles contained within the fundamental dimension of any particular ideology may or may not be congruent with their corresponding counterparts in the operative dimension. Also, principles may not be congruent with one another in the same dimension. For example, interdependencies between fundamental ideology (FI) and operative ideology (OI) in a simple two principle (P) system can be schematically described as follows:

$$FI\ (P_1 \rightleftarrows P_2 \ldots\ldots\ldots\ldots\ldots\ldots\ldots\ldots\ldots\ldots\ldots P_n)$$
$$OI\ (P_1 \rightleftarrows P_2 \ldots\ldots\ldots\ldots\ldots\ldots\ldots\ldots\ldots\ldots\ldots P_m)$$

Contradictions and inconsistencies between principles are inevitable. The 'ideal' supportive matching of principles in organizations is both a rare and unstable condition. Principles collide and diverge within and between dimensions. Yet, there are legitimating forces and mechanisms that may restore coherence. Contradictions and inconsistencies which may give rise to demands for ideological change can be reduced by mythologizing of institutional rules (Meyer & Rowan, 1977), rational justifications (Anthony, 1977), legitimizing myths (Kamen, 1977), and mediating myths (Barthes, 1972).

Principles that are protected when challenged preserve ideological identity. Principles that change in deference to circumstance ensure survival. We may hypothesize that fundamental principles will not significantly change unless there is a major strategic shift.

An example. The question "what is to be done?" is invoked given an ideological commitment to a 'cause' that serves as a 'call to joint action.' In 1901, Lenin designated the answer to this question as the crucial determinant for success or failure in the socialist-revolutionary movement:

> It is not a matter of choosing the path we are to travel . . . but of the practical
> measures and the methods we must adopt on a certain path. What we have in mind
> is a system and a plan of practical activity.

For Lenin, the path was self-evident. Organization was to be instrumental but subservient to fundamental ideology. The practice of Bolshevism serves to exemplify the separation-in-action of the difference between the *operative ideology* and the *fundamental ideology*. What can and is to be done according to Lenin entails a response that may (some would say did) require a deviation from the fundamental and a priori principles of communism and socialism (a non-alienative way of life) toward statism. In this case operative concerns dominate fundamental concerns resulting in some rather glaring ideological contradictions.

Members, by virtue of their commitments to first principles often agree not to disagree about fundamental ideology. The fundamental ideology is a version of the moral order to which the organization is committed. It represents what remains to be done (the aspired or the ideal) yet it need not necessarily be grounded in the practical, but rather held as that against which the practical is still recognized as incomplete. Thus, an organization could be said to be what it does, and it does what remains to be done (Hegel, 1966, p. 794).

The distinction between the two dimensions could be represented by the following 'matched pairs'.

Fundamental ideology	*Operative ideology*
(what remains to be done)	(what has been done)
version of the moral order	version of organizational life
limitless	limited
aspired	achieved
ideal	practical
desirable	available
sacred	legitimate
mythical	official
an idea	its enactment
ends	means

Organizational success does not necessarily depend on a direct isomorphism between its fundamental and operative ideologies. Conflicts and inconsistencies are both inevitable and analytically unresolvable. The bifurcation of the two dimensions of ideology allows for different kinds of logic or thought processes to be applied and maintained at some distance from one another. The following four sources of potential inconsistency between fundamental and operative concerns have been identified by Meyer and Rowan (*AJS*, Vol. 83, 1977):

1. The domination by categorical rules derived from fundamental moral prescription over operative efficiency requirements (technical prescription).

   "A sick worker must be treated by a doctor using accepted medical procedures; whether the worker is treated effectively is less important. A bus company must service routes whether or not there are many passengers. A university must maintain appropriate departments independently of the departments' enrollments. Activity, that is, has ritual significance: it maintains appearances and validates an organization" (p. 355).

2. The problem of giving priority to long-term, delayed benefits as opposed to immediate, short-term operative considerations.

   "For example, hiring a Nobel Prize winner brings great ceremonial benefits to a university. The celebrated name can lead to research grants, brighter students, or reputational gains. But from the point of view of immediate outcomes, the expenditure lowers the university's ability to solve immediate logistical problems. Also, expensive technologies, which bring prestige to hospitals and business firms, may be simply excessive costs from the point of view of immediate production. Similarly, highly professionalized consultants who bring external blessings on an organization are often difficult to justify in terms of improved productivity, yet may be very important in maintaining internal and external legitimacy" (p. 355).

3. The difficulties of applying higher levels of generalization associated with the fundamental ideology to concerns that vary with specific, unstandardized and possibly unique circumstances encountered in the operative dimension.

   "A governmentally mandated curriculum may be inappropriate for the students at hand, a conventional medical treatment may make little sense given the characteristics of a patient, and federal safety inspectors may intolerably delay boundary-spanning exchanges" (p. 355).

4. The problem of inconsistency between ideologically pluralistic participant groups who may have jurisdictional rights.

   "Professionals are incorporated although they make overlapping jurisdictional claims. Programs are adopted which contend with each other for authority over a given domain. For instance, if one inquires who decides what curricula will be taught in schools, any number of parties from the various governments down to individual teachers may say that they decide" (p. 356).

Inconsistencies and contradictions cause great uncertainty. Meyer and Rowan propose and reject four partial solutions that are basically unsatisfactory, because they do not resolve the basic contradictions but instead camoflage them.

Partial solutions	*Problems*
1. *resistance to fundamental ideology* by reliance on efficiency and output measurement	difficulty legitimating efficiency and neglect of important resources and sources of stability.
2. *rigid conformity* to fundamental ideology by cutting off external relations	inability to manage boundary-spanning activities and to demonstrate that the fundamental ideology actually works.
3. *cynically acknowledge* inconsistencies.	denies validity of fundamental ideology and sabotages the legitimacy of the organization.
4. *promise a future* of fundamental and/or operative reforms.	makes the organization's current structure and ideology illegitimate.

Instead of relying on such partial solutions, Meyer and Rowan argue for the use of "decoupling" and of the "logic of confidence." Decoupling acts to create sub-ideologies which reduce the incidence or magnitude of internal contradiction and conflict. They facilitate not only specialization of technical work such as sales and production, but also the formation of distinct custom-tailored sub-ideologies that can co-exist within an organization. Meyer and Rowan suggest that "human relations", as a managerial technique, may bridge contradictions of the following nature:

> The organization cannot formally coordinate activities because its formal rules, if applied, would generate inconsistencies. Therefore individuals are left to work out technical interdependencies informally. The ability to coordinate things in violation of the rules—that is, to get along with other people—is highly valued (Meyer & Rowan, 1977, p. 358).

For example, salesmen, supervisors, and campus Presidents are often evaluated for their ability to get things done and may even be admired more for those rules not honoured in the breach than in their observance. The practice of confidence and good faith in the organization may be maintained by an avoidance of juxtaposing irreconcilable issues, by overlooking anomalies, and by the use of discretion in selecting and implementing courses of action about which there is substantial consensus (Meyer & Rowan, 1977, p. 358).

Both "decoupling" and the "logic of confidence" are, nonetheless, partial mechanisms. They contribute to getting on with pursuing objectives by buffering contradictions through collective concealment. Under the auspices of getting on with the work at hand, the use of the "logic of confidence" moves toward the pre-ideological. Pre-ideological beliefs merely generate feelings of security due to an absence of ideological contradiction. The very effectiveness of getting on with the work makes "good" sense and "good" practice. However, organizational faith in what is "good" requires ideological justification and support. In the case of individuals having complete confidence and good faith, ideology becomes virtually non-existent and, hence, unproblematic. As such, individuals with merely practiced beliefs have delegated ideological work elsewhere.

This kind of delegating is not possible for the collectivity or the organization. Organizations, unlike individuals, cannot afford the luxury of non-ideological practice. In order to survive, they must have a solid ideological base. The inevitable contradictions emerging between the fundamental and operative dimensions of the ideology are mediated by various myths. The use of mediatory myths is essential to our continued ability to carry out unproblematic action in a world of incongruity.

PROCESSING CONTRADICTIONS: THE WORK OF MEDIATORY MYTHS

A dialectical tension between fundamental and operative ideology, that is, the idea and its enactment, results in concrete and unique versions of organizational life. Ideology is continuously required and reinforced by organizations. Concrete versions of organizational life demand commitment, preference, and decisions that leave signs and traces (outcomes), which together constitute the organization. The organization can be viewed as a regenerative residue that is a result of a dialectical process, requiring legitimation and justification. Such articulation defines ideology as it unfolds in numerous ever-changing circumstances (Benson, 1977).

For many, the work of "ideological" membership in an organization is part of the mundane, the obvious and the assumed. Contradictions are not recognized. In such cases a myth that encompasses the fundamental and operative has effectively mediated contradictions. The individual then enacts merely practiced beliefs. He lives in a simple pre-ideological, myth-mediated and unproblematic world. On the other hand, members who recognize contradictions, who doubt or question their own faith in previous commitments, must carry on a recurring struggle. They may admire or despise the unquestioning believer, the unwavering faithful. Their own fate may be recurring doubt and questioning of the "essentials" of living. Few organizations can tolerate such uncertainty and non–commitment, and survive. The process by which organizations negotiate and reaffirm their version of the moral order as on-going practice demonstrates the 'ideological' work of membership.

Nonalienating organizational practice requires that a process of reconciliation take place between mundane work practice, the official rhetoric of the organization, and its vision of the future. This can be accomplished by permitting covert transcendence to become open and normative, and, as a result, not subversive, but rather constructive for purposes of the organization (Brown, 1978, p. 372). Most organizations do not ritualize overt emotional release (Japanese stress-release activities are an interesting exception). Often they encourage the creation and maintenance of mediating myths.

The mediating work of myths serves to reconcile the fundamental with the operative. The word myth designates a story about past, present, or future events. The truth of these events is asserted as dogma or taken for granted (Robinson, 1968, p. 294).

Myths are the most appropriate instruments for the inversion of ideological contradictions which man can internalize without upsetting organizational requirements. They help us to get on with our work. Roland Barthes (1973) powerfully describes the functions, the structure and the process whereby myths become tangible and effective instruments of ideological inversion.

> Myth does not deny things, . . . it gives them a clarity which is not that of an explanation, but that of a statement of fact . . . myth acts economically: it abolishes the complexity of human acts, it gives them the simplicity of essences. . . (p. 143).

Myth creation is universal. Barthes even suggests that to the pleasure-principle of Freudian man could be added the clarity-principle of mythological humanity, for whom clarity is euphoric (p. 143). Barthes describes the relation which ties the concept or form of the myth to its meaning as essentially a relation of deformation.

> . . . in the mythical signifier . . . its form is empty but present, its meaning absent but full. To wonder at this contradiction I must . . . pass from the state of reader to that of mythologist (p. 123–124).

Furthermore, man's relationship with myth is not based on truth, but rather on use. The apparent disconnectedness between a collection of ideas, events, or objects can be given meaning, if not coherence, by way of myth.

Myth can easily impose itself on objects, language, processes and situations. But what are the principal mechanisms by which myth gains ascendency? Barthes (1973) identifies several such mechanisms:

1. *The innoculation.* This consists of identifying the evil, pettiness, injustices, vexations and imperfections of the ideology and then at the last moment, saving the ideology by reference to a greater and more important good that is available in spite of, or thanks to the heavy costs of its own blemishes.

2. *The privation of history.* History disappears along with contradictions when things are prepared and displayed so that all we have to do is enjoy this beautiful object without wondering where it comes from.

3. *Identification.* Otherness or uniqueness is reduced to sameness (generalizing) or relegated to an ideal type, a pure object, a spectacle or a clown (stereotyping) which then no longer threatens the security of the home, the sacred or the desired.

4. *Tautology.* When at a loss for an explanation this device consists in defining like by like or in taking refuge in the magical, totalitarian response of authority: 'Because that's how it is,' or even better: 'Just because, that's all.'

5. *Neither-Norism.* This consists in stating two opposites and balancing the one by the other so as to reject them both, that is, one magically flees an intolerable reality by dismissing both alternatives— because it is embarassing to choose, and thus reinforcing the status quo ideology.

6. *The quantification of quality.* This is the mechanism through which myth 'understands' reality more efficiently by reducing quality to quantity, and then validating its truth by quantitative effects such as success, popularity, citations, etc.

7. *The statement of fact.* Here objects and relationships are already prepared as in maxims and proverbs which claim for example, universality or 'an unalterable hierarchy of the world' and thus refuse to provide any explanation.

These mechanisms sustain myths. They can be used under different circumstances and purposes, singularly or in combination. The mechanisms available to sustain a myth can be readily summoned by the faithful or their leaders. It is the individual who uses the above sustaining mechanisms. Individuals believe in 'truth' and subscribe to certain values. The organization as a unit seeks legitimacy and a reduction of contradictions. Organizations engage certain myths that come to be institutionalized. The institutionalized organizational myth can not be viewed strictly as an individual phenomenon. It is an important organizational phenomenon. In the following, case examples are used to describe a variety of organizational myths.

CASE EXAMPLES OF THE MEDIATORY WORK OF MYTH

Mediatory myths are ubiquitous. However, ubiquitousness does not necessarily imply that myths are easy to identify. Identification is sometimes self-evident, while sometimes it requires extensive detective work. Four examples are described below. First, the fundamental and operative ideologies are described; next, any contradictions or inconsistencies between them are identified; and finally, the *institutionalized myth* that effectively reduces or eliminates contradictions is located. The first three cases are simple; they relate to International Business Machines, the Federal Bureau of Investigation, and a large U.K. public sector organization. The final example is a more complex myth found in an intentional community; in it a series of myths are shown to be effectively interlocked.

International Business Machines

IBM under T. J. Watson Jr., wanted to change perceptions of the corporation's demands for conformity. In Martin and Power's article (this volume) we have a description of Watson's attempt to improve the functioning of the corporation and to leave his personal mark on its culture. He wished to encourage employee individuality, intellectual freedom and the rights to express disagreement. Thus in IBM's official rhetoric, freedom and independence of employees become part of the fundamental ideology. In Watson's favorite story concerning wild ducks, the moral was "You can make wild ducks tame, but you can never make tame ducks wild again". That is, IBM, like any business, needs its wild ducks and wouldn't try to tame them.

But operationally IBM carefully screened and trained its employees to conform to an all encompassing IBM view of the world that included dress codes, the use of alcohol, sexual relations, appearing busy, etc.

'Are wild ducks really wild?" asks Dick Ott (1979). In IBM freedom is the freedom to fly in a particular collective formation but not to select the migratory route. In other words, employees should not tamper with fundamental or operative ideology. According to IBM rationality, freedom and opportunity are inexorably linked with its brand of structure and conformity. You cannot have one without the other, that is, freedom comes with constraint. This constitutes the organizational myth at IBM. It is this myth which allows the employee to reconcile organizational rhetoric—"we do not try to tame wild ducks"—with concrete work requirements such as 'proper' dress and 'proper' behaviour.

Federal Bureau of Investigation

Edger Hoover spoke of the FBI as a "we organization", a team, a human organization, never far from the crossroads of America, either spiritually or physically. The FBI was identified with the higher values of America; law and order was opposed to change and chaos. Such an identification with higher American values was encouraged: law, order, stability and national security are necessary if America is to survive and thrive.

Nonetheless, the FBI was very concerned about its image and reputation. Hoover stated, "I tell my associates repeatedly that one man did not build the reputation of the FBI—but one man can pull it down" (Ott, 1979b, p. 20). Those who criticized the organization were punished, and driven away in disgrace. If they persisted in their criticism after they left they were considered "enemies". Furthermore as "enemies" they were equated with outsiders who wished to change, diminish or expose the Bureau. The FBI's enemies included members of the counter-culture of the 1960s, the Nazi Party, the Communist Party and, in addition to ex-employees, Soviet spies and certain social science professors. In terms of organizational rhetoric, "enemies" could include anyone who was designated as threatening to America and especially to the Bureau. How is it that a "we", human organization at the crossroads of America can exhibit excessive suspicion as well as mystification and secrecy in its operations? How is it that a "we" human organization uses power to disrupt the lives of individuals designated as "enemies"?

The answer is that this is not just any organization. The FBI is no less than the protector of the-American-way-of-life. The FBI equates itself with the American ideology. It is this identification with the greater good that transforms vigilence into license. Better to be too careful at the cost of harassing a few suspect individuals than to risk the security of all. Because it stands for America, the FBI is on the side of goodness and "right". It can do no major wrong. That was its myth under Hoover.

Public Sector Organizations in the U.K.

Silverman and Jones (1976) in a fascinating study of recruitment and socialization processes in a large public sector organization in the U.K. attempted to expose the system of intelligibility whereby employee recruitment decisions made sense to the members of the selection committee. The study contains a good example of one bureaucratic myth operating within a larger organization.

In the selection process described, the degree of acceptability is based on selection operations which attempt to match the qualities of the candidates with the qualities required in the available positions (Silverman & Jones, 1976, p. 47). It appears that the candidates' display of "acceptability" is the crucial element for selection. However, when the researchers played back an interview tape to committee members some time after the committee had conducted the selection interview, members predicted that the candidate involved was probably hired when, in fact, he was not. The selectors were surprised! The researchers concluded that the organizational work of recruitment could not be fully understood if viewed only as practice in-accord-with-a-rule based on the logical matching of 'acceptability' displayed with established requirements. If selection were merely rule-governed (the committee uses standard forms to evaluate candidates) selection outcomes would be replicable, at least by those performing the selection. Evidently this is not always the case. Hiring outcomes are obviously influenced by an additional, invisible factor: a myth held in common by those carrying out such organizational work.

Very simply, the myth is, "Because we are rational, acceptable members of the organization ourselves, *we know what we are doing* and we are best suited to perform important organizational work, in this case to select new acceptable members". Because the myth is sacred territory, it will be closely guarded and protected if challenged. But, as a rule, the myth is usually not challenged. The fact that the selection committee would not have duplicated *its own* decision some time later does not lead to the conclusion, "We might not know what we are doing". Instead, the incident is shrugged off; the selection work is viewed as demanding and challenging; the selectors enhance the importance of their work; the myth remains intact. All agree not to disagree and organizational work carries on.

An Intentional Community

This particular intentional community has about twenty members. The stated nature of the organization is three-dimensional. The community is alternative, therapeutic and spiritual. Consequently, three fundamental ideologies are apparent. The "alternative" ideology manifests itself primarily in the fact that the community has self-sufficiency goals which are taken very seriously by all members. On the operational level, however, the effort that goes into self-sufficiency activities is sporadic and amateurish, leaving no doubt that the goal is not likely to be achieved. The members are fully aware of this, yet show unwavering loyalty to the ideal of self-sufficiency as a 'good' alternative to the consumer life-style. The gap between the inadequate implementation of self-sufficiency plans and their expressed fundamental value is bridged by the following mediatory myth: "Self-sufficiency is important, but we must remember that we are here primarily to provide therapeutic services for both outsiders and ourselves. After all, we are a therapeutic community."

In its therpay-providing role, the community's fundamental ideology states that therapy and personal growth are important. Operationally, however, intense concentration on personal problems and introspective processes is seen as misguided self-indulgence and is, therefore, discouraged. This rather glaring contradiction is negotiated by means of another mediatory myth: "Personal growth is important, but, fortunately, the burden of accomplishing it doesnot rest on our shoulders alone. We have the faith necessary to relinguish personal control to a higher source. We must remember that spiritual growth is the ultimate aim. And since spiritual and personal growth are synonymous (a statement often made by members), if we strive towards a higher awareness we automatically attend to personal growth. After all, we are a spiritual community."

As a spiritual community, the fundamental ideology of the organization is trust in a guiding force beyond Man. Simply stated, this ideology says, "We put ourselves in God's hands. He is the doer." In daily practice, however, members take action to maintain and protect their life-style. They even choose courses of action which contradict their trust in a benevolent Protector. For example, a decision was made to invest in insurance because simple faith could not be relied upon to prevent all accidents. Obviously, operationally Man is the doer.

This conflict between fundamental tenets and enactment require-ments is bridged by the following mediatory myth: "When we act on our own behalf, we do so as God's helpers, remaining always attentive to His guidance. He is the primal doer. But we can trust ourselves to deal appropriately with mundane matters without losing ourselves in the mundane because, after all, we are different. That is why we came to-gether to build this alternative community."

And so we come a full circle, the contradictions in each aspect of organizational life being negotiated by a myth which owes its effective-ness to presenting the organization in one of its other two aspects.

CONCLUSION

The mediating work of myths in the analysis of ideological contradic-tions has been developed and applied to several cases. Analysis of institu-tionalized myths helps interpret organizations so that they can be viewed within the terms of their ideological bases. The aim has been to demon-strate the important role of myth in organizational analysis and to pro-vide a basis for the interpretation of organizational actions within the limits of the organization's own ideological commitments. These consid-erations are important to the theory of organizations.

Four brief case studies of varying complexity have been used to ex-plore and demonstrate the role of myths in organizational analysis. The method can be applied to any organization. The basic hypothetical ten-ets on which the framework rests are: (1) that organizational ideology consists of two contradicting concerns; namely, the fundamental and the operative, and (2) that organizational myths mediate the contradictions so that the tasks of the organization can be more effectively accomp-lished.

Particularly interesting ideological interpretations require sharp, ac-curate and sensitive descriptive data. The analytical framework defines ideology in such a way that it structures and limits the infinite capacity of case data to extend itself and become overwhelming. The task at hand is to re-present organizational data so that its ideological content can be recognized. If the framework presented is adequate to this task, in-terpretation of organizations can then proceed in a way which incorpo-rates the ideological concerns identified.

REFERENCES

Anthony, D. *The ideology of work*. London: Tavistock, 1977.

Barthes, R. *Mythologies*. St. Albans: Granada Publishing, 1973.

Benson, J. K. Organizations: A dialectical view. *Administrative Science Quarterly*, 1977, *22*, 1–21.

Berger, P. L., & Luckmann, T. *The social construction of reality*. Garden City, N.Y.: Doubleday, 1966.

Brown, H. B. Bureaucracy as praxis: Toward a political phenomenology of organizations. *Administrative Science Quarterly*, 1978, *23*, 365–382.

Geertz, C. Ideology as a cultural system. In D. Apter (Ed.), *Ideology and Discontent*. London: The Free Press, 1964.

Hegel, G. W. F. *The phenomenology of mind*. (J. B. Baillie, trans.) New York: Harper & Row, 1967.

Kalberg, S. Max Weber's types of rationality. *American Journal of Sociology*, 1980, *85*, 1145–1179.

Kamen, D. Legitimating myths and educational organizations. *American Sociological Review*, 1977, *42*, 208–219.

Malinowski, B. Myth in primitive psychology. In B. Malinowski (Ed.), *Magic, science and religion and other essays*. Garden City, N.Y.: Doubleday, 1955. (Originally published, 1926.)

Meyer, J. W. & Rowan, B. Institutionalized organizations. *American Journal of Sociology*, 1977, *83*, 340–363.

Ott, R. *Are wild ducks really wild*. Unpublished manuscript, Northeastern Anthropological Association, 1979. (a)

Ott, R. *Nobody shorts Santa Claus*. Unpublished manuscript, Organizational Symbolism Conference, 1979. (b)

Schurmann, F. *Ideology and organization in Communist China* (2nd ed.). Berkeley: University of California Press, 1968.

Seliger, M. *Ideology and politics*. Winchester, Mass.: George Allen & Unwin, 1976.

Silverman, D. & Jones, J. *Organizational work*. London: Collier MacMillan, 1976.

Robinson, M. S. The house of the mighty hero. In E. R. Leach (Ed.), *Dialectic in practical religion*. Cambridge: Cambridge University Press, 1968.

Weber, M. *Economy and society*. (G. Roth and C. Wittich, Eds.) New York: Bedminister, 1968.

Wilson, J. *Introduction to social movements*. New York: Basic Books, 1973.

AUTHOR INDEX

295

SUBJECT INDEX